To

From

Message

Published by Christian Art Publishers
PO Box 1599, Vereeniging, 1930, RSA

First edition 2019

Designed by Christian Art Publishers

Cover designed by Christian Art Publishers

Images used under license from Shutterstock.com

Printed in China

ISBN 978-1-4321-2889-0 (Hardcover)
ISBN 978-1-4321-3097-8 (LuxLeather)

19 20 21 22 23 24 25 26 27 28 – 10 9 8 7 6 5 4 3 2 1

Strength for Your Soul

KAREN MOORE

CHRISTIAN ART PUBLISHERS

January

God Holds You Close

Be strong and take heart, all you
who hope in the LORD. *Ps. 31:24, NIV*

One of the amazing gifts of God is that He opens the lines of communication for us at any hour of the day. We always have a place to go when life overwhelms us, or our spirits take a nose-dive, or we simply don't have one earthly place to turn.

When we find ourselves growing weaker, longing for God's Presence, hoping beyond hope for new direction and answers, we can be assured that He draws near to us. He sees our frustration and understands our yearning, and He picks us up as gently as a mother scoops up her baby, and He holds us close.

He never lets us go! He lets us rest in His grace and mercy. Things may not immediately change, but we are comforted, stabilized, and embraced by His Spirit.

If your spirits are sagging and your heart is wondering where to turn, then know there is strength for your soul because God is near, and you can count on His amazing Spirit each time you call His name. He will renew your heart with His great love.

There is not a heart but has its moments of longing, yearning for something better. ~ *Henry Ward Beecher*

Worth the Wait

I say to myself, "The LORD is my portion; therefore I will wait for him. The LORD is good to those whose hope is in him, to the one who seeks him." *Lam. 3:24-25, NIV*

As human beings, one of our least favorite activities is waiting. We don't like waiting for nearly anything. Long lines at the supermarket make us cringe. Waiting for important information frustrates our eagerness to get things done. Sitting in a big traffic jam tries our patience. We don't like having to wait!

Perhaps we're more comfortable when these two words are put together, "wait and hope." When we wait for the Lord, the long line at the grocery store gives us time to reflect on other important things. When life slows us down, even if it was not by our own design, we may have an opportunity to see God's hand at work in a way we would have missed. As we wait, hope comforts us, and causes us to seek God more intentionally.

We move from a circumstance that is all about us, to one that is all about God. Once we have our priorities straight, we can smile at the waiting because hope is alive and well once again. The Lord is good to those who hope in Him. Now, that's worth the wait!

All human wisdom is summed up in two words—wait and hope.

~ Alexandre Dumas

Fear Not

"Don't be afraid, for I am with you. Don't be discouraged, for I am your God. I will strengthen you and help you. I will hold you up with my victorious right hand." *Isa. 41:10, NLT*

We all get discouraged sometimes. Pursuing hopes and dreams is a risky business. Nothing comes easily and as a person who believes that God is in your heart's desires, you can grow restless and weary waiting for things to come together.

Those moments of feeling discouraged are temporary though and usually based on a situation that feels out of your control. The good news is that everything is out of your control, and that's how you want it.

The best thing for you is to surrender every hope, every desire, and every circumstance to God. He's in control. He knows what to do.

Today, He reminds you to have no fear. Let Him help you get back on your feet and feel the sun on your face. He sees you and He knows the best path for you to walk. Trust your concerns to Him and He will lead you to victory. That's His promise.

Fear not!

Fear knocked on the door. Faith answered, but no one was there.

~ Author unknown

JANUARY 4

Wait on the Lord!

Wait on the LORD; be of good courage, and He shall strengthen your heart; wait, I say, on the LORD! *Ps. 27:14, NKJV*

Did you ever wait for a visit from a good friend? Maybe you hadn't seen them for a long time and finally an opportunity came up for the two of you to meet again.

Excited to see your friend, you made plans to go to dinner or to show them around your town. You may have bought a little gift to welcome them to your home, all the while imagining the fun you would have catching up on old times and replaying favorite memories.

However, a conflict arose, and your friend's visit was delayed. You were polite, but disappointed, because you were so looking forward to seeing them. You had to make a new plan to get together later.

Most of us wait patiently for a little while, but sometimes waiting takes more than patience. We try to keep busy and not get discouraged or fall into despair. If we wait for someone a long time, we can lose heart and become fearful, wondering if they will return.

Have courage when you wait and ask God to be with you. He knows how hard it is to stay strong when you feel alone. He will guard you and protect you. Wait on the Lord! He will strengthen your heart.

Lord, keep me strong and brave as I wait patiently by Your side.

~ *Amen*

JANUARY 5

Be of Good Cheer

"These things I have spoken to you, that in Me you may have peace. In the world you will have tribulation; but be of good cheer, I have overcome the world." *John 16:33, NKJV*

Each new year brings out your desire to leave the past behind and forge ahead into a brave new world. You want to, but the old year clings to you, still hanging on, trying to get your attention. It disrupts your new plans.

If the old year drags you down, stop everything and focus your heart and mind on the One who can help you. Seek the peace that only Jesus can offer because He has overcome the tumult and chaos of the world. He invites you to simply stand next to Him, breathe in His Spirit, His peace, and His love. He's there for you, ready to help you begin again at a pace you can handle.

Be of good cheer and put your burdens from the past on His shoulders and He will carry them. He will renew you and give you strength to get through today. Remember, you're not trying to find the strength to carry half of last year and some of this year. You only need strength and peace of mind for today. With Jesus, you can do it, one day at a time. Be of good cheer!

Christ alone can bring lasting peace—peace with God—peace among men and nations—and peace within our hearts.

~ *Billy Graham*

Continue in Hope

But I will hope continually, and will yet
praise thee more and more. Ps. 71:14, KJV

You may recall a time when you had a more childlike hopefulness. You anticipated an event, perhaps graduating from school, or getting married, or beginning a new job. You had hope for a new kind of satisfaction, a possibility for good that you might never have experienced before. That kind of hope brought great joy.

Today, you don't feel quite so innocent, quite so capable of that childlike hope you once possessed and yet God has not changed. God is still there for you, every bit as much interested in your well-being as ever. He wants all good things for you and so He asks you to continue in hope. What you started a long time ago has not been completed. Your faith, and your hope, and the challenges of life are all intertwined, but each one brings you closer to the goal of knowing the love of your Heavenly Father and knowing the peace He gives when you surrender to Him.

The psalmist says that he will not only hope continually, but he will praise God continually. Pick up today wherever you left off with joyful hope in all that God desires to fulfill in you. He holds your life lovingly in His hands.

Practice hope. As hopefulness becomes a habit, you can achieve a permanently happy spirit. ~ *Norman Vincent Peale*

God Goes Before You

The LORD himself will go before you. He will be with you; he will not leave you or forget you. Don't be afraid and don't worry. *Deut. 31:8, NCV*

There are at least eighty references in the Old Testament that remind people not to be afraid. Like it or not, we all suffer from certain fears. Some of us fear an uncertain and unpredictable future. Some fear chronic illness, or job loss, or losing someone we love. Whatever causes us to spin endless stories of woe in our heads, there's only one solution, and it's as true for us now as it was in the days of the patriarchs.

God is with you. God goes before you into the future and if you are interested in getting His guidance and receiving His plans for your well-being, then He will never leave you or forsake you. He will continue with you, even if you wander off without Him.

Remember that if you surrender your ego and your will to God, you will never have to worry about anything again. Now doesn't that sound good? You can put your hand in His hand today and start walking side by side. Oh, and you don't have to worry about the future either because He goes before you. He prepares the way just for you, knowing exactly when you will arrive.

Lord, I give You thanks and praise for going on ahead of me to strengthen my path.

~ Amen

JANUARY 8

Encourage One Another

Whoever has the gift of encouraging others should encourage. Whoever has the gift of giving to others should give freely. Anyone who has the gift of being a leader should try hard when he leads. Whoever has the gift of showing mercy to others should do so with joy. *Rom. 12:8, NCV*

You are so gifted! You have been blessed with a sound mind and a happy heart. You have the kind of smile that brings light into any room and a spirit that is always ready to lend a hand. Since God knows all these things are true about you, He has only one request.

He wants you to remember to share the bounty of gifts He has given you. Someone you know needs your compassionate heart and your ability to listen with kindness to their troubles. Someone needs your prayers or your witness or simply the chance to connect with you.

Everything about you that nurtures and encourages those around you is a gift from God. He knew that if He gave you those gifts that you would use them well. Your gentle and generous presence is a gift. When others draw near to you, they see and affirm God's Presence as well. Just hold up the gifts God gave you and others will receive them wrapped with a bow. You offer encouragement, hope and love and kindness, and nothing can be better than that. Go on! Encourage others today.

Encouragement is oxygen for the soul. *~ Author unknown*

God Bless You

May God himself, the God of peace, sanctify you through and through. May your whole spirit, soul and body be kept blameless at the coming of our Lord Jesus Christ. *1 Thess. 5:23, NIV*

If this Scripture was a greeting card, it would have a beautiful design of some extraordinary landscape or a lush field of flowers. It would take your breath away with its beauty and cause you to sing praises to your Heavenly Father. Why? Because this Scripture is a wish like no other. It is a blessing to your soul, offering you wholeness and peace, purity of heart and spirit, and the gift of God's grace. It doesn't really get better than this. You're sanctified, approved of, blessed beyond measure because of all that Jesus has done for you. God started where you were, and He's been making you more beautiful ever since.

Let this generous thought erase any concerns you have about your day and help you breathe in the matters of Heaven. In fact, keep in mind that when it comes to Heaven, you are what matters. God has already stamped you with His seal of approval, working to refresh your spirit with His breath. He wants you to walk in peace and joy, knowing full well that He holds the victory over any concern you may have. It's your day to feel His blessing like sunshine on your soul.

The renewal of our natures is a work of great importance. It is not to be done in a day. ~ *George Whitefield*

God Sets Things Right

But as for you, you meant evil against me;
but God meant it for good, in order to bring it
about as it is this day, to save many people alive.
Now therefore, do not be afraid. *Gen. 50:20-21, NKJV*

Joseph's brothers sold him into slavery because they were jealous. They didn't like the way their father doted on him. They resented Joseph's dreams. Getting rid of him seemed like a good idea.

God had other plans though. He had his eye on Joseph from the beginning and He knew what He wanted Joseph to accomplish in his lifetime. He knew that Joseph's brothers would one day meet him again. Only this time, they wouldn't be jealous or spiteful. This time, they would need his help.

Sometimes things happen in our lives that we simply do not understand. Something that feels wrong or downright evil makes a mess of our lives. We wonder if we'll always be a slave to the mess we made. The thing to remember though is that God designed you for good. He knows His purpose for your life and if you allow Him to use you, and mold you and shape you, your life will turn out better than you could ever imagine. God knows how to set things right in your life. Trust Him!

The saint never knows the joy of the Lord in spite of tribulation, but because of it.
~ *Oswald Chambers*

The Upside Down Good

And we know that all things work together for good
to those who love God, to those who are the
called according to His purpose. *Rom. 8:28, NKJV*

We love sharing our stories of success or accomplishment. We love the feeling that life is working out and if we just keep going after it, the good path will be ours. The truth is God loves it too when we enjoy the rewards of our labors and reap the benefits of a job well done. He's cheering us on!

The problem is that when something turns our world upside down, we don't feel like everything is good. We don't even imagine our crisis can have a good thing about it. Yet, the writer of Romans keys in on something worthy of our reflection. All things work together for good. It isn't just the good things that make us grow and live more fully, but it's all things. Everything we experience has value when God's hand is in it and when we surrender the circumstance that challenges us over to Him, He works with us to make a difference. He strengthens us and encourages us when we lose sight of life's good things.

Give God thanks in every circumstance, even when things are upside down, and He'll work with you to continue to fulfill your glorious purpose.

God sees every one of us; He creates every soul…for a purpose.

~ *John Henry Newman*

And the Winner Is...

But thanks be to God! He gives us the victory through our Lord Jesus Christ. *1 Cor. 15:57, NIV*

Sometimes when you feel unmotivated or uncertain or even in peril, it makes you want to skip a few chapters of your story and go right to the end. After all, you're anxious to see how things turn out. Some of us are even tempted to try to read the ending before we go through the beginning chapters of a new book because we don't want to waste time on anything that makes us miserable.

That's all well and good except for most of us, the ups and downs of life are what make it interesting. Learning how to manage a crisis or a tragedy or a heartbreak is how we learn about ourselves, about who we really are. Not only that, but we often need a calamity to remember to lean on God. Of course, God is ready for us to lean on Him through every aspect of our story, but we're not always mindful of His Presence.

Today, it may help to remember that the eternal story is already written, and we know the ending. Jesus has the victory, and because of His life and death and resurrection, you have the victory too. He already knows your story. Let Him help you move toward greater victory in your life right now!

Lord, lead me on to victory in You today. ~ *Amen*

What Will You Choose?

Who, then, are those who fear the LORD? He will instruct them in the ways they should choose. *Ps. 25:12, NIV*

Most of us are still on a learning curve when it comes to making choices. Sure, we make better ones now that we're more mature spiritually and emotionally because God is good and helps us move forward. He rewards those choices we've made with a tender and surrendered heart.

The fact is, we must choose God first with every decision we make. When we don't, the consequences become apparent. We have to own that we chose unwisely, and eventually we must admit we made a bad choice of our own free will.

So what will you choose today of your own free will? How about this? How about starting your day by choosing to praise God for all that He has done to help you make your life journey so far? What about choosing to spend time with Him in conversation or in reading His Word so that His Spirit can guide you?

Often, we choose to blame God when things don't go our way. Perhaps today, you could choose to praise Him instead for all that you are and all that you are yet to be. Choose to put your life in His hands and He will teach you how to follow Him.

Destiny is no matter of chance; It's a matter of choice.

~ *William J. Bryan*

Turn on the Light, Please!

Let the one who walks in the dark, who has no light, trust in the name of the LORD and rely on their God. *Isa. 50:10, NIV*

When you read the news of the day, you can wonder if the whole world has eclipsed into darkness. Gray skies hover and even your own light feels like it's growing dimmer. When that happens, switch things up and turn on more light. How?

Start with a simple prayer. "Lord, please shine the light of Your love on my life today. Help me to see You every place I go." Then, rest in God's light. Stay still and listen for His voice. Don't move until you feel warm again, light-hearted and ready to step back into the world. It will make all the difference, and not just to you, but to everyone who encounters you today.

Some people will not even know why, but they will realize that your presence made them feel better. You made their day seem brighter because you connected them to the Light of the World, the glory of God. You brought them closer to all that God can do for them.

Wherever you are today, turn up the light! It will cause your face to be more cheerful and your heart to rejoice. Trust in the name of the Lord!

The night shall not hang its darkness forever over our souls; the sun shall yet arise with healing beneath its wings.

~ *C.H. Spurgeon*

Getting Busy Signals?

He does not ignore those in trouble. He doesn't hide from them but listens when they call out to him. *Ps. 22:24, NCV*

Hello? God, are you there? Do you ever feel like you have prayed and prayed about your difficulties, but nothing changes? You've called on God, but it feels like He must be busy with other customers because He doesn't appear to be answering you.

When you wonder if God is there or not, you might want to stop everything, even your prayers. Stop and rest. Stop and wait. Stop and listen for your heart to tune into God's frequency. Open the airwaves of your mind so that every uttered syllable from your lips to God's ear comes through with clarity. God is there! He's always there and He never puts you on hold. He never ignores your pleas for help. He listens with love.

When you align yourself with God, heart to heart and spirit to Spirit, it won't be long before you feel His amazing Presence. He promises that when you call sincerely on His Name, He is there. If you're getting a busy signal, check your line. It may be coming from your end of the call.

God never ceases to speak to us, but the noise of the world without and the tumult of our passions within bewilder us and prevent us from listening to Him. *~ F. Fénelon*

Working Off the Stress

"The seed cast in the weeds represents the ones who hear the kingdom news but are overwhelmed with worries about all the things they have to do and all the things they want to get. The stress strangles what they heard, and nothing comes of it." *Mark 4:18-19, MSG*

You may remember in the above parable that some seeds are sown in the weeds. The weeds choke out the seeds and don't allow them to take root and grow. That's what worry does. It comes into our lives and strangles us even when we know better than to plant its seeds.

Worry has no benefits. It does not change the story you're dealing with. It doesn't make someone else act in a better way because you chose to worry about them and their behaviors. It doesn't pay your bills and it doesn't treat you to a story with a happy ending.

Worry means that you've taken God's possibilities out of the equation. You've forgotten who is in control. You can go to the gym and try to work off your stress and that may be productive. You can simply choose not to worry, but better still is that you hand over everything that keeps you in the weeds and seek the Sower. He'll do all that He can do to help your situation. The smallest thing He can do is far greater than the biggest thing you can do. Trust Him!

Lord, I hand over all my worries to You right now. ~ *Amen*

Overcome Your Unbelief

Immediately the boy's father exclaimed, "I do believe; help me overcome my unbelief!" *Mark 9:24, NIV*

When things aren't working out well, it causes doubt and worry. You may wonder if you've been making wise decisions or if you've been doing those things that please God. The questions are disconcerting, but you are out of sorts and not quite on your game.

Perhaps this is a good time to simply check in with your belief system. How much of what you are doing right now depends on you and your strength and your passion? How much of what you're doing depends on God?

It's easy to get caught up in a "business as usual" lifestyle and find yourself out on the skinny branches, not feeling as safe and secure as you were. What you believe doesn't depend on you. What you believe determines how much you are willing to depend on God. You are called to surrender.

The father from the story in Mark knew what he believed. He knew Who he believed in, but he still was afraid as his son's life hung in the balance. He still needed help to overcome his unbelief. Don't let anything stand between you and Jesus. Jesus has overcome the troubles of the world so you can trust in Him. He's on your side today. He'll help you overcome your unbelief.

Lord, help me to trust You in every way and for all things in my life.

~ *Amen*

Time to Power Up!

For our struggle is not against flesh and blood, but against the rulers, against the authorities, against the powers of this dark world and against the spiritual forces of evil in the heavenly realms. *Eph. 6:12, NIV*

It's important to be realistic and practical. Those things help you get through your daily chores. Your common sense guides you to make good choices and as much as it depends on you, you're able to manage life pretty well.

This message from Ephesians though is about the uncommon things, the ones that are even other-worldly. They are things you may be aware of, but they are not the things that occupy your mind daily. However, in the present darkness, it's good to remember the only Source of power you have. Your weakness is made strong in this power alone. You are wrapped in the armor of God.

The dark and evil forces that are part of this world are everywhere, lurking in places and spaces that you don't even think to look. The reminder here then is to stay connected to your Savior, the One who has already defeated the demons of this world. You are protected and loved and armed for battle. God's only request is that you will stand with Him. When you do, His love keeps you firmly in His grasp. With Him you can always get more power!

The greatest trick the devil ever played was convincing the world he didn't exist. *~ Author unknown*

Your Forgiving Heart

Instead, be kind to each other, tenderhearted, forgiving one another, just as God through Christ has forgiven you. *Eph. 4:32, NLT*

Issues around forgiveness may cause your heart sadness, or even make you fearful. You may have people that still cause you to grow angry as you think of them. Something they did that offended you or wounded your pride way back when, wounds you again with each thought as the incident comes freshly to mind. You imagine that it's no big deal because, after all, it happened years ago.

The thing is that any sense of unforgiveness that lingers in your soul causes you pain. It shrinks your spirit and takes away your peace. It has power over you that does not serve you well. So what can you do?

Start by recalling all the times that God has forgiven you. You may not even be able to create a laundry list of your offenses, but it could be time well spent. After all, you want to seek His forgiveness so that those errors of judgment, those unkind deeds, or angry words can be wiped away, expunged from your record. God wants you to forgive others the same way that He forgives you. Be free and be kind, not just to others, but to yourself. Forgiveness brings healing to your heart.

Lord, please help me to be forgiving to people in my life in the same way that You are so often forgiving to me. *~ Amen*

JANUARY 20

Shipwrecked Faith

Cling to your faith in Christ, and keep your conscience clear. For some people have deliberately violated their consciences; as a result, their faith has been shipwrecked. *1 Tim. 1:19, NLT*

Ever felt like you're just drifting from day to day? Maybe you find something that interests you here and there, but for the most part you are just floating along without purpose or plan. You know it would help if you could pray. You could seek God's help, but for some reason, you can't bring yourself to do it. Your energy and your spirit are just not lined up properly.

If some version of this happens to you, then you have to look for an anchor and the quicker the better. It doesn't take long to become totally shipwrecked when you are tossed about by every storm life can throw at you and simply don't know where to turn.

Take heart! God sees you and He knows what to do to calm those stormy thoughts, those endless noises in your head that keep you from hearing His voice. He's got a life preserver for you and His Son, Jesus, is waiting to help you receive it. Grab on and hold fast. Cling to your faith for dear life and God will bless you with everything He has. He is ready to rescue you right now.

Faith is a living, bold trust in God's grace, so certain of God's favor that it would risk death a thousand times trusting in it.

~ *Martin Luther*

The Trouble with Patience

My brothers and sisters, when you have many kinds of troubles, you should be full of joy, because you know that these troubles test your faith, and this will give you patience. Let your patience show itself perfectly in what you do. *James 1:2-7, NCV*

Sometimes you have to reorganize your thoughts. You must step aside from the way you normally view your issues and concerns and see if God wants to show you something new. This passage from James is a good example because it reminds you that even your troubles give God a chance to grow your faith. If you never stumble or fall, the chances are good that you might totally forget to look up. God wants you to always look up and seek His face. In fact, He wants you to look up before you look anywhere else.

Troubles serve to bring clarity and strength to your faith because when faith is your focus, you leave your troubles in God's hands. Patience and peace return and things begin to look better. Sure, it isn't easy. It takes a lot of courage to surrender all your cares and give them over to God. That courage will serve you well though because God will stand with you through every difficult time in your life.

Take your eyes off your troubles today and look at the only Source available to you to strengthen and revive your faith.

God can only relieve your troubles if you in your anxiety cling to Him.

~ *Augustine of Hippo*

Raising Your Hopes

My aim is to raise hopes by pointing the way to life without end. This is the life God promised long ago—and he doesn't break promises! *Titus 1:2-3, MSG*

Those of us who cling to God's promise of everlasting life have a choice to make every day we're on earth. Will we live today with the hope of eternity in our hearts, or will we live today as though every effort we make depends on our own ingenuity?

Our hope in eternity means that we believe in the promises of God. It means that we trust that one day, according to His timing, we'll go to Heaven.

The point here is that the hope you have of Heaven starts right now. God's promises to make you new every morning, give you a listening ear when you pray, and deliver you into His Kingdom are real opportunities; hopes that will come to fruition. All you have to do is live each day as a redeemed child of God. When you do, He draws near to you, listening to the desires of your heart and opening the vast windows of hope that only He can provide.

Rejoice in all that you are and all that you can be as you embrace God's love for you. Your hope for tomorrow comes from every seed of faith you plant today.

The prospects are as bright as the promises of God.

~ Adoniram Judson

Don't Look Back

But one thing I do: Forgetting what is behind and straining toward what is ahead, I press on toward the goal to win the prize for which God has called me heavenward in Christ Jesus. *Phil. 3:13-14, NIV*

When you're training for something, let's say running in a marathon, you do it because you need to build up your strength and your energy. You want to get better at doing small things so that you can take on bigger things. Without the training, you most likely won't win the day.

When the big day of the race finally arrives, you've trained, you're ready, and as soon as the whistle blows, you're off and running. What would happen if you started running backwards? How far behind would you get if you could not see where you were going?

Hold those thoughts and think about the way you are running your life. Are you willing to spend time in training, that is with God in prayer and in His Word so that you're stronger and have more of His Spirit to guide you? Once you have been fortified with renewed energy, you can take on all that is ahead of you. If you keep your eyes on the Lord, you will always take the straight path ahead. Looking back will never serve you well.

Lord, help me please to keep my gaze fixed on You so that my heart and my faith are always ready for what is ahead. *~ Amen*

God Is My Strength

My health may fail, and my spirit may grow weak,
but God remains the strength of my heart;
he is mine forever. *Ps. 73:26, NLT*

David was a man after God's own heart, because David was so human on one hand, and awestruck by God on the other. David was sinful, but despite himself, he held on to his Redeemer. He knew he had to run to God with his heart in his hand when he disappointed his Heavenly Father. David knew only God could renew his strength.

Today, before you leave your home to go out into the world, step in front of your mirror. Look at the person you see there and then say aloud, "God remains the strength of my heart; He is mine forever!"

If God is the strength of your heart, not just today, but forever, then every day of your life you will know that you can trust Him with your biggest fears, your deepest needs and your worst sins. You can count on Him to heal you and to protect you and to guide you out of the mire you get yourself into because He loves you always.

May that thought carry you through the day, brighten your step, and bring you ever closer to the God of your heart.

There is a God-shaped vacuum in the heart of every man which cannot be filled by any created thing, but only by God, the Creator, made known through Jesus. ~ *Blaise Pascal*

God Bless and Keep You

Now all glory to God, who is able to keep you from falling away and will bring you with great joy into his glorious presence without a single fault. *Jude 1:24, NLT*

You're a witness to life's little miracles. You see the seasons change and the frozen ground renew itself into springtime flowers. You see people change their hearts and seek God's face. You see the work God has done in your own life, drawing you closer to Him, nourishing you and providing for your daily needs. Yes, God is with you at every turn, with every step you take. Even before you know you need Him, He's there for you.

Isn't it glorious to truly recognize what that means? The God who created the tallest tree and the tiniest insect and the brightest star, also created you. He created you because He knew you would be a beautiful example of His work. He's proud to show you off. He sees you rise to each new day with the determination to try again, to do what you can to grow in His strength.

Today, remember Him. Thank Him for protecting you from falling away, from guarding your heart and renewing your spirit so that you can one day return to Him as a light of love, standing in His Presence without a single fault. Now won't that be a glorious day!

May God bless you and keep you wherever you may go today.

~ *Amen*

JANUARY 26

Good Discipline

No discipline seems pleasant at the time, but painful. Later on, however, it produces a harvest of righteousness and peace for those who have been trained by it. *Heb. 12:11, NIV*

What is good discipline? What can be good about being punished, chastised, left to feel badly about something you've done?

You already know the answer! You know that a course correction can strengthen you and put you on a better path. You may not like criticism, but if you heed thoughtful advice, you see the benefit. In fact, you make wiser choices from that point on. That's what God wants for you. If He intervenes in your life to show you that you need to change a behavior or a direction, then the sooner you listen to His advice, the faster He can put you on a better path. He'll help you, but He must know He has your attention first. He must know that you are listening.

Good discipline is like training, it's a chance to keep improving your game. You can make the effort to change, and keep trying, and God will step up and step in to strengthen you to achieve the goal. He's there for you even when He has to suggest a way to correct the path you're on. Thank Him for loving you so much that He won't let you fall too far from His side.

The goal of God's discipline is restoration—never condemnation.

~ Author unknown

Becoming More Effective

Make every effort to add to your faith goodness; and to goodness, knowledge; and to knowledge, self-control; and to self-control, perseverance; and to perseverance, godliness; and to godliness, mutual affection; and to mutual affection, love. For if you possess these qualities in increasing measure, they will keep you from being ineffective and unproductive in your knowledge of our Lord Jesus Christ. *2 Pet. 1:5-8, NIV*

We are list makers. It's how we get things done. We think it makes us more efficient, or at least less forgetful.

This passage from Peter is a kind of efficiency list as well. If you heed it, your work for the Lord will be more productive and you'll have a definite effect on the lives of others. If that's one of your personal goals, then this list is a good one. Of course, it's not a bread and butter list, one that you can check off once and call it done. This is a life-long list, one to be embraced with all your heart. This is a list you may never accomplish, but that doesn't mean you won't reap amazing benefits from your efforts.

If you are trying to move from faith to knowledge to self-control to love, then you are making progress. Be encouraged. God rewards your progress with greater gifts of joy and contentment and peace. Keep going, you're doing great!

Lord, help me to keep this amazing list in front of me each day.
~ *Amen*

God Is Your Refuge

As for God, his way is perfect: The LORD's word is flawless; he shields all who take refuge in him. *Ps. 18:30, NIV*

When you need a safe place to stop your head from spinning and your heart from jumping, try God. Try slipping away from the office for a few minutes, stepping aside from your daily chores and find an oasis.

God is your oasis. He is a place of rest and peace. He never leaves you nor forsakes you because He knows you need Him. He does everything He can to remind you of His Presence. He whispers to you during your prayers and lifts a Scripture passage right off the page for you to consider. He sends a friend to your side. He allows you to bask in the shadow of His love and reflect more clearly on the things that weigh on your heart and mind. An oasis moment is available to you any time you need it. You don't have to make a reservation. You don't have to plan each thing you'll do there. You simply have to desire God's Presence and He'll bring the oasis to you.

The Lord is your refuge when life burdens your soul. Look to Him. Any time you do, you will surely find Him waiting for you. Ah, now that brings a sigh of relief!

The house of my soul is too small for You to enter: make it more spacious by Your coming. It lies in ruins: rebuild it.

~ Augustine of Hippo

God Blesses Your Work

So, my dear brothers and sisters, be strong and immovable. Always work enthusiastically for the Lord, for you know that nothing you do for the Lord is ever useless. *1 Cor. 15:58, NLT*

Did you ever spend months on a project at work only to have the project cancelled just about the time you were finished with it? Or perhaps you had a home project and when you got it half completed, you didn't like it nearly as much as you had hoped you would and so you had to start again. When you go through times like that, it can feel like a huge waste of resources and effort and time itself. You can begrudge the loss.

This portion of the letter to the Corinthians may offer us a new perspective. What if we began that project at work as though we were doing it for God? You would put your heart into it, pray about each step, and whatever happens to the project, you would still feel engaged, and pleased with the effort you made because you would trust God's guidance as you took each step. The same is true for home projects or other ways that you spend your time and effort. Working for anything in the world may be a waste of time. Working in the world for God, can be an enormous Source of joy. You get to choose how you wish to make the effort.

Work becomes worship when it's done for the Lord.

~ Author unknown

Don't Worry!

"That is why I tell you not to worry about everyday life—whether you have enough food and drink, or enough clothes to wear. Isn't life more than food, and your body more than clothing? Look at the birds. They don't plant or harvest or store food in barns, for your heavenly Father feeds them. And aren't you far more valuable to him than they are? Can all your worries add a single moment to your life?" *Matt. 6:25-27, NLT*

Sure, you try not to worry. You know that it doesn't really serve you and that most of the time the things you worry about, don't happen. Yet, here it is, another worry has lodged itself inside your brain and no matter what you do, you can't seem to shake it.

Matthew records practical advice that Jesus gave His followers about worrying. He says we don't have to worry about our resources, whether we have enough of the things we need. We simply must trust God will provide. We must go about our business, do our best and let God do the rest.

Remember that if God takes care of the birds and your favorite dog then He can surely take care of you. Devote your time to peace and prayer and love. Count your blessings instead of your troubles. If you do that, you'll simply have no time to worry.

Blessed are you if you are too busy to worry during the day, and too sleepy to worry at night. ~ *Author unknown*

A New Thing

"See, I am doing a new thing! Now it springs up; do you not perceive it? I am making a way in the wilderness and streams in the wasteland." *Isa. 43:19, NIV*

Do you remember what it was like when you loved to try new things? You know, you were curious about the world and you wanted to learn as much as you could because everything was fascinating. If you're thinking that you haven't had that experience since you were about seven, then maybe God wants you to try again.

When you're curious about life, you put yourself out there to discover what else there is. When you're curious about God, you dive into His Word and you devote time to prayer because you know that you have many things to learn. Imagine that today, God is talking directly to you. Imagine that He is suggesting to you that He wants to begin a new thing in your heart. He wants you to discover more of what He has for you. Would you be ready to receive His gift to you?

If you've been living in a way that is no longer flourishing, no longer feeling vital and new, then open your heart and your mind to all that God can do. He may truly want to do a new thing in you!

Lord, open my eyes to any new things You may want to do in my life. Thank You, Jesus! *~ Amen*

February

Making Progress

And let God bless all who fear God—bless the small, bless the great. Oh, let God enlarge your families—giving growth to you, growth to your children. May you be blessed by God, by God, who made heaven and earth. *Ps 115:13-15, MSG*

This Psalm reads like a prayer that echoes across the hearts and minds of believers everywhere. No matter who we are, what our job is, or what status we might hold, God blesses us greatly when we trust in Him.

What would it mean to you for God to enlarge your sense of family? Perhaps it means you would be blessed with more children or grandchildren. Perhaps it means He would fill each member of your family with His Spirit, so each person grows to understand and perceive His ways more fully. Perhaps it means that He would walk beside the people you love each day as they work and travel and manage their lives, connecting your hearts in new ways.

We are each a work in progress and with God's help we grow to become a little wiser and a little more complete in Him. The only secret is that we must hold God in reverence and esteem, praising His name and giving Him the glory for all that we are and all that we yet will be. May God bless your progress as you draw near to Him today.

Lord, I thank You for helping me to grow and for the blessings You alone have given me. *~ Amen*

Learning from Mistakes

Every part of Scripture is God-breathed and useful one way or another—showing us truth, exposing our rebellion, correcting our mistakes, training us to live God's way. Through the Word we are put together and shaped up for the tasks God has for us. *2 Tim. 3:16-17, MSG*

You did it again! Another mistake. How many times can God forgive you? You may wonder whether your sins have piled up too high for God to be able to wipe the slate clean again. After all, you know what a mess you've made, and you can barely forgive yourself. God knows that about you, and about all the rest of His children as well. He knows we need Him every hour of the day and we prove it to ourselves repeatedly. Every time we fall, He lifts us up again.

If you worry about your mistakes, seek God's counsel. Pray for His healing for the things you simply cannot overcome on your own. Get your Bible out and pour through the pages with a hunger to know more of what God wants from you. His Word brings insight and His Holy Spirit brings instruction to help you live completely in God's care.

If you're the kind of person who really likes to dive in to things, jumping in with both feet, going all the way, then let that be your attitude about studying God's Word. You'll be blessed beyond measure.

Lord, teach me to be enthusiastic about learning from my mistakes.

~ *Amen*

Tripped Up

The godly may trip seven times, but they will get up again. But one disaster is enough to overthrow the wicked. *Prov. 24:16, NLT*

Sometimes you work hard, and you can see the fruit of your labors. Things are shaping up in the direction you want, and your goal is clearly in sight. Then, out of nowhere an obstacle looms in the path. You can't see around it and you can't understand where it came from. It's upsetting because you're so close to the goal.

If you've ever come in second when you thought you'd win, or you missed the mark that seemed right in front of you, you'll understand this Proverb more clearly. Obstacles will show up, and times will happen that you'll get tripped up even when you're doing great work, but the gift is that you'll rise again. You'll get up, dust yourself off and keep moving forward.

God sees you. When you stumble, He puts out His hand to steady your step. He knows what you need, and He goes ahead of you so that He can prepare the way. If you focus on the obstacles, they will get bigger and bigger. If you focus on the One who is in the lead, He will help you get back up and get going. He wants you to win at those things He has called you to do. Get up! You're good to go.

God loves us not because of who we are, but because of who He is.

~ Author unknown

A Bit of Humility

Always be humble and gentle. Be patient with each other, making allowance for each other's faults because of your love. *Eph. 4:2, NLT*

Human beings are quirky. We each are quite capable of doing little things that easily annoy others. We do them so naturally that we probably don't even give them any thought. The problem is that those around us think about our little faults all the time. They start out as splinters and become logs, not in our eyes, but in theirs.

So, what do we do? We probably are best served by stepping in front of a mirror and asking God to help us see ourselves more clearly. We must seek His help to look at those things we do that require others to be patient with us, forgiving us, and often simply overlooking our foibles. Once we've done that, it's a little easier to extend grace and love to others. After all, God overlooks countless faults of His children because He aims to love them into doing better next time. We can do the same for the people around us. Let's make allowance for each other's faults.

Lord, I ask You to help me to be patient, not only with the annoying things I imagine others to do, but with the ones I do as well.

~ *Amen*

Strength and Courage

If your faith is not strong, you will not have strength enough to last. *Isa. 7:9, NCV*

How do you measure strength? What images come to your mind when you think about ideas or people or things that are strong? Okay, now make it more personal. What are your strengths? What keeps you strong?

Perhaps a strength finder for your faith would reveal areas where you are especially gifted and areas where your weaknesses show up. For example, you may be a prayer warrior, continually aware of the needs of others and genuinely able to offer heartfelt prayers to God. That's a matter of your faith and a place where you are strong.

However, you may be less willing to step out into the world and be a witness to your faith, choosing instead to keep faith a personal matter. Like any strength analysis, a few simple tests can help determine your greatest assets and your less developed ones. It's important to know what your strengths are because those are the areas you will continue to exercise and develop. You will serve God with all your heart, mind, soul and strength.

Think about your gifts, assets, and strengths as you serve Him today so that you will stand firm. God will strengthen you with His Spirit every step of the way.

All the resources of the Godhead are at our disposal.

~ Jonathan Goforth

Walk Faithfully

See, the enemy is puffed up; his desires are not upright—but the righteous person will live by his faithfulness. *Hab. 2:4, NIV*

Sometimes arrogance is obvious. We can spot it in those who flaunt their self-importance. We encounter it in some who have attained wealth or status or position in society in one way or another. No matter where we see it, in others or even now and then in ourselves, it means we're puffed up by a lie. We believe that we've accomplished something that others should envy. We imagine we've done it all by ourselves.

The thing is we don't have anything to be puffed up about no matter who we are. We may have succeeded in our jobs or our life work, but we didn't succeed on our own. We succeeded by the grace of God.

A believer understands that in their humanness, they don't have much to offer to God or the world. In their faithfulness though, they have infinite opportunities to bless others through the work God has given them to do.

You know the work you've been called to do, and you know that God alone is your Source of possibility, the One who keeps you moving forward. Boast only of your success in doing His will with love. That's what it means to walk faithfully.

Make God proud of you today!

~ Author unknown

A Troubled Heart

Answer me when I pray to you, my God who does what is right. Make things easier for me when I am in trouble. Have mercy on me and hear my prayer. Ps 4:1, NCV

Your heart is troubled, and everything feels like it's falling apart. You have no control over your circumstances and you wonder if God is even aware of all that's going on in your life. It's not easy, but deep down you trust that God does know. You realize that only He can make a difference, but you struggle with a sense of overwhelming need for help. You hope and pray for God's mercy.

When your heart is troubled, it may help to review some of Jesus' promises. He reminded His followers He would always be with them, even to the end of the age. He said that He would send them the comforter, the Holy Spirit, who would guide them.

God is never too busy to hear your concerns. He's not slow to answer. He does not want you to suffer, for He is only mercy and love. When circumstances drag you down, then go to the only place that can strengthen your soul. Go to your Father in Heaven who knows what you need. Nothing about your life is too hard for Him to handle. He loves you and He's with you every moment when your heart is troubled.

He can only give according to His might; therefore, He always gives more than we ask for. ~ *Martin Luther*

FEBRUARY 8

You Are Strong

Be alert. Continue strong in the faith. Have courage, and be strong. Do everything in love. *1 Cor. 16:13-14, NCV*

Signs are everywhere! Traffic signals tell you when to stop or go. Libraries tell you to talk softly. Office buildings show you how to get to the exit. You're alerted to the latest news. The writer of Corinthians wants to keep you on the alert too. He wants you to keep moving forward with strong faith, courageously and intentionally.

Your faith brings you Divine signs that help you discern when to stop and when to keep going. You move closer to God's Presence as you consider the steps you need to take. You know that He sees you and keeps you in His care.

Be alert to what God is doing all the time. He wants His children to be awake, to see His hand at work, and hear His voice. You don't want to do anything alone. You are strong, but your strength comes from the Lord and so the most protected place to be is close by His side.

His strength will give you courage. His voice will give you a deeper desire to share His love with others. Look for signs of His Presence in everything you do today. You may be surprised at how often you will see Him draw near to you.

We may ignore, but we can nowhere evade the presence of God.

~ *C.S. Lewis*

Living by What You Believe

So we always have courage. We know that while
we live in this body, we are away from the Lord.
We live by what we believe, not by what we can see.
So I say that we have courage. 2 Cor. 5:6-8, NCV

What you think changes all the time. Thoughts are fleeting and subject to the influence of the environment or your mood. Sometimes you're not even sure where a thought comes from as it flits through your mind exiting almost as quickly as it came.

What you believe though is very different. Your beliefs are much more solid, built on a foundation of experience or expertise. What you believe is an effort of your heart and mind and sometimes even your soul. You may not always be certain of what you think about a particular matter, but you are convicted about the things you believe.

God has given you the courage and the faith to believe in Him. That faith is more than a thought, more than an impression or even a vague hope. Your faith makes you strong because God keeps showing you who He is and He keeps inviting you to come closer to Him.

You stand on what you believe, and those beliefs are anchored to your soul. Believing is living courageously in the Presence of God's grace and mercy.

Keep believing in the One who always believes in you!

The Good Fight of Faith

Fight the good fight of the faith. Take hold of the eternal life to which you were called when you made your good confession in the presence of many witnesses. *1 Tim. 6:12, NIV*

Remember when you were asked to give a report in front of the class, or the first time you were called to bat when the bases were loaded? When you are called to perform a task, you react differently than when you choose to do something yourself. Being called is about answering when someone else chooses you to come forward.

You were called to faith. You didn't just volunteer. God chose you and you answered and that makes all the difference. So what do you want to do with that call on your life? How do you want to respond?

Of course, God is gracious and once you've given Him an initial answer, He nurtures you toward making a bigger commitment. He looks to you to keep choosing to fight for your faith, standing up for it when it counts, hitting a home run for Him when you get the opportunity.

God called you to the good fight of faith because He knew you would make a difference to your family, and your community and perhaps even in the world. Thank you for answering His call.

Lord, please help me to stand firm in my faith and honor my calling to You. *~ Amen*

Keep Believing

And without faith it is impossible to please God, because anyone who comes to him must believe that he exists and that he rewards those who earnestly seek him. *Heb. 11:6, NIV*

This Scripture offers you a mini formula for success, or at least a "How-to" approach to God. The first step is for you to simply believe that God exists. Okay, that sounds easy enough, but is it? Do you believe God exists for you all the time, every day, and in every way?

Believing God exists is not an intellectual task, but a heart imperative. Once you are certain of His existence, you can grow your faith and do the work that pleases Him. The more you and God know each other, the better chance He has to let you know how pleased He is with your work.

God actively participates in your relationship. You believe He exists, He's pleased with what you do for Him, and so He takes the opportunity to reward you for your efforts on His behalf. Your faith in Him has benefits you can never measure. His rewards are beyond anything your mind can fathom. His big-ticket gift is eternal life. Everything else is just a perk designed to make you happy. The love of God is greater than anything you can understand. Oh, how blessed you are in believing!

Good works will never produce salvation, but salvation should produce good works. *~ Author unknown*

Hold Fast

"Behold, I am coming quickly! Hold fast what you have, that no one may take your crown." *Rev. 3:11, NKJV*

At times life can feel like a contest, perhaps the one where you and your team are pulling on one side of a heavy rope and some other team is pulling just as hard from the opposite end. It's difficult to say who will win because both sides are pulling as hard as they can. When the winner is declared, it's because there is finally only one team still holding fast to the rope.

What pulls at you during the day? What makes it hard for you to simply hold on to your faith and your convictions? The world pulls at your beliefs without ceasing. People lob their opinions like tennis balls, hurling them like insults to confuse your heart and mind. Evil lurks and kindness wanes. You aren't even sure how to hold up your end of things, much less, pull everyone else in the right direction.

Eternity is sure. You're not juggling to see whether you'll win. You're simply holding on because no matter which way the rope may pull you, as long as you're attached to it, holding fast, you'll reap the rewards. God knows how hard you're clinging to Him. He's got your back today.

Endurance is not just the ability to bear a hard thing, but to turn it into glory.

~ *William Barclay*

Faith Is the Substance of Hope

Now faith is the substance of things hoped for,
the evidence of things not seen. *Heb. 11:1, NKJV*

What gives anything substance or significance? According to the writer of Hebrews, faith is the substance, the material, the essence of what causes you to have hope in the things you cannot see.

Faith then is the power, the engine that drives the whole train called Hope. What that means then is that hope is based on something significant. You can have hope in the unseen things because your hopes are not just pie in the sky wishes, or dreams that vanish into thin air, they are very real things. Your hopes are real because they are built on the foundation of faith.

Whatever you're going through, you have the hope of things getting better. You have the hope that there will be a brighter day. You have every reason to take heart because good things will come. How do you know? You know because God promises that through faith, you can conquer anything. With faith, you can move mountains. With faith, you can reach up and reach out. God will take your hand and lift you out of whatever hardship you are facing. Your hope is built on a powerful substance. It's called faith!

A little faith will bring your soul to heaven, but a lot of faith will bring heaven to your soul. *~ Dwight L. Moody*

Don't Be Afraid

He says, "Don't be afraid, because I have saved you.
I have called you by name, and you are mine." *Isa. 43:1, NCV*

For some of us, this is love day, the day we give Valentines to people we are fond of so that we can share our hearts with joy. It's a nice idea, of course, to have a day to express love, but as it turns out, Valentine's Day should be every day.

The beauty of this Scripture from Isaiah is that it's a message of love. It's a Valentine from God. He reminds us that we don't have anything to fear because He loves us so much that He has called us to be His own. He loves us so much that He knows our names and He went to all the trouble of purchasing us at Calvary. We are His and that's an amazing thing. In fact, there probably couldn't be a more powerful love letter given to human beings than to know God loves us, saves us, and knows us by name.

As you celebrate the day of hearts and flowers, say a special gratitude prayer to your Savior who gave His life for yours, all because of love. You might even break out into a song of praise.

Lord, I am overcome with joy because of what You have done to save me. Help me to share Your love courageously with everyone I meet today.

~ Amen

Heart Trouble

Jesus said, "Don't let your hearts be troubled.
Trust in God, and trust in me." *John 14:1, NCV*

Everyone has some form of heart trouble. The problem with your heart may not send you to the hospital for a triple bi-pass, but it's trouble all the same. In fact, most of the things that trouble your heart come from fear and fear comes from a lack of trust.

God the Father, God the Son, and God the Holy Spirit are the three reasons your heart can be at peace. You are covered from head to toe with the greatest power in the universe. All you must do is trust.

Dwight L. Moody gave us some guidelines for trust that are great words of wisdom for today. He basically said that if we trust in ourselves, we'll be disappointed. If we trust in our friends, a time will come when they will leave us. If we trust in our money, it may all disappear, and if we trust in our reputation, someone will surely try to put us to shame. Therefore, the best thing we can do is trust in God because only then will we be blessed from here to eternity.

If your heart is troubled in any way today, go to the One you can rely on, the One you can trust always with your heart and with your soul.

Faith is not a once-done act, but a continuous gaze of the heart at the Triune God.
~ *A.W. Tozer*

More Faith Please

Jesus replied, "Truly I tell you, if you have faith and do not doubt, not only can you do what was done to the fig tree, but also you can say to this mountain, 'Go, throw yourself into the sea,' and it will be done." *Matt. 21:21, NIV*

You're more likely to achieve a goal when you are confident in yourself and go after it, believing you can do it. Your belief then motivates you to complete your task.

When Jesus' disciples were marveling over the things Jesus could do, like speaking to the fig tree and causing it to dry up, they couldn't understand how He could do it. How does someone speak to nature and have nature listen to them? It seems like a fair question and Jesus gave a fair answer. When you know what you can do, you do it. Jesus knew what He could do and didn't have a shred of doubt to derail His actions. He was so aligned with God that He could do anything.

What about you? Ah, there is the question. When your faith is totally aligned with the Spirit of God and you believe that He has ordained you, called you to do a certain thing, you can do it. When God is with you, you can do anything through Him. You simply need more faith.

Lord, I pray that You will move my faith past all doubts that may linger in my heart and help me do more for You. *~ Amen*

FEBRUARY 17

God Is Everywhere

"All people everywhere, follow me and be saved. I am God. There is no other God." *Isa. 45:22, NCV*

The Creator of the Universe, the God who Is, the One who has always been and always will be continually inserts Himself into the human family. He strives to show us He exists right now, today. He has not gone anywhere. In fact, God is everywhere.

For some, it's clear. God is picture perfect, and part of everything they do. For others, it's vague and they can sense that God is somewhere, but they're not sure where to find Him. Of course, there are also those who are simply blind to God's Presence because they have rejected Him so many times, they can no longer feel that He has anything to do with their lives.

Regardless of how He is received, the fact remains that there is only one God and there is no other God. No technological advance, no Pulitzer Prize winning scientist or brilliant politician has all the answers to life on earth. No one even comes close to knowing the mind of God. The best possibility you have is to enlarge your heart to fit more of God into your life. When you do, you will see Him everywhere.

If the work of God could be comprehended by reason, it would be no longer wonderful, and faith would have no merit if reason provided proof. ~ *Gregory the Great*

Have Eyes of Faith

And let us run with perseverance the race marked out for us, fixing our eyes on Jesus, the pioneer and perfecter of faith. *Heb. 12:1-2, NIV*

What's in front of you today? Perhaps you've got your to-do list ready and waiting on your desk calendar or the refrigerator. You've set some goals and you have an idea of where you should go, but you may not be all that certain how you'll get there. After all, you have too many items on that list and something will surely have to fall by the wayside, along with the ones still waiting there from yesterday.

Our lives are crowded with responsibilities to our work and family and perhaps even to our community. The race before us is not well marked, so we need Jesus to run ahead of us. In fact, we might not even know what track to be on if we haven't kept our eyes on the One Source that makes everything else in our lives possible.

It's always a choice. You can decide that your list is too long to take the time to pray or read the Word or seek counsel from your Heavenly Father. You'll see your path more clearly and run more effectively with the Perfecter of your faith by your side. You're always on a good path with Him.

Faith must trample under foot all reason, sense, and understanding.

~ Martin Luther

Fragile Faith

What they trust in is fragile; what they rely on is a spider's web. *Job 8:14, NIV*

Trust can only be built on a strong foundation. It must hold you up no matter what else happens. The last thing you want is for your safety net to be torn apart the moment you land on it.

Scripture often refers to God as the rock. We would likely agree that a rock feels solid. It can hold you up and when the winds of life come along, it doesn't blow away. That's a good analogy and one that helps us identify with God's ability to keep us firmly in His grasp.

What might be fragile then is not the Rock, but the person standing on the Rock, the one who is still weak in faith. If you feel weak today, uncertain as to where to go from here, or how to get a better hold on the things of God, stop everything and simply sit down and pray. Ask God to show you how to draw nearer to Him. Ask Him to hold you up and help you build your trust in Him so that your faith grows strong.

What you rely on is important. You have no strength in yourself. God is the Rock and He will fortify you for each new day. That's a promise.

Lord, help me to trust in You for all I do today so that I stand firmly on Your Rock of grace and mercy. *~ Amen*

Bread for Today

"Give us this day our daily bread. And forgive us our debts, as we forgive our debtors." *Matt. 6:11-12, NKJV*

It's interesting that in the Lord's Prayer, our first request is for daily bread. Give us this day our daily bread is surely a discussion of God's provision. We pray God will supply those things that nurture and sustain us through life.

We also pray that somehow God would forgive the debt that we have accumulated, or the sins we have committed. We need His help with that debt, a debt we could never repay on our own, and we want Him to forgive us as we forgive others. We may not be especially good at forgiveness, but the One who is the Bread of life, forgives us all our sins when we come to Him with contrite hearts.

Today, may God bless you with your daily bread, providing for all your needs, blessing your health and your finances and those things that sustain your life. May He then fill you with such joy that you are able to forgive any who have offended you, knowing how often you have been forgiven yourself. The bread of life is yours and He alone will sustain your soul.

Lord, thank You for being the Living Bread, the One who keeps me well fed by Your grace and love. *~ Amen*

When You Are Brokenhearted

The LORD is close to the brokenhearted, and he saves those whose spirits have been crushed. *Ps. 34:18, NCV*

Heartbreak happens! Overwhelmed by grief, we let days go by, chained to our misery, and wondering if God knows what we're going through. Nothing makes up for the loss, or the shattered hopes and dreams, but one thing can help. If we rest in the comfort and care of our Savior, clinging closely to His side, waiting patiently for His healing, we will see that the sun rises again.

God knows that we need Him more than ever when we feel crushed and defeated and so He leans in, lovingly sharing our pain and doing what He can to strengthen and renew our spirits. He understands the human heart and puts in a request for the Holy Spirit to guard and comfort us.

It takes time for broken hearts to heal and if you're going through an experience of grief or loss, breathe in God's Spirit, rest in His care and allow yourself the opportunity to go through the process. You may be weary now, but God promises to lift you up again and sustain you. Let Him in. Cast your burdens on Him and He will give you a renewed sense of peace.

No one ever told me about the laziness of grief. Not only writing, but even reading a letter is too much. Even shaving. What does it matter now whether my cheek is rough or smooth? ~ *C.S. Lewis*

FEBRUARY 22

You Can Do It!

Blessed is the one who perseveres under trial because, having stood the test, that person will receive the crown of life that the Lord has promised to those who love him. *James 1:12, NIV*

You can't do everything, at least not on your own. God doesn't expect you to give until you're so depleted you can't breathe. Instead, He expects you to come to Him when you're feeling stressed, talk to Him when you can't figure out just what else to do and keep your chin up.

The gift of going through struggles doesn't seem apparent at the time, but you may later realize how much you grew during the rough times. You gained confidence in your ability to handle things and you have a sense of pride about owning your responsibilities and doing a good job. Sometimes even your faith is tested. When you've been challenged about your beliefs, or belittled because of your faith, you may want to walk away. You may wonder if it's all worth it, but stay strong, and God will lead you forward.

We're told in James that if we persevere and pass the tests, we'll receive the gifts that God gives to His own. That sounds like quite a promise. Persevere through the tough spots and it will pay off.

Lord, I don't always feel like I can make it through the difficult times I'm facing. Help me to stay close to You every step of the way.

~ Amen

The Stories in Your Head

How long must I wrestle with my thoughts and day after day have sorrow in my heart? *Ps. 13:2, NIV*

Like most of us, David had stories in his head. He had thoughts that perplexed him and caused him sorrow. He had enemies and he worried that God might not show up in time to help him, and then he would simply die. You may have experienced that feeling. Does God hear my prayer? Does He know how hopeless I feel?

See what David did when he was worried. At the end of Psalm 13, after bemoaning the concerns of his heart, he changed his attitude. He created a new story in his head. David was special to God because he always returned to God in praise. David shared his troubles, but he didn't stop there. He changed his message to God to one of praise. He remembered what God had done for him in the past and he believed God would help him again.

Whatever you are going through, it's good to express your cares and concerns to God. It's okay to tell Him how defeated and alone you feel, but it's better to end your prayer with praise. Thank God for the many times He's been there for you and trust that He will show up again to provide what you need. After all, love is His only response to you.

Prayer is love in need appealing to love in power.

~ James Moffatt

Know and Believe Today

Know and believe today that the LORD is God. He is God in heaven above and on the earth below. There is no other god! *Deut. 4:39, NCV*

Who do we really know? We may think we know the people in our families, only to have them do something that is so out of character, we can't believe they did it. We can think we know the people we work with but be surprised at their behavior when we see them in a totally different setting.

When it comes to God, we surely have things we think we know about Him. What we think may well be true. What we believe may well be something different. God is always trying to appeal to our hearts in a way that may cause us to give up what we think we know and surrender to His guidance so we can truly know Him. He wants us to know Him more each day so that He can bless our work and our families and our lives. He never stops trying and He hopes we won't stop trying either.

Today, check in with your heart to see what you really know and believe about God. If you find any holes in your theories, or your theology, then ask Him to help you know the truth. Get to know Your Savior in a personal way.

God often visits us, but most of the time we are not at home.

~ *Joseph Roux*

Your Point of View

So we have stopped evaluating others from a human point of view. At one time we thought of Christ merely from a human point of view. How differently we know him now! *2 Cor. 5:16, NLT*

Did you ever make a poor first impression? People make assumptions about others based on hearsay or their own life experience. They may share an opinion of them before they know the truth. The New Testament Christians had an opinion of Jesus. For some, He was the son of a carpenter. For others, He was the Son of God, the Savior.

Maybe you had the wrong impression when you first met Jesus. You may have passed Him by a time or two. When you finally invited Him into your heart you felt free to become all that He would have you become. You knew the truth about Him.

Now you see Him as important to every decision you make. You look to Him for comfort when you need help and for His Divine favor when things are not going well. Your human point of view is becoming more spiritually aligned and so you see Him differently than you did at first. Praise God! He's working in your heart and mind to shape all that you do.

Lord, I thank You with all my heart for helping me get to know You. I pray that our relationship will grow stronger each day of my life. ~ *Amen*

When You're Smiling

May the Lord bless you and protect you. May the Lord smile on you and be gracious to you. May the Lord show you his favor and give you his peace. *Num. 6:24-26, NLT*

This is one of the sweetest blessings in all of Scripture. It's sweet because it is truly a prayer that we would offer for our children and our friends and others in our families. It's a prayer that we are delighted to receive from those who care about us.

Perhaps today, you could make it your intention to offer this prayer, this blessing, either verbally or in your heart for those around you. Offer it for the vagrant who sits on the corner in rags. Offer it for the business person who leads those at work and must make important decisions. Offer it for the leaders of our country and for the people who have enormous influence over the lives of others.

With this prayer, you're asking God to intervene in their lives, make His face known to them and grant them favor. You're asking for His protection and His peace that passes all understanding. You may discover that this is not simply a sweet blessing, but an important prayer to offer for people everywhere.

May God bless you and keep you and show you His favor today.

We do good deeds, but God works in us in the doing of them.

~ Augustine of Hippo

The Light in Your Heart

For it is the God who commanded light to shine out of the darkness, who has shone in our hearts to give the light of the knowledge of the glory of God in the face of Jesus Christ. 2 Cor. 4:6, NKJV

When Jesus is in your heart, your light is always on. It can't be helped. The longer you keep His light on, the more energy you derive from Him. You don't even have to pay the energy bill because He already did that before He came to dwell with you.

The question then is what will you do with His light today? How will you shine for those around you so they can feel His Presence and desire to have what you have; Christ in their heart? It's a persistent question and each day you can choose how you will answer it. As always, Jesus is ready to respond, ready to help you share His love. He will go with you because He wants to be your lifetime companion. He doesn't ever want you to walk this life alone.

His relationship with you is the key to everything else that you think and do. It is a gift of joy that comes from His Presence. As you continue to walk with Him and to share His light, your knowledge of His love will grow. You will be forever Light-hearted! What a glorious reason to give Him thanks and praise.

As we let our own light shine, we unconsciously give other people permission to do the same. ~ *Nelson Mandela*

No Need to Fear

Where God's love is, there is no fear, because God's perfect love drives out fear. *1 John 4:18, NCV*

If we had to list our fears we would probably see that we share many of the same fears.

What if we took every list we have, every fear we've written down and put them at the feet of our Savior, one by one? That would mean that we are no longer carrying those fears around in our heads, but that we've intentionally chosen to give those to God, the One who has an answer for every fear we might imagine.

Once we've set our fears down, we might be able to pick up courage, the kind of courage that only comes from God's Spirit. We might hold on to Divine hope and peace, so that new stories replace the ones that kept us paralyzed in the past.

God is real; most of your fears are imagined. The ones that truly exist in your life still need a response that allows God to help you. That means you persevere in prayer and you seek God's favor for all that causes you despair. God's love is perfectly poised to drive every fear from your heart and mind.

The wise person in the storm prays to God, not for safety from danger, but for deliverance from fear.

~ Adapted from Ralph Waldo Emerson

No Timid Souls

God did not give us a spirit that makes us afraid but a spirit of power and love and self-control. *2 Tim. 1:7, NCV*

You are so brave! Each day you rise, manage your household, walk out into the world and do your very best. You live with intention and purpose, and that's a bold move.

This Scripture reminds us that when God comes to live within our souls, creating a space in our hearts to help us grow, we have no reason to be timid. After all, we have incredible power if we allow the love of Christ to shine through us.

You may have been a wall flower in the seventh grade, or you may have been the last person to be picked for the football team, but those days are gone. You are not a timid soul because God is with you. God's work requires strength of heart and soul because that work is never done. You'll never be out of a job until the day He calls you home.

Give God praise today for investing in you. Thank Him for giving you the only power you will ever need, the kind that faces adversity, loves unconditionally, and seeks to know more of Your Creator. Yes, you are very brave indeed.

Lord, I pray today that You would release me from any fear that causes me to feel timid, but instead renew my heart with the courage to press on for You. *~ Amen*

March

Breathe In, Breathe Out!

The Spirit of God has made me; the breath of the Almighty gives me life. *Job 33:4, NIV*

Whatever obstacles we face, or whatever troubles have come our way, few of us will experience the countless tragedies that Job did. Oh, we can feel like we've had days like Job experienced, but by the grace of God we have not had one tragedy after another.

This Scripture is a good one to note though because it helps us understand why God honored Job at the end of this story and restored everything to him. Job never gave up his trust in God. Even in the worst of his situations, he was ready to breathe in the Spirit of God. He knew that he was alive in God alone and that nothing else really mattered.

Imagine having that kind of faith! As you go through the day, experiencing the ups and downs of life, remember to simply keep breathing in the Spirit of your Father in Heaven. Breathe in! Breathe out! He will honor all that you are and all that you will yet be as you stay closely connected to His love and grace.

Ask God to be with you, helping you breathe in His kindness and comfort. He's there! You can trust Him!

Do not lose heart in pursuing your spiritual life.

~ *Thomas à Kempis*

Listen and Lean In

Wise people can also listen and learn; even they can find good advice in these words. *Prov. 1:5, NCV*

Most of us can be hard of hearing. We hear what we want to hear, drowning out or ignoring the things we don't care to hear about. We listen half-heartedly to our spouse or our children assuming we know what they are going to say. We even do the same thing in church. After all, we know the Scripture reading and we've heard the stories before, so what can be new?

Listening is primarily about quieting our minds enough to take in what someone else is sharing. We must get the noises out of our heads, the white noise out of the background and lean in, focusing on each word, listening for more than the words themselves so we discover the intent and the desire behind them.

God listens to you with His whole heart. He doesn't get confused by your words and He doesn't wait for you to be brilliant, He simply hears how your heart speaks. When He talks to you through Scripture or prayer, He wants you to seek His heart alone. You are having a conversation that means the world to Him because you mean the world to Him. Lean in and really listen to each person you encounter today. You may learn some amazing things.

Lord, help me to listen more fully to You and to the people that I love today.

~ *Amen*

Look Up!

LORD, I look upward to you,
you who live in heaven. *Ps. 123:1, NCV*

When you hear news that makes you sad, you may weep, or look down as your face loses its light. Your overcast appearance reflects your mood. The gloomy feeling you have clings to you and weighs you down.

The psalmist wants to remind you that there is another approach you can take when difficulties happen, sad news envelops you, or your heart is depressed. You can look up. You can seek the face of the One who knows you and everything about the situation you now face. You can sit quietly at His feet and share your sorrow and your broken heart.

Intellectually, you may know that this is true, but emotionally, it is not easy. That means that you must come to Jesus with your heart in your hand, share that you are lost and that you need Him to help you find the way. He will offer His comfort through the Holy Spirit and bring you the peace that passes all understanding. Why will He do that? Because you are so important to Him and He won't leave you. When your spirits are low and you're feeling down, there's only one thing to do. Look up! Look up and God will draw near.

The basic command of religion is not, "Do this!" or "Do not do that!" but simply "Look!" ~ *P. Toynbee*

MARCH 4

Reach Out

In my trouble I called to the LORD. I cried out to my God for help. From his temple he heard my voice; my call for help reached his ears. *Ps. 18:6, NCV*

When something is just out of your reach, you must stretch yourself or move closer to the object you're trying to grasp. You may even have to get up from your chair to get what you wanted.

Some days, you may feel that God is out of reach. God is near you, but you may have to change your position, your thoughts, or your feeling of hopelessness. You may even have to look for Him in Scripture. When you do, it won't take long before you realize that God has heard you and that you can now reach Him.

Sometimes we call for help and we're uncertain if anyone truly hears our cries. We feel alone and vulnerable. The beauty of God's Spirit though is that He can be everywhere Present, everywhere available to those in need. He hears you from His Heavenly realm as you call Him from your earthly place. Reach out to Him whenever you have troubles that overwhelm your spirit and complicate your life. God will answer in every way that is best for your soul.

You called, You cried out, You shattered my deafness: You flashed, You shone, You scattered my blindness: You breathed fragrance, and I drew in my breath and I pant for You!

~ Augustine of Hippo

The Last Straw

That was the last straw. God had had enough of Herod's arrogance and sent an angel to strike him down. Herod had given God no credit for anything. *Acts 12:23, MSG*

One thing we learn about our relationship with God as we continue to walk with Him in faith is that He wants us to share His stories. He wants us to give Him thanks and praise for the life He has given us. He wants us to acknowledge His goodness!

So why do we hesitate to praise Him? We know that we did not create the ground we walk on. We did not create the life we are living because everything we have comes from God's endless mercy. Though God is slow to anger, it appears that with Herod even His Divine patience was worn thin.

Herod was a bully, arrogant and self-serving. You know what it feels like when you've suffered little injustices or bullying. When it goes on for some time, you finally come to the end of your forbearance. You finally hit the last straw.

God is slow to anger, but we don't want to test His patience. We want to thank Him for every blessing, big and small, that He has given us. Glorify His name!

Lord, I thank You for the gifts You've lavished on my life and on my family. Thank You for Your steadfast love!

~ Amen

You Make a Difference

I ask that you give me a heart that understands,
so I can rule the people in the right way and will know
the difference between right and wrong. *1 Kings 3:9, NCV*

Consider embroidering this prayer on a pillow or putting it on a plaque that you see every day. It's a prayer that Solomon prayed as he began to rule over Israel after the death of his father, David. God had asked Solomon what He could do for him and this was the new king's response. He didn't ask for money and power and long life. Instead, he prayed for the right heart, the kind of heart that would help him understand his people so that he could rule over them with wisdom.

You may not be ruling over anyone, but the prayer is still a good one for you to consider. Pray that you will have the right heart with your family as you help them make choices and plans.

Pray that you would have the right heart to listen intentionally at work to your boss and to the people you work with so that you could bring light to any situation. Pray that you would have the right heart for God so that you would seek to know Him even more than you do today. With the right heart, you will continue to make a difference!

It is only with the heart that one can see rightly; what is essential is invisible to the eye. *~ Antoine de Saint-Exupéry*

Why Should You Worry?

"And which of you by worrying can add one cubit to his stature? If you then are not able to do the least, why are you anxious for the rest?" *Luke 12:25-26, NKJV*

Remember how you got out a tape measure when you were a kid to see whether you were taller than your brother or your sister? Or maybe you put a little pencil mark on the wall every six months, so you could track how fast you were growing.

The example from Luke is one that reminds us that we have no power over how fast we grow, or how tall we become. In fact, we cannot influence things to happen because we want them to. We know that truth, but that information doesn't keep us from worrying.

Spending countless hours in fearful contemplation does not serve us well. In fact, no matter how hard we worry or how much sleep we lose, we cannot by sheer mental effort effect any change in our situation. In fact, worrying does the opposite thing because it saps our energy and makes us even less able to do those helpful things that we could do.

Worry is simply not productive. Worry drains your strength. So, what is your choice? You can pray and surrender all things into God's hand, or you can sit up half the night and needlessly worry. For today, choose to pray!

I worry until bedtime and then after that, I let God worry.

~ Author unknown

MARCH 8

Trouble with a Capital T

But when you hear of wars and rumors of wars, do not be troubled; for such things must happen, but the end is not yet. For nation will rise against nation, and kingdom against kingdom. And there will be earthquakes in various places, and there will be famines and troubles. *Mark 13:7-8, NKJV*

Earthquakes and tsunamis and hurricanes have devastated cities all over the globe. Drought has left some without food and water for months on end, and floods have left others seeking shelter on higher ground. These troubles are everywhere, and human beings may be able to predict them, but we can't control them. We can't keep them from happening. The only One who can control the elements of nature is the One who created them.

Troubles with this kind of disastrous scope put everything in life in perspective. They make our concerns of the day seem almost unimportant. They cause us to remember who oversees life on earth.

Trouble may land at your doorstep and when it does, take the same approach you would take if you heard a hurricane was approaching. Prepare as best you can for what's ahead, pray for protection, and leave the rest to God. He guards your life in the big things and in the little things.

Lord, be with me today as I face the troubles that surround me. Bless me with understanding to surrender all I can to You.

~ Amen

God Still Loves Me

But I am like an olive tree flourishing in the house of God;
I trust in God's unfailing love for ever and ever. *Ps. 52:8, NIV*

The olive tree is symbolic of peace and good will, as in the olive branch that the dove held in its beak when it returned to Noah. Waving an olive branch has come to mean forgiveness and peace.

The olive tree is a beautiful example of something that God created that is good and will flourish forever. David wanted to be steadfast in his faith and worthy before God. He pictured himself then as something that nourished the lives of others. God put him in a position to serve, to be strong, and to do good things. He was like the olive tree.

In our day, we might hope to be like a mighty oak, or a golden aspen, creating a sense of community as we root ourselves in the Spirit of God. Whatever the case, it's a delightful symbol of faith as we seek to grow closer to God each day. When you are rooted in His love, you can branch out and share His gifts with those around you. All you must do is plant your heart in His unfailing love and trust Him for every step you take. May God bless you with bounty beyond measure today.

Trials are the winds which root the tree of our faith.

~ C.H. Spurgeon

MARCH 10

Self-Reflection

For by the grace given me I say to every one of you: Do not think of yourself more highly than you ought, but rather think of yourself with sober judgment, in accordance with the faith God has distributed to each of you. *Rom. 12:3,* NIV

The right balance of humility and self-reflection guides us in our choices and makes a difference in how we treat others and how we worship God.

God called you to the work you do, the place you live and the lifestyle you've adopted for one reason. He wants you to know Him and to tell others what He has done. He wants you to be His ambassador in the world and extend the light of His Spirit to those around you.

Now and then, it's good to take a little inventory to see where you are in the process of spiritual growth. Are you surrendering your heart, mind, and soul to your Creator? Are you willing to seek His advice and then heed His counsel with the concerns of your heart? Do you tell others how much He means to you and give Him thanks and praise?

Those kinds of questions added to your prayers and your daily Scripture readings are what keep your faith active and alive. They keep your perspective balanced by the grace of God to continue to do all you can to honor Him with the things you do.

The longest journey is the journey inwards. ~ *Dag Hammarskjöld*

Words Will Not Fail You

Good people speak with wisdom, and they say what is fair.
The teachings of their God are in their heart,
so they do not fail to keep them. *Ps. 37:30-31, NCV*

It's embarrassing to realize that we have no excuse for being unkind or unfair. We cannot claim to not understand God's commands to love one another or to treat others in the ways we want to be treated. We are without excuse because God put His teachings in our hearts. He put a portion of Himself within us from the moment of conception, before our first steps were taken on earth. He knew we would need to be connected to Him from our first breath to our last breath.

So what does that mean to us? How does that help us with everyday living? Perhaps one thing it does is remind us to play fair. Offer hope. Give others the benefit of the doubt and be aware of our judgments and perceptions that may not tell the whole story. Pray for wisdom. Seek God's help in saying and doing the right thing wherever you are and in every circumstance.

When you're prepared to say the right thing then words will not fail you. When you're prepared to do the right thing, then God will honor your efforts. These are the things that contribute to others knowing you as a good person.

Lord, help me to speak with thoughtful words and a kind heart today.

~ Amen

Give What You Can

"Give, and you will receive. You will be given much. Pressed down, shaken together, and running over, it will spill into your lap. The way you give to others is the way God will give to you." *Luke 6:38, NCV*

You're generous! You give your time and your money to help those in need. You give advice to your friends when they ask you for it and you pray continually.

This Scripture focuses on what happens when you act in generous and giving ways. It suggests that when you give, you receive, and so giving inspires a response. It causes God to take notice of what you are doing, and He repays you in kind. He may offer you even more than what you've given to others, so much more that it will spill over into your lap. The point is that when we're generous to each other, God is also generous to us.

You don't give so that you will receive, but when you give, God wants you to get something back. He wants you to receive the richness of friendships and relationships at home and at work and in the neighborhood. He wants you to receive more of His grace and mercy and love. Give God the praise today for all He has given you. It will bring joy to your heart and renew your spirit.

The world says, "The more you take, the more you have." Christ says, "The more you give, the more you are."

~ *Frederick Buechner*

MARCH 13

Don't Give Up!

But you should be strong. Don't give up, because you will get a reward for your good work. *2 Chron. 15:7, NCV*

The thought of achieving a goal or getting a reward makes the effort worthwhile. When you start something new, you're excited and you could work at your project for hours because it means so much to you.

About midway through to the finish line, you're faced with obstacles. You begin to have doubts about the direction and the strength of your work. It takes perseverance then to keep at it and not give up.

When your spirits are lagging and you're wondering whether it's worth it to keep going, go back to the beginning. Remind yourself why you thought this work was so important. Review your motives and your intentions and then take it all to God in prayer. Sure, there are projects that are best put aside midstream, but most of the time, you simply need to stay strong. Stay focused on your original goals and God will help you to succeed. He knows what you are trying to accomplish and if you've asked for His blessing and guidance, then you will get to the goal.

When you work toward goals as though you are working for God, He will reward you beyond measure.

Lord, help me to never give up on those things that You have blessed and inspired me to do. *~ Amen*

Forgive Others

"Yes, if you forgive others for their sins, your Father in heaven will also forgive you for your sins." *Matt. 6:14, NCV*

When someone offends us, we believe we have a right to expect an apology. We imagine they owe us some sign of regret or remorse for their actions. We want to be sure that they understand how much they have hurt us.

Here's the thing. Though your thoughts may well be correct in the sense of the circumstance in question, they leave off a critical element. They continue to point fingers at the other person, keeping the story of the offense freshly brewing in your mind. In fact, left to only wait for the apology, your spirit is wounded over and over again.

God wants to free you of the pain caused when someone hurts you and so He wisely sets up a condition. It's pretty sweet when you think about it. He says, "Forgive the offender. When you do, I can forgive you for one of the times you offended Me."

If there's even the slightest chance that you've done something to offend your Father in Heaven, then this is one way to rectify things. Forgive your enemies with your heart and mind. Forgive others as swiftly as you can, and your heart will be blessed, and your spirit will be lighter... because God will have forgiven you!

Forgiveness doesn't change the past, but it changes the future.

~ Author unknown

Delivering Heartfelt Prayers

For I know that as you pray for me and the Spirit of Jesus Christ helps me, this will lead to my deliverance. *Phil. 1:19, NLT*

When you're struggling with a personal matter that you simply can't resolve on your own, you may seek the prayers of people close to you. When you ask them to pray, you are sharing your heart and letting them know you feel vulnerable and uncertain. It's not always easy to make that kind of prayer request.

Today, you may seek heartfelt prayers, or you might consider being one of the friends who offers to do the praying. When a friend or associate specifically asks for your prayers, make a commitment to them. Commit to pray, not just once, but on a regular basis for the needs that they have. Your prayers then combined with others of like mind rise to the throne of God.

You know the prayers of others make a difference. They usher in the Spirit of Christ and bring hope for deliverance. Whenever anyone requests your prayers, honor them, and honor God by committing to pray. Your heartfelt and loving prayers usher in the help of Heaven.

Prayer offered in holiness from a faithful heart rises like incense from a holy altar. *~ Augustine of Hippo*

That Does Not Compute

Trust in the LORD with all your heart, and lean not on your own understanding. *Prov. 3:5, NKJV*

As a Christian, you have a desire to understand more fully the things of God and so you keep praying and reading Scripture and learning from those who have gained insight and wisdom. It's all good!

The interesting thing though is that to really understand the things of God, you have to step aside from things that you can memorize or challenge in a debate or read about. You can fill your head with great gobs of knowledge, but you won't understand much at all until your heart is engaged. Your heart is the place where you first accepted Jesus as your Lord and Savior and so it is the center of truth and understanding for you. It is the place where you can lean in and learn from His Spirit.

Everything you do, requires that you trust the Lord. You trust that He'll protect you as you go to work or take your children to school. You trust that He knows your situation at home and that He sees you right where you are. Your head may not always recognize His hand at work, but when you trust Him, your heart will know that He is with you always, providing, protecting, and guiding your way.

Lord, when things in my life simply do not compute, I lean on You and trust You with all my heart. *~ Amen*

Faith of Our Fathers

My ancestors Abraham and Isaac served our God,
and like a shepherd God has led me all my life. *Gen. 48:15, NCV*

You didn't come to faith totally on your own. God initiated the gift of faith and hoped you would respond. It's likely also that someone in your family influenced your path of faith. If it wasn't a family member, then by the grace of God, you connected with someone who helped you understand more about faith.

God depends on people we know and on the believers, the ones who came before us, to guide our faith experience. Your ancestors in faith may not be related to you, but they are part of your family nevertheless. They are the ones who prayed for you before you were born, seeking God's love and mercy for the generations that followed them on earth.

The faith exhibited by the fathers and the mothers who came before you are part of the foundation of all that you believe today. They nurtured you to walk in the path of God, so that He could one day Shepherd you one to one.

Today, give thanks and praise to God for the people who came before you and paved the way for you to discover the One true guardian of your soul.

The family was ordained by God before he established any other institution, even before he established the church.

~ *Billy Graham*

The Good Old Days

Don't ask, "Why was life better in the 'good old days'?"
It is not wise to ask such questions. *Eccles. 7:10, NCV*

Probably most of us can think back to a time in our lives where we felt a measure of contentment and a sense that all was right with the world. Granted, it may not have lasted long, but still the memory is there and every now and then you picture that moment. So, what's wrong with looking back and wishing you could be there again?

Solomon in his wisdom offers the thought that it is better to just not go there. Don't ask such questions. Perhaps the wisdom in it has to do with realizing that the precious present is really all we have. The moment we're living in is the one that God has ordained and since He always wants us to keep our eyes on Him to help us move forward, looking back challenges our progress. After all, we still remember what happened to Lot's wife. We don't want to be permanently stopped in our tracks. Looking back tends to keep us from desiring to move forward no matter what is going on.

The "good old days" may well be worthy of a smile and some reflection, but the good present days need your attention right now. Make them as smile worthy as you can. With God at your side, they are likely to be blessed.

It's always a good day to make new memories.

Don't Be Afraid

"Don't be afraid, I've redeemed you. I've called your name. You're mine. When you're in over your head, I'll be there with you. When you're in rough waters, you will not go down. When you're between a rock and a hard place, it won't be a dead end—Because I am God, your personal God." *Isa. 43:1-2, MSG*

Life is full of drama and most of it is not in your control. The good news though is that your own personal life preserver has your back. He knows your name and He will not let you get in over your head. All you must do is acknowledge Him and He will help you hold on.

God has not only redeemed you, but He knows you by name and He has claimed you as His own. That means that you're His child and He does not forsake you. He wants only what is best for you and He's always looking out for you. It's personal for Him. Your relationship matters, and He does not want you to venture out into the world alone.

Whatever you must do today, remember that you have an invisible means of support, a life raft, and it's always there for you. There may be rough waters, but you are assured that peace will prevail.

The relationship between you and God is more private and intimate than any possible relation between two people could ever be.

~ *Adapted from C.S. Lewis*

In Happy Harmony

Be happy with those who are happy, and weep with those who weep. Live in harmony with each other. *Rom. 12:15-16, NLT*

Our sense of family and community connection is never greater than when we are celebrating together. We love to share in the joy of a new baby whose parents beam with delight. We applaud as newly married couples walk back down the aisle. It's glorious because we relate to each moment with joy and warm memories of our own experiences.

Hearts that play together, also grieve together when a loved one has passed into the arms of Jesus, or some misfortune requires a commitment to prayer. God has designed us to be people of compassion with hearts that truly can love our neighbors as ourselves.

These moments that are shared are ones that bring harmony to our souls and joy to our spirits. We recognize how blessed we are to have each other and how gracious God is to help us establish loving relationships.

Today, take a moment to pray for the people who are closest to you. These are the ones who will be there when you are totally happy, and who will comfort you when you need the gift of their strength and presence. You know who those people are in your life. Thank God for each one.

Lord, I give You the glory for the amazing people You have put in my life.

~ *Amen*

You Know You Blew It!

For the kind of sorrow God wants us to experience leads us away from sin and results in salvation. There's no regret for that kind of sorrow. But worldly sorrow, which lacks repentance, results in spiritual death. *2 Cor. 7:10, NLT*

This Scripture causes us to focus on the difference between those things that grieve our hearts as human beings, and those things that grieve our hearts in our personal relationship with God. Both kinds of grief are meaningful, but only one results in spiritual renewal.

Chances are good that you've lived long enough to make a huge mistake. All you can think about is that you know you blew it. You did it all by yourself and no matter how many excuses you might give, or how hard you might try to blame others for your indiscretion, there's only one truth. You were wrong!

Worldly sorrow may motivate you to change so that you behave differently than you did before. Spiritual sorrow though will bring your heart straight to the throne of God, the place where forgiveness prevails, and you can be changed inwardly by His Spirit. Only in God's Presence, can you experience saving grace.

It's a new day. Forgive yourself for the things that are past and give God the glory for redeeming you with great love.

God loves us not because of who we are, but because of who HE is!

~ Author unknown

Foolish Me

"But everyone who hears these words of mine and does not put them into practice is like a foolish man who built his house on sand." *Matt. 7:26, NIV*

You've got some sand between your toes because you've done a foolhardy thing a time or two. The good news is that the love of Christ has gotten you past your craziness and He's washed your feet with mercy. You stand on a firm foundation that will never fail you.

We can stand on our Savior's grace and love, firm in our direction and motivated by all the right things and still have days of being, oh, so foolish. We may not even be certain why, but we know it happens. We make one seemingly insignificant decision, tell a little white lie or omit something too uncomfortable to discuss with our spouse, only to have that small thing come back to cause disgrace. Our foolish ways make us stumble, probably because we have too much sand on our feet.

As you walk with the Lord today, ask Him to help you remain steady and strong in your pursuit to do the right thing. Seek His protection against your own foolishness and allow Him to guide your steps.

Save all the sand for a walk on the beach. That way, the tide will continue to favor you and those you love. Be wise!

He is truly wise who looks upon all earthly things as folly that he may gain Christ.

~ *Thomas à Kempis*

Life Is Sticky

"Behold, I am the LORD, the God of all flesh. Is there anything too hard for Me?" *Jer. 32:27, NKJV*

Sometimes we try to help God along. Our prayers are not as much about surrendering to let God's will be done, as they are apt to give suggestions about how God might handle our troubles. It's a natural thought, but maybe not the best thing we can do. Maybe we'd do better to remember the question posed here to Jeremiah. "Is there anything too hard for Me?" Is there anything too hard for God to handle?

Of course, it's not a trick question. The answer is simple. There is nothing that's too hard for God to handle. Today, see what you can do to take your sticky life situations and truly put them in God's hands. Don't leave some of the problems you face, stuck to your fingers so that you try to act on them, but let your troubles go. Let them roll off your shoulders and cast them on the only One who can truly carry them. After all, He's carried the weight of the entire world for generations.

It's your day to let God be God. Draw near to Him and share your deepest concerns and then go out in total trust that He will do all that He can to help you. When you do, your heart will no longer be troubled.

Lord, I know that nothing is too hard for You. I surrender my current troubles to You. *~ Amen*

MARCH 24

Following in the Steps of Faith

The steps of a good man are ordered by the LORD,
and He delights in his way. *Ps. 37:23, NKJV*

God delights in our walk with Him. He orders our steps, organizes our thoughts, and helps us to move in ways that please Him. We only have to follow the path He has set for us.

Imagine a parent who plans a scavenger hunt for their child, giving special clues to help the child get to each goal. The parent cheers vigorously as the child finds each special clue. If you could apply that image to your life in Christ, you might imagine Him going ahead of you on the path of life, delighted as He notes the places you will go, beaming with pride as you discover the gifts that He has designed just for you. No one will cheer more enthusiastically than He will when your path finally leads right up to His door. What fun it will be for both of you!

Sometimes we think that we must go about our work and carry out our plans all by ourselves, but the truth is, God has already gone before you, planning each step and delighting in your way. Thank Him today for helping you discover more of Him as you stay on the path of salvation.

Lead kindly light, amid the encircling gloom;
The night is dark and I am far from home.
Keep Thou my feet, I do not ask to see,
The distant scene: one step is enough for me! ~ *J.H. Newman*

MARCH 25

Power Talk

Men shall speak of the might of Your awesome acts,
and I will declare Your greatness. *Ps. 145:6, NKJV*

No doubt you've heard some powerful speakers in your life. You may recall portions of their speeches because their words impacted you in a significant way. There's nothing like a good power talk.

You're a power speaker too. Every time you choose to share the stories that demonstrate God's awesome acts in your life, you are blessed with power. You are blessed with messages that ignite the hearts and minds of your listeners wherever you happen to be. God honors you each time you whole-heartedly share His greatness.

Think about your life in the past few days. Do you have a story to tell about how God showed up and made a difference in the direction you took, or in the results you obtained from your work? Do you have a story of how your child said a fervent prayer that made your heart rejoice? You have lots of power talks you could give to those around you. Just know that when you share your stories, you're paving the way for someone to think more intentionally about God's magnificence. You're helping the story to continue.

Keep on talking!

Lord, I will declare Your greatness to people I know today.

~ *Amen*

Don't Panic

"'I've picked you. I haven't dropped you.' Don't panic.
I'm with you. There's no need to fear for I'm your God.
I'll give you strength. I'll help you. I'll hold you steady,
keep a firm grip on you." Isa. 41:10, MSG

You can get a little panicky when too many things go wrong at once. It can feel like your world is crashing down around you and there's nothing you can do to stop it. Whatever it is that strikes fear in your heart, God wants you to know this one thing. He's with you.

This Scripture from Isaiah is beautifully put in *The Message* Bible. It says in no uncertain terms that God has your back. He sees what is happening and He will not leave you to handle your circumstances or situation all alone. He's there with you, around you, above you and holding on to you. He will never let go because He is stronger than any force, or any fear, or any disheartening story you may be dealing with.

Today, just hold on and trust that God is near and that He has plans to care for you and protect you and watch over you all the days of your life. You are important to Him. You always have been, and you always will be. Just trust Him with your whole heart.

To hold to God is to rely on the fact that God is there for me, and to live in this certainty. ~ *Karl Barth*

MARCH 27

Don't Beat Yourself Up

He said to her, "Daughter, your faith has healed you. Go in peace and be freed from your suffering." *Mark 5:34, NIV*

Remember the story of the woman who touched the garment of Jesus as He walked through the crowded streets? People pressed near Him from every side. The woman was in the crowd. She had been hemorrhaging for nearly twelve years. When she heard that Jesus was passing through the town, she could only think of one thing. She believed with all her heart that if she simply could touch the hem of His garment, she would be healed.

She knew that she was considered unclean and that she could never enjoy peaceful and loving relationships with family and friends. She had been an outcast and yet she had done nothing wrong. She simply was ill, and no doctor of her day had a cure. She needed Jesus.

Her strong faith guided her toward the man she had heard so much about. Despite the harsh looks she probably received from those who knew of her, she pressed on and finally got close enough to reach out to Him and touch the hem of His robe. She was healed in an instant. Such faith and trust are rewarded by our Heavenly Father. Let your faith insist that you walk closer to Him today.

Let us keep to Christ, and cling to Him, and hang on Him, so that no power can remove us. ~ *Martin Luther*

MARCH 28

A Work in Progress

Be diligent in these matters; give yourself wholly to them, so that everyone may see your progress. Watch your life and doctrine closely. *1 Tim. 4:15-16, NIV*

Most of us are a work in progress when it comes to our faith. We learn a bit more about what it means to be a Christian and walk with God each day. Sometimes we enjoy the learning process and other times we wonder if we're the only ones who still need tutoring. Of course, we all need teaching and studying and reflecting on God's Word to grow. It's not easy, but it's good for the soul.

Timothy suggests we be diligent, meticulous, and work hard to learn as quickly as we can. We must give our whole hearts to the work, praying often and turning to Scripture for guidance so we can apply it to life.

As you pursue your life in Christ, your light shines and others are more aware of who you are. They look to your example of what it means to be a person of faith. They may take their own faith walk more seriously. Keep learning and pay close attention to all the things God has shown you. You're working hard and you're making great progress!

You can go anywhere, do everything and be completely curious about the universe. But only a rare person now and then is curious enough to want to know God. ~ *Adapted from A.W. Tozer*

MARCH 29

Your Inheritance

Now I commit you to God and to the word of his grace, which can build you up and give you an inheritance among all those who are sanctified. *Acts 20:32, NIV*

Perhaps one of the most humbling and amazing thoughts for believers is the understanding that God has already set aside our inheritance. He already knows what He plans to give each of us. How can He know what to give each one of us? He knows the same way that you know the members of your family. He knows who you are and what you do, and He knows how much you love Him.

The beautiful thing about His legacy is that it never ends. It won't die out a few generations from now. It surpasses any DNA test because you have been adopted and are an heir of His grace and mercy.

When your earthly life disappoints you or confuses you, it can be helpful to think joyfully about your eternal life, the promise of what will yet come. God wants you to continue to live all your days joyfully, covered by His Spirit. Live in His light and in His grace and mercy and offer Him a heart of gratitude for the things He does, even now to help you. He loves to see you smile.

This is all the inheritance I can give to my dear family. The religion of Christ can give them one which will make them rich indeed.

~ Patrick Henry

MARCH 30

One to One

Draw near to God and He will draw near to you.
Cleanse your hands, you sinners; and purify your hearts,
you double-minded. *James 4:8, NKJV*

Perhaps when we read a Scripture like this one, we're tempted to think of people we would imagine James would talk to even today. We recognize those who appear to operate with double standards, or who seem to say one thing, but do another. Like Pontius Pilate, their hands are dirty, and they may have trouble removing the stains.

Once we get past those thoughts, it's worthwhile to check in with our spirits and seek God's face. Have we done anything that might appear double minded? Are we in need of cleansing for jealous or wrongful or even unkind thoughts? The chances are that our personal inventory will cause us to admit we have done those things. We have walked away from God.

The blessing God offers though is that when we draw near to Him, He will quickly move closer to us. When He is near us, we can seek His help in making wise decisions, and in not yielding to even the smallest temptations. God will cleanse us from head to toe so that we can shine for Him wherever we may be. Take heart! God is near you even now.

Lord, I pray that You would stay so close to me today that nothing can come between us. *~ Amen*

Pack Up Your Troubles

The righteous cry out, and the LORD hears,
and delivers them out of all their troubles. *Ps. 34:17, NKJV*

We can spend our time counting our troubles, or we can spend our time counting our blessings. The tug-of-war that we experience though is a matter of trust.

When things are going well for us, we can easily give God the glory. When things are not going well for us, we tend to wonder if God is still available to us, or if He even knows the trouble we're in. Then we get lost in worry and we forget who we are. We forget that we are sons and daughters of the Living God, the same God that we read about in the Bible. This God created the universe. This God does miraculous things! This God knows us intimately and this God loves us so much that He sent His Son to redeem us.

When the Son redeemed us, God counted that as our righteousness. That's not something we could achieve on our own. We've been delivered out of all our troubles, because we've been delivered from sin and death. Now that you know you are truly delivered, it's a great day to simply count your blessings! The first blessing is knowing that you can always count on God!

What a world this would be if we could forget our troubles as easily as we forget our blessings. *~ Author unknown*

April

Make a U-Turn Here!

Why, then, have the people of Jerusalem gone the wrong way and not turned back? They believe their own lies and refuse to turn around and come back. *Jer. 8:5, NCV*

It would be helpful to have clear signs in life, perhaps like the ones we see on the highway: "Wrong Way" or "No U-Turns!" Signs like that might help when we're getting ready to make a foolish decision, or when we're walking in the wrong direction.

God has been providing signs for us since He created us. Jesus performed miracles in plain sight of the people of His day. The Holy Spirit puts up signs all over the planet and often whispers directly into our ears, saying, "Wrong way. Make a U-turn!"

We don't need bigger billboards. What we need are eyes to see and ears to hear. We need a willingness to turn around and seek after God. God will guide and direct us, but He will not force us to do the right thing. He will not make us listen or follow Him. He will wait patiently for us to wake up and see Him.

If it's time for a U-turn in your life, then don't wait. Do it today. When you do, you'll be surprised at the peace you'll have in your heart. You can believe that things will turn for the better!

Lord, You are the only one who can turn my life around, I pray that You will be with me as I hasten to come to You. ~ *Amen*

Need a Safety Net?

I will say to the LORD, "You are my place of safety and protection. You are my God and I trust you." *Ps. 91:2, NCV*

When you are going through difficult times, the thing you want most is to simply get through them, get to the other side so you don't have to deal with them anymore. You want to get safely past the messes and not have any cause to worry.

Perhaps what the psalmist is trying to say here is that you can walk your tightrope, hoping you won't fall, hoping the rope will hold you up, or you can put your trust in God. You can place your situation in God's hand and He will support you. He will be your safety net, ready to catch you any moment if your foot should slip. He sees you and He wants you to rest in Him.

Sure, you can stay up on the tightrope if you want, but God has better plans for you. He wants you to come on down and trust Him and allow Him to keep your heart and your mind on solid ground. Nothing can separate you from Him. Nothing can draw you away from His protection.

When you need a safety net, just know that you don't have to worry. You simply must step forward in faith and God will be with you no matter how tight a spot you're in.

If you don't place your foot on the rope, you'll never cross the chasm.
~ Author unknown

APRIL 3

The Source for Good

There I will go to the altar of God, to God—the source of all my joy. I will praise you with my harp, O God, my God! *Ps. 43:4, NLT*

If you're counting more troubles than joys, it might be good to remember the One who is your Source of hope and possibility. The shadows of adversity can cause the blessings in your life to be dimmed, but they can't erase them. Adversity may bring temporary blindness, but God is anxious for you to see His Light again.

Perhaps today, you could take the opportunity to thank God for every good thing you can imagine. Thank Him for a warm bed where you can safely rest. Thank Him for family and friends and caregivers and those who minister to your spirit. Give Him praise for the opportunities He gives you every moment of the day to reach out to Him, share your troubles and seek His guidance.

Your Light, your Source for good far outweighs the things that would bring your spirit to despair. Move those shadows aside and turn your face toward the sunlight. The Holy Spirit will comfort you and bless you and fill your heart with peace. God always seeks your good and He is close beside you every moment of the day.

Lord, thank You for drawing near to me when I am uncertain and afraid. I know that You are watching over me and that all good things are possible with You. *~ Amen*

Pushing Against the Boundaries

Obviously, the law applies to those to whom it was given, for its purpose is to keep people from having excuses, and to show that the entire world is guilty before God. *Rom. 3:19, NLT*

Human beings are always pushing the boundaries. We like to know where the limits are so we can step around them or go over them. We imagine that somehow, we won't get caught and that we have matters well in control. Both things are wrong.

We are not in control and we will always get caught. It's a lifelong lesson and God continues to make every effort to help us understand His guidelines, His boundaries for our lives. It would be entirely frustrating to Him and to us, except for one thing. God knows us so well that He planned a way for us to be forgiven, to be redeemed, each time adversity comes to our door. He opened His heart to us and like a mother protecting her child, He draws us close, even when we fall or walk away from Him.

If you have pushed against the boundaries, ask God to guide you safely to the place He would have you be. He will hold you close and help you do better next time. There are no boundaries around His love for you.

God, who needs nothing, loves into existence wholly superfluous creatures in order that He may love and perfect them.

~ C.S. Lewis

When Storms Are Brewing

When the storms of life come, the wicked are whirled away, but the godly have a lasting foundation. *Prov. 10:25, NLT*

Most of us would probably opt to evacuate our home if we heard a hurricane was heading straight for our beach house. After all, we know the kind of devastation a hurricane can bring as winds and tornados and ocean surges whirl with fury. We can make a good choice when storms are brewing.

We may find ourselves in a kind of storm in our spiritual life surrounded by people and ideas and temptations that might cause us to spin out of control and fall. We don't want to be swept away by forces that we don't even understand.

The good news is that we don't have to be. We can stand on the firm foundation of God's promises and His love. He will hold fast to us and protect us when we're faced with difficult choices and people are pressuring us to move in directions that don't feel safe or even right. When a spiritual storm comes up, you can evacuate the danger zones and move closer to safety as you draw near to God. Remember that you are never alone and that God Himself will quiet the storms of life that come up. Rest in His care today.

Lord, please protect me when I feel pressured or tempted to step aside from Your strength and love. Let me always stay safely in Your hand. *~ Amen*

Obstacles and Opinions

Instead, make up your mind not to put any stumbling block or obstacle in the way of a brother or sister. I am convinced, being fully persuaded in the Lord Jesus, that nothing is unclean in itself. But if anyone regards something as unclean, then for that person it is unclean. *Rom. 14:13-14, NIV*

Chances are good that on any given subject, you'll discover a wide variety of opinions. Some people deliver their opinions with such authority that it is hard to resist believing them. If the opinions they share are based on truth and wisdom, then it's probably good to listen.

Sometimes though, people with strong opinions are skilled at throwing meaningless roadblocks into their discussion. They offer you a stream of imagined facts that can leave you reeling with uncertainty.

Generally, a range of opinions is fine. You can safely believe and operate in the ways that seem best to you. When it comes to God though, the best course to take is to go straight to the Source, to the One who holds the truth in His hands. When in doubt, stay alert and give your spirit a chance to discern what is true through God's Word. He will meet you there.

Lord, thank You that within the boundaries of Your love, we can hold a variety of opinions and still not offend You. Help me to trust You in all ways. *~ Amen*

Faith and Promises

And we desire that each one of you show the same diligence to the full assurance of hope until the end, that you do not become sluggish, but imitate those who through faith and patience inherit the promises. *Heb. 6:11-12, NKJV*

You've probably got as many plates spinning in the air as you can possibly manage. Parts of your world are going well, but other parts are turned upside down, spinning out of control, and you're not sure how to balance them again. It makes you weary to keep trying and you wonder if God is even aware of all that you're going through.

Take heart! God knows your struggles and He recognizes how difficult your days can be. He stands close to you, holding on to you with His strength to bring peace to your soul. Rest in His care. He invites you to put all those spinning plates at His feet.

When you just don't know how to unravel the mess, lean on the One who can smooth things out. Continue in hope, knowing that He works for your good and that He has a plan for a brighter future.

Don't give in to anxiety, or the stress that feels like a weight on your shoulders. Stop juggling things by yourself. Simply wrap your heart around Jesus, and let Him work out the details of your challenges. He is with you now.

Jesus did not come to make God's love possible, but to make God's love visible. *~ Author unknown*

Do Good Things

And you shall do what is right and good in the sight of the Lord, that it may be well with you. *Deut. 6:18, NKJV*

You're the answer. You're the answer to the person who needs a smile, a kind word, or a gesture of human decency. You're the one who can reach out and change the gloom that permeates the air. How is that possible?

You're a child of God, someone who knows that with God all things work together for good. You're the one who has been nurtured to do good things for others. He needs you to be His smile, His glimmer of hope to the people around you.

You do good things all the time because you want to please God and because He has put a measure of His love inside your heart to share with others. The more you share, the more you will have to give away. In fact, God will be sure that your heart overflows with His goodness and love and you will never run out of what He offers you.

Today, be encouraged, because you're doing great works with love and humility. Go out and do good things, simply because God has put His love in your heart. As you do, it's sure to be an awesome day.

No individual has any right to come into the world and go out of it without leaving something behind.

~ George Washington Carver

No More Excuses

"But they all with one accord began to make excuses. The first said to him, 'I have bought a piece of ground, and I must go and see it. I ask you to have me excused.'" *Luke 14:18, NKJV*

Some of those Jesus called to be His followers dropped everything and simply followed Him. Others were excited about Him and said they'd love to join Him, but… but, they had things to do first. They answered "Yes, but…"

They were just like us! Some days, we are on fire for the Lord, ready to follow Him and be His light. We're inspired to do all we can to help others see Him and come to Him. Other days we're still saying yes,we want to follow Him, but we've got a few other things to attend to first. We give Him our excuses as though those excuses make sense to Him.

God is not asking you to leave your home and your work and your responsibilities behind, but He is still seeking followers. He's still looking for those people who would willingly dedicate their time and their lives to Him.

When He calls you today, how will you answer? Are you willing to simply follow Him wherever He leads? He promises to guide you with love all your life.

Lord, forgive me when I give You my own small excuses for not following You. Let me always be a willing and loving servant.

~ Amen

Prayer Poppers

Lord, listen carefully to the prayer of your servant and the prayers of your servants who love to honor you. *Neh. 1:11, NCV*

Most of us haven't quite figured out how to pray "without ceasing" as it says in 1 Thessalonians. We often find it helpful to say quick prayers, many times throughout the day. These simple prayer poppers are meant to remind you that you can turn to God in heartfelt prayer any time you want and as often as you want. It is one of His most amazing gifts God gives to His children. He hears you whenever you pray.

When your heart is heavy, it can feel good to simply offer quiet reflective prayers, thanking God for being with you, giving God praise for all that He does and all that He has yet to do to help your situation.

Prayer makes you feel better. It turns the light of hope back on. It gives you something to do that will benefit you and those you are concerned about. You probably know by now that worry brings no benefit whatsoever. It's not even a good way to pass the time, but prayer is always helpful.

Send out a few prayer poppers today, just little thoughts and opportunities to put your worries in God's hands. He knows your heart and He will hear every word you speak.

Prayer is faith in God, not faith in prayer. *~ Author unknown*

APRIL 11

Life Lessons

GOD, teach me lessons for living so I can stay the course. Give me insight so I can do what you tell me — my whole life one long, obedient response. *Ps. 119:33, MSG*

By now your book of life lessons is probably pretty well written. Oh, you've got several entries left to make, but the ones you've already written down and taken to heart have done a good job of guiding you through life. Most of those lessons weren't easily understood, so you've learned to observe others to get a good sense of what God would have you do in a similar situation. As you mature spiritually, your learning curve isn't quite as steep.

Even though you've learned a lot, God isn't done with you yet. In fact, He will be teaching you some of the most important lessons of your life in the days ahead. He wants you to understand His ways so that you can stay the course from here to Heaven.

Today, seek God's guidance and pray for insight to understand a circumstance that you have not understood before. Let Him show you what He wants for you and from you so that you can continue to walk with Him and learn from Him each day. He's always ready to share more time with you.

Lord, help me to look for You in all that I do today so that I can walk the path You designed for me. *~ Amen*

APRIL 12

Teach Me How to Live

You will teach me how to live a holy life.
Being with you will fill me with joy; at your right
hand I will find pleasure forever. *Ps. 16:11, NCV*

When you consider the opportunities God gives you each day, guiding you and teaching you how to live, do you find His ways challenging? Do you find that His support and love make a difference in the ways you understand life and the choices that you make?

The psalmist wanted God to teach him how to be holy, how to live a life that was intentionally, reverently, holy. He wanted that because he knew that when he stayed close to God, he felt good. He felt protected and loved and there was nothing that gave him more joy than knowing God was a continual presence in his life.

When you walk with God, you realize that there's nothing more amazing in this world than knowing He is by your side, comforting you in the hard times, lifting your spirits and returning you to great joy. Give God thanks and praise for all that He is doing in your life right now. Seek to be holy as He is holy!

In the morning, prayer is the key that opens to us the treasures of God's mercies and blessings; in the evening, it is the key that shuts us up under His protection and safeguard.

~ *Henry Ward Beecher*

Wandering and Wondering

Remember the miracles he has done,
his wonders, and his decisions. *1 Chron. 16:12, NCV*

Sometimes you have to let the dust settle from the past and look for new direction and opportunity. It's good to take a little inventory about where you are and where you want to go.

During that time of wandering and wondering, remind yourself about the things God has done for you personally. His miracles may not be as obvious as parting the Red Sea, but you have been a recipient of His miraculous ways. See His hand in the most mundane things, the ones you may take for granted. The very fact that you can live and breathe and think for yourself and make choices every day for how you will live, are part of His design, part of His plan for you. He made you and He put you in the family you have because He had wonders to perform. He made incredible decisions just for you.

He opened your heart to the love of Christ, and He caused your spirit to rejoice in knowing your salvation is assured. Remember today, that God is still making decisions that will influence and affect your life and He is still in the miracle business. He is with you wherever you go.

Lord, I get lost now and then and it helps me to think about all You've done for me in the past. I know You are with me now and I thank You.
~ *Amen*

APRIL 14

Blinded by the Light

My companions led me by the hand into Damascus, because the brilliance of the light had blinded me. *Acts 22:11, NIV*

Imagine that blinding light that hit Paul as he walked toward Damascus, intending to do what he could to stop the followers of Christ. Jesus had stopped him in his journey and temporarily put Paul in the dark so that Paul could adjust his vision toward the light.

Perhaps you've wandered in the darkness before, and stumbled along, waiting for more direction. You've wondered if anyone would be there to help you and guide you to the place you wanted to go. The thing is that when you're in spiritual darkness, you need a Divine guide because you can't find your way alone.

Be assured that you can always reach up to Heaven and ask Jesus to draw near to you. Reach out to believers around you and let them know you feel blind and you're praying to see God's hand at work in your life again. Open your heart to the One who calls you by name. Temporary blindness happens to all of us. The gift of God is that He has ushered us into the steadfast Light and love of His Son.

If I stoop into a dark tremendous sea of cloud, it is but for a time; I press God's lamp close to my breast; its splendor, soon or late, will pierce the gloom: I shall emerge one day. ~ *Robert Browning*

Listen to Your Heart

Listen to his instructions, and store them in your heart. *Job 22:22, NLT*

Products that require some assembly, usually come with instructions. You may follow those instructions word for word and step by step. If you've assembled an item before, you may skip the instructions and just get to work. Of course, you may find yourself referring to the manual for that one thing that you forgot.

When you think about all that Job went through, not to assemble a product, but to understand life, it is amazing to realize that he still waited to hear God's instructions. He knew that he didn't understand what was going on. He knew that even if he tried to build something that might make sense to his mind, it didn't make sense to his heart. He knew that if he was going to get his life fixed, once and for all, he had to wait and listen to God's instructions.

It's important to note though that Job's instructions weren't going to serve him well if he simply tried to listen and understand. He had to take the step of keeping God's words in his heart. Only then would he be able to rebuild his life. Whether you are building a DIY project or a foundation for your faith, remember to listen for God's voice. When you listen God can make all things new.

Lord, help me to take Your Word to heart today and listen to Your instructions for my life. *~ Amen*

The Antidote

So you should certainly obey him when he says simply, 'Go and wash and be cured!' *2 Kings 5:13, NLT*

If you don't feel well, you may finally give in and go to the doctor. The only cure for your malady is to fill the prescription the doctor gives you and be diligent about it. After all, you want to get better.

Some of us refuse to take the doctor's advice. We prefer to live with the ailment or hope it will somehow go away on its own. We resist the antidote, the solution, the cure, even though it's a rather simple path to getting better.

This attitude may be why some of us resist the idea of salvation. We can see the world is ailing, and that we have personal diseases that simply can't be healed, sins that can't be wiped away with intervention and yet, we don't want to go for the cure. We don't want to wash away our sins by the gift of God's Son. It's hard to imagine why anyone would choose to remain in the muck that life brings, when we can be healed. We simply have to ask for the cure.

No matter what your body may go through in this life, with Jesus, you're healed. You have life eternal by God's love and mercy. Stay healthy and strong in His love today. With Him, you'll be made perfect.

Before an individual can be saved, he must first learn that he cannot save himself.

~ *M.R. DeHaan*

What God Wants

Be shepherds of God's flock that is under your care, watching over them—not because you must, but because you are willing, as God wants you to be. *1 Pet. 5:2, NIV*

You have a flock, people who are in your care and keeping. It may be your family, or your friends at work or at school. It may be your siblings or the group you work out with on Tuesdays. Wherever it is, you have a sense that you want to protect them and watch out for them.

The difference between those that take care of others because they must, and those who watch out for people around them because they want to, is important to recognize. The person hired to watch the sheep may take off when troubles come. The person who is watching out for others because they want to, never considers the cost or the inconvenience. They do it because they have a desire to shepherd those around them.

What God wants from you then is to know what flock you are willing to shepherd. What group would you watch over with your whole heart? Once you pick a flock to watch over, He'll give you the strength and the love and the compassion to do the job well. He simply wants your heart to be in it. Since you're already part of His flock, He gives you all you need to help those around you.

The world doesn't care what you know until they know that you care. ~ *David Harvard*

Plant More Seeds

"But the seed falling on good soil refers to someone who hears the word and understands it. This is the one who produces a crop, yielding a hundred, sixty or thirty times what was sown." *Matt. 13:23, NIV*

Do you ever feel like you're out of options? You've tried everything you can think of to fix a problem or to take initiative in your job, but the results are never what you hoped for. You don't get a good return on your investment. When that happens, you must consider what else to do.

One solution is simply to plant more seeds. You don't want to plant just any seeds, because you want to expand the possibilities, and find new soil. When you take the time to plant more seeds, you may discover that some of them open doors you never dreamed could open. Some of them will give you a lead or spark an idea toward something you had not considered before.

You're never stuck. You're never out of choices. God has created you with skills and talents that allow you opportunities to grow and change and begin again. If you're looking for better soil to plant new seeds, seek God's direction. He planted you right where you are, and He will surely help you grow.

Lord, thank You for giving me new seeds to plant so that I grow stronger in You.

~ *Amen*

APRIL 19

Glimmers of Hope

Now hope does not disappoint, because the love of God has been poured out in our hearts by the Holy Spirit who was given to us. *Rom. 5:5, NKJV*

Hope is one of the essential building blocks of life. It moves us forward and motivates us to try harder. It renews our energy as we launch a new project or try a different direction. It lives in our hearts and it thrives there.

Yet, sometimes the things we hope for don't happen, or at least they don't happen in the way that we expected. Does that mean we are disappointed by hope? Perhaps at first, we would say yes, but then we realize that it isn't hope that disappointed us at all. Hope was there for us, cheering us on, helping us want to do better.

We need the glimmers of hope that make life more meaningful and we can trust that hope exists because it comes from God Himself. God poured His love into our hearts and He gave us hope and instruction and comfort from the Holy Spirit to keep us moving with purpose to fulfill His plans for us. If anything, perhaps we need to give hope a wider berth, give it more opportunity to play out in our lives. After all, it's built on the foundation of God's love and His incredible Spirit. Hope is alive and well.

There is no medicine like hope, no incentive so great, and no tonic so powerful as expectation of something tomorrow.

~ *Orison Swett Marden*

What You Trust In

But let all those rejoice who put their trust in You; let them ever shout for joy, because You defend them; let those also who love Your name be joyful in You. *Ps. 5:11, NKJV*

Thomas Brooks once wrote, "Everything that a person leans upon but God, will be a dart that will certainly pierce his heart. He who leans only on Christ, lives the highest, choicest, safest, and sweetest life."

We must take note of where we place our trust. Considering Brooks's sentiment, we might look at adjusting our list of the places we think are trustworthy. The message is that anything apart from Christ becomes unsteady, perhaps even leading to sorrow. Bank accounts run out of money, stocks fall short, and love disappears, but Jesus stays the same. Jesus wants us to lean on Him for support because He is our Rock, the One who will always be there for us.

The psalmist advised us to celebrate, be happy, and shout out loud when we trust God. He will defend us to our dying day. If you are still not certain about this, look at those things you may have trusted in the past and see where they are now. God who is the same yesterday, today, and tomorrow is steadfast and holds you in His hand. Trust Him and you will have more reasons for joy than you could ever imagine.

Lord, thank You that I can trust You completely with my heart, mind, and soul. *~ Amen*

Let's Be Practical

Practically everything that goes on in the world—
wanting your own way, wanting everything for yourself,
wanting to appear important—has nothing to do with
the Father. It just isolates you from him. *1 John 2:16, MSG*

Is there anything we can say or do that could separate us from the One who loves us more than we can even comprehend?

The world does not see faith as a very practical thing. People of faith put their trust in this One being whom they cannot touch or feel, yet they recognize as being more real than anything else in their lives. Yes, faith does not really stack up as practical from an earthly view. It may not get you ahead or make you prosper in the ways of the world.

From a Heavenly view, nothing on earth compares with the richness of God's promises and the depth of His love. Nothing can fill your heart and mind and soul the way the love of Christ can do. In fact, nothing can separate you from the love of God. When you look at it that way, the most practical thing to do is to draw close to your Creator and do everything you can to love Him in return. With His love, you can do beautiful things that even the world will applaud!

There is no other method of living piously and justly, than that of depending upon God. ~ *John Calvin*

More than a Mustard Seed

Then He said, "To what shall we liken the kingdom of God? Or with what parable shall we picture it? It is like a mustard seed which, when it is sown on the ground, is smaller than all the seeds on earth; but when it is sown, it grows up and becomes greater than all herbs, and shoots out large branches, so that the birds of the air may nest under its shade." *Mark 4:30-32, NKJV*

If you can imagine that tiny seed growing so large that it provides shelter and a place for birds to build their nests, then maybe you can imagine the kind of impact you might have on the world.

Your tiny seed of faith is contagious. It grows more important in your daily life and changes the way you think and feel. It makes others draw nearer to God so they can experience the faith they see in you.

Your mustard seed faith is important. You are part of God's plan to help people come to know Him. He expands your territory and gives you wisdom and grace.

God opened your heart and planted His seeds of love within you. He wants you to enrich the soil where others can grow. He sustains you and strengthens you through difficulties and celebrations because He wants you to bloom continually. Thank God for giving you mustard seed faith.

The smallest seed of faith is better than the largest fruit of happiness.

~ Author unknown

White Flag Day

"You must give your whole heart to him and hold out your hands to him for help." *Job 11:13, NCV*

You can choose to give God a little space in your day, or you can choose to make Him the CEO of your life. You can hold on to the things you want to keep apart from Him, or you can put up the white flag and simply surrender everything you are and everything you hope to be. Surrender may be the best idea.

What part of your life would you imagine to be something you can manage better than God can? You can try to tough things out and go on your own, thinking that this is just the way life is, or you can stop. You can stop trying to be the leader. You can stop trying to have all the answers. You can stop getting in the way of the real plans God has for your life.

Hold out your hands for help today. Surrender every worry, every bad habit, every concern you have for your family, your friends, or yourself and let God take over. He knows who you are. Nothing is hidden from Him. You can confide everything to your Creator, the One who loves you and has marvelous plans for you. Just give Him your whole heart and do it every single day.

Lord, please lift me up and hold me tight. I surrender my whole heart and mind and soul to You. *~ Amen*

Turn this Thing Around

But God warned the wise men in a dream not to go back to Herod, so they returned to their own country by a different way. *Matt. 2:12, NCV*

Have you ever planned your route for a journey, only to discover you could not go back the same way you came? Sometimes, for reasons only known to God, He wants you to turn things around. Don't go further without hearing His voice. Don't go back on the original route.

This example from Matthew was God's way of keeping the wise men from returning to Herod and revealing where the baby Jesus was. Herod meant to harm the child.

Turning around can be a wise choice when we find ourselves going down a path that is not good for us. When you're going the wrong direction, something in your spirit sends a signal to your heart. That signal means "turn this thing around." It's not good for you to keep moving forward.

If God is directing you to turn around or turn over some part of your life to Him right now, then do what the wise men did. Listen for His voice and go in the direction He tells you to go. He'll always keep you on the right path.

The will of God will never take you where the grace of God cannot keep you. ~ *Author unknown*

APRIL 25

When God Shows Up

Strong God, I'm watching you do it, I can always count on you. God in dependable love shows up on time. *Ps. 59:9, MSG*

Often in our prayers, we seek help with something we want God to take care of today. We don't want to wait. We want God to show up now!

On the other hand, we have said prayers where we realized our blessing was that God did not show up and do what we wanted. With the benefit of time, we were able to see God's wisdom in not answering our prayer according to our desires. We are thankful to God for knowing what was good for us.

God shows up every time you pray. He hears your voice and He notes what you need. He looks at what is behind you and what is ahead of you and begins to immediately look for the best solution.

You should know though that God's greatest desire is for you to share in a relationship with Him. He wants the two of you to know each other well, so He works to answer your prayers according to His will and purpose.

The more you connect to each other, the more you'll understand His timing. It is God's intention to always answer you with love.

The steady discipline of intimate friendship with Jesus results in men becoming like Him.

~ Harry E. Fosdick

Starting a Fire

"I've come to start a fire on this earth—how I wish it were blazing right now! I've come to change everything, turn everything rightside up—how I long for it to be finished! Do you think I came to smooth things over and make everything nice?" Luke 12:49-50, MSG

You may not picture Jesus as the One who came to earth to change things up, set them ablaze and get the world back in order. Most of us have a "nice" Jesus in our minds. One reason for that is that we don't understand His Holy power. We don't really get what it is that He came to do then, or what He wants to do now in our hearts.

The Spirit of God is often depicted in images of fire. A pillar of fire went before the Israelites as they followed Moses through the desert. The fiery bush drew the attention of Moses as God called Him to come closer. The followers of Jesus were given tongues of fire as the Holy Spirit descended upon them. Maybe there's a message in all of this. Maybe God wants us to be more than nice, more than people pleasers. Maybe He's calling us to set hearts aglow.

Create a Holy fire wherever you are. It's clear that the world is desperately in need of being set right side up.

Lord, help me to be intentional about speaking Your name and setting a little holy fire in those around me today. ~ *Amen*

APRIL 27

Turn It Over...to God

"Seek first God's kingdom and what God wants.
Then all your other needs will be met as well." *Matt. 6:33, NCV*

What might be different in your day if you started seeking God's direction and counsel before your feet even hit the floor in the morning? What if you took every big decision to Him before you signed any agreements, or you made any promises?

You may not know exactly what it means to seek God's Kingdom, but you do know what it means to seek God. You know that He wants you to come to Him with everything so that He can help you carry your burdens.

God knows everything about you. When you come to Him for help, you let Him know that you're glad to be in a relationship with Him and that you want to live your life in ways that please Him. You want to do what God wants you to do and that is all that matters.

God will guide you to understand more of what it means to feel His Presence and His Kingdom here on earth. He is your Provider and the one who is ready to meet your needs every time you call Him. He's never too busy to hear from you.

To want all that God wants, always to want it, for all occasions and without reservations, this is the kingdom of God which is all within.

~ *F. Fénelon*

Restoring Your Joy

Now may the God of hope fill you with all joy and peace in believing, that you may abound in hope by the power of the Holy Spirit. *Rom. 15:13, NKJV*

No matter what you are going through, you can gain strength for your soul and trust God is with you. He knows what you need, and He offers you hope and peace.

Will you take it? If you do, then you will have every reason to feel the sunshine on your face. You have hope in the Only One who can make a difference in your life. Why?

The Holy Spirit offers you comfort, and He fills you with certainty that your life in its infinite detail is all in God's hands. Those are the most powerful hands available to humankind. They are without exception.

Today, let your hope be restored and let the power of God's love renew you, energize you and keep you close. He protects and provides and cares about you more than you can even understand.

Let go of whatever keeps you away from Him and let Him fill you with new joy and with peace in believing. He's there for you. Always has been. Always will be!

Joy is the serious business of Heaven. ~ *C.S. Lewis*

God Is for You

What then shall we say to these things?
If God is for us, who can be against us? *Rom. 8:31, NKJV*

Is God still there for you? After all, the world is a mess and it seems to spiral out of control.

The best way to get the answer, is to go to God Himself. Stop what you're doing and get on your knees. Seek His face. Ask Him to allow you to feel His Presence. Wait. Wait some more.

Before long, you will most assuredly know that He has drawn near to you. He hears your voice. He loves you and He wants to give you peace and comfort. He's with you in all things, no matter how complex your life may be. He can help you simplify things and get them back on track.

Your sins may feel like a pile of rubbish too big for you to even carry to the junkyard. If so, don't try to carry it yourself. Give up! Give in! Go directly to Jesus and ask Him to forgive every sin you have ever committed.

Nothing can save you from yourself and your sins like His holy forgiveness. His steadfast love is always available to you. Why? Because He's always for you every moment of the day.

Lord, You are the joy of my heart. Thank You for bearing my sins and always being there for me. ~ *Amen*

APRIL 30

Resisting the Devil

Therefore submit to God. Resist the devil and he will flee from you. *James 4:7, NKJV*

The devil's plan is to separate us from God. He knows that when we're connected to God he can't get in. He can't get through that armor of protection God has provided.

Sometimes though, he hovers around anyway. He looks for any little sign that you could be vulnerable. Maybe you're filled with self-doubt. That invites him in. Maybe you think your sins are too big for God to forgive you. That lights him up!

You see his plan is to make you feel that you are not worthy of God's love and that you are just not one of those people God really cares about and forgives. He'll bait you and tempt you and try to squeeze between you and God any chance he can get. When that happens, here's what you do.

You resist, fight back, speak God's name aloud, pray with all your heart, and simply tell him to go away and he will run from you. He just doesn't like being in God's Presence and if you're filled with God's Spirit that just gags him. Submit, surrender, praise God with all your heart.

The greatest trick the devil ever played was convincing the world that he did not exist.

~ Author unknown

May

Worry Is a Brain Drain

"Therefore do not worry about tomorrow, for tomorrow will worry about itself. Each day has enough trouble of its own." *Matt. 6:34, NIV*

Many of us are worriers, so we hardly take note of when we're doing it again. So how can we avoid worry's endless brain drain? Jesus told us not to worry. He didn't say don't worry right now, or sometimes. He said don't worry about tomorrow or today. You've got more important things to do.

Prayer is the first answer to worry. Simply take every worry you can think of and tell God about your fears. Tell Him what you think and what you hope for and what you want Him to do for you in the current situation. Look to Him to help you.

The big thing about worry is that it undermines your faith. It treats you as though you don't have a Source for your troubles. It deceives you into thinking that you are supposed to be able to come up with the answers for your life or someone else's. It's fake news! Let worry go and hand everything over to your Father in Heaven. He knows just what to do.

Blessed are you when you're too busy to worry during the day, and too tired to worry at night. *~ Author unknown*

The Thing to Know

God says, "Be still and know that I am God. I will be praised in all the nations; I will be praised throughout the earth." *Ps. 46:10, NCV*

What do you really know? You imagine you know your neighbors, until something strange happens with them that shocks you. You think you're doing a great job at work until your job is suddenly downsized.

So, what does it mean when God asks us to be still and know Him? Perhaps God is asking for something more than recognition, or even a confession of faith. Perhaps He is asking us to know His heart, His desires for our lives, and to know His steadfast love.

We often confess our faith in church. We acknowledge our belief in the Supreme Creator of the universe. We sing His praises and we leave the building feeling like we've spent time with God.

The challenge then is to consider in the quiet of your heart and mind how well you know God. How often do you seek to know more of Him? God knows everything about you and He truly desires a relationship with you that is eternal. He wants you to know one another in every possible way. Be still! Seek Him today.

Lord, I ask that You quiet my heart and speak to my soul. Help me to know You a little bit more each day. ~ *Amen*

Poverty Stricken?

I know your afflictions and your poverty—
yet you are rich! *Rev. 2:9, NIV*

Most of us work hard, but we may not feel we have everything we need. If we lose the job that pays our bills, we wonder how we'll survive. If our health takes an unfortunate turn, we're not sure how we'll get back on our feet. Setbacks are difficult and they can last a long time. But setbacks can remind us that we may not be as poor as we think we are, because God is with us.

Our Father in Heaven strengthens and renews our faith during any crisis and remembers that we are His. He holds the door open for conversation any time we're ready to talk. He walks ahead of us and prepares the way so that we can move more easily. He holds us tight, never giving up on who we are and what He knows we will yet be.

God sees you right now. He is there with you no matter what you're going through, and He knows your future. Things will get better. He knows that He has plans for you in this world and the next and you are richer than you may yet understand. You're in the hands of not just a king, but THE King. Nothing can separate you from His love and His resources. Look for Him to show up in special ways.

Prayer is taking our troubles to God. Faith is leaving them there.

~ Author unknown

MAY 4

Worship God

And when they heard that the LORD was concerned
about them and had seen their misery,
they bowed down and worshiped. *Exod. 4:31, NIV*

Do you recognize the fact that God is concerned for you, about your life and your well-being? God knows when something is wrong, and He acts to help you. You may tell yourself that God cares about you, but still not truly take that idea to heart so that it gives you comfort and peace.

When the Israelites realized that God saw their misery and that He was expressing concern for them, they responded by bowing down and worshiping God. They were grateful for His Presence and wanted to let God know what a difference He made in their lives. They respected and trusted Him.

We understand the idea of worship when we are at a church service or a gathering of people with like minds, but we may not consider worshiping God in the stillness of the morning sunrise or the quiet of a starry night. Worship means love and adoration. Worship shows respect and enlarges the heart. Worship fills you up and over so that when something is wrong, you can take it to God, and He will begin to make it right. He wants only your good.

Your chief work is the praise of God. ~ *Augustine of Hippo*

Make It Right

"Whom have I cheated? Whom have I oppressed? From whose hand have I accepted a bribe to make me shut my eyes? If I have done any of these things, I will make it right." *1 Sam.12:3, NIV*

When we create a mess in our lives, most of us want to make things right. Even if we weren't entirely to blame, we feel responsible. A moral code in our hearts and minds beckons us to do the right thing.

The world may not share your concern about fixing mistakes or admitting being wrong. It may even cause you to question whether you really must own this mess.

Integrity is God's gift to your spirit. It helps others to see Christ within you. Your responsible actions and intentions to right the wrongs of life, are character builders. They are part of your natural light that shines every place you go. God knows He can rely on you to do things with honor. He knows you trust Him in all ways. He considers you to be righteous before Him.

It's important then to maintain your good character and be honest with those around you. Your example will be a light to others, and you can be sure, God will always work to make things right for you.

Lord, I pray that I will always own my mistakes, and that I will seek to make amends in ways that please You. *~ Amen*

What's the News?

Then he told John's disciples, "Go back to John and tell him what you have seen and heard—the blind see, the lame walk, those with leprosy are cured, the deaf hear, the dead are raised to life, and the Good News is being preached to the poor." *Luke 7:22, NLT*

The news didn't always come streaming into people's homes on a variety of electronic devices. It had to rely on one thing, word of mouth. The news of the day was shared person to person. For the news to go viral, it had to go on foot.

Even if you're a news junky, you may find yourself wondering if there is ever any "good" news. Daily news focuses on things that are unkind, unfair, or unusual. We seldom read the good news of medical breakthroughs, or of people reaching out to help each other.

So, here's a thought. What if you do just what the people in ancient times did? What if you walk over to your neighbor and share wonderful news? You could carry a word of encouragement, or the story of your faith or simply listen to them with interest. You could become the bearer of good news. If each person in each town across the planet spoke about the good news of Jesus Christ, it would be a whole new world in no time.

I am to become a Christ to my neighbor and be for my neighbor what Christ is to me. *~ Martin Luther*

Are You There, God?

LORD, why are you so far away?
Why do you hide when there is trouble? *Ps. 10:1, NCV*

When you feel like God is simply out of reach, you must keep in mind that He has not stepped aside, nor is He sleeping or hiding from you. He does not think your difficulty is too hard for Him and He's not trying to ignore you. In fact, He hasn't gone anywhere. He's right there with you.

When God is silent, keep praying. Keep trying to connect. Keep looking for Him to show up in unexpected places. Keep your heart and mind focused on Him and pray without ceasing. When you do, God will see you and He will observe your faithfulness and, in His mercy, look for ways to communicate with you. Stand firm and trust Him.

Imagine how hard it must have been for Job as he prayed and prayed for relief from his troubles. His friends just made him feel worse as they pretended to comfort him. Job did not understand what God was doing as he waited in the silence, but he did understand one thing. He knew that God was aware of everything he was going through and at some point, He would answer Job's prayers.

May your faith sustain you while you await God's guidance in your life.

God is always near you and with you; leave Him not alone.

~ Brother Lawrence

MAY 8

It's Not About You

Love is not rude, is not selfish, and does not get upset with others. Love does not count up wrongs that have been done. *1 Cor. 13:5, NCV*

When you are the object of someone else's anger and you're not even sure why, it's easy to feel angry in return. It may cause you to react in negative ways.

The writer of Corinthians reminds us about something we can easily forget in those situations. As people who aspire to demonstrate Christ-likeness and what it means that God is love, we have to consider our responses. We must act in love.

Love doesn't give us a chance to be rude or selfish. No, it expects more of us because love, the kind that we hope to emulate, sees past all those tricks of the world. Love isn't taken in by rudeness or alarmed at selfishness, because love understands a greater purpose. Love doesn't act out any time it feels wronged. We know this is true because God is love and He has borne our rudeness and our selfishness and our anger more times than we can count. He continues to be all that He can be to us. He continues in love. Love is the only measure that counts so when in doubt, don't make it about you, make it about God, and make it about love.

God loves past our rudeness, past our selfishness, and past our wrongs, so that we can learn by His example.

God Is on Your Side

"The LORD your God is with you; the mighty One will save you. He will rejoice over you. You will rest in his love; he will sing and be joyful about you." *Zeph. 3:17, NCV*

Today as you drive to your job or walk through town, imagine that you've got the greatest force ever known to any planet, walking right beside you. Imagine that you are surrounded by His holy angels and that He is watching out for everything that happens to you. He's with you as you begin your new project, as you give advice to your friend, and as you take off on an airplane. He holds you up and encourages you to stay confident that He knows right where you are.

You can relax then. You can continue in good faith. You can rejoice that He loves to guide you and guard you as you go on your way. When you have God on your side, all things are possible. He only needs your prayers, your permission to bring you even closer to Him so that you can hear His voice. Sing with joy or give Him praise for all that He does and all that He will do for you. You have a powerful team; more powerful than anything on earth. It's good to have God on your side.

Lord, I am so grateful to know that You are with me everywhere I must go today. I praise Your name for all You've done to bless my life. *~ Amen*

Stay the Course

I have taken an oath and confirmed it,
that I will follow your righteous laws. *Ps. 119:106, NIV*

Sometimes you make heartfelt promises you intend to keep, but life happens. You suffer a big setback, or you struggle with health and before you know it, nothing seems to work out right. You lose heart.

You must keep seeking God's face, and His direction for what to do right now. Look to Him to create a new path. Once you've chosen to follow Him, He only asks you to "stay the course." Stay on the path He gives you until you see the changes, the healing, the purpose He has designed for you.

When you promise to follow Him, He'll stick with you until the end. If you slip and slide, He'll hold on to you. If you wander and get lost, He'll stay close by your side. He won't leave you unless you ask Him to do so. He heard your request, the one you made with your heart, asking Him to come in and live with you. He came in and He's been there ever since. He knows what you need and despite how things may feel, He has not forgotten you. You're on the path of love and life and redemption. Don't turn back. The best is yet to be.

Lord, thank You for being with me and picking me up when I fail to stay on course. Help me to get stronger in You. *~ Amen*

MAY 11

Be Alert

And pray in the Spirit on all occasions with all kinds of prayers and requests. With this in mind, be alert and always keep on praying for all the Lord's people. *Eph. 6:18, NIV*

What puts you on the alert, checking back often to see what's going on? Oftentimes, when we feel alerted, it's because we anticipate something foreboding. That's not what the writer of Ephesians is suggesting though.

We're being told to be on the alert for those who need our prayers. Be watchful! Look out for those who desperately need you to pray for them. Let the Spirit come in to every part of your life. Let the Holy Spirit lead you to those who need to connect with God but may not know how. You do know how, so God wants you to be a prayer intercessor or a champion for His Kingdom. Come before Him with endless requests for others.

Prayer is your ministry and it's something you do with compassion. You open the windows of Heaven for others because you're willing to see them as they are and be alert to their needs.

Today, offer heartfelt prayers for family, friends, and people across the world that you will never meet. It will do you good.

To make intercession for others is the most powerful and practical way in which we can express our love for them. ~ *John Calvin*

MAY 12

Jump

He jumped up, stood on his feet, and began to walk.
He went into the Temple with them,
walking and jumping and praising God. *Acts 3:8, NCV*

Most of us take being able to walk for granted. That is, until we can't walk easily! If you've ever been laid up, you know what it's like to have to depend on others. You must watch what you do, where you go, and how you travel. At best, it's inconvenient. At worst, it's painful.

Imagine the guy who was unable to walk his entire life. He gets carried to the healing pool every day in the hope he will get into the waters. He watches for his opportunity to be healed, focused on the moment when he'll finally walk, barely able to think of anything else.

Finally, Peter comes along and offers to heal him. He agrees to the healing, the moment he's waited for with amazing anticipation. Suddenly, he realizes he cannot only get up, but he can jump up. He jumps up on his feet. Can you picture him enjoying every step he takes? Finally, he goes walking, running, jumping all the way to the temple to give God the glory.

Thank You, God for feet that can walk and legs that support me and arms that can hug those who are near. I will take nothing for granted today.
~ Amen

Get Moving

After all this had come to a head, Paul decided it was time to move on to Macedonia and Achaia provinces, and from there to Jerusalem. "Then," he said, "I'm off to Rome. I've got to see Rome!" *Acts 19:21, MSG*

Traveling is a gift because we see others with new perspective. We experience life in new ways. When Paul was traveling and preaching from town to town, he met with people and shared the gospel. Sometimes he was met with enthusiasm and excitement; other times they wanted to beat him and asked him to leave them alone. Either way, he moved on. After all, he was on a mission!

Perhaps you need to move on too. It may be time to move past old heartaches that keep replaying in your mind and simply give them to God. It may be time to give up a bad habit or let go of a toxic relationship. Go beyond the safety zone you're so comfortable in and stretch your faith. Move on and forgive yourself. Move on and start over again with a clean slate. It's time to do something new.

Whatever your destination might be, echo with Paul the excitement of getting there with the opportunity to gain a new perspective. God is with you wherever you choose to go, so get moving!

Lord, help me move with joy and seek Your face today. ~ *Amen*

Grateful

And the Lord God prepared a plant and made it come up over Jonah, that it might be shade for his head to deliver him from his misery. So Jonah was very grateful for the plant. *Jonah 4:6, NKJV*

Some people believe in fate and coincidence, but Christians believe in God's favor. God favored Jonah when he was overwhelmed by the desert sun. He prepared a plant to cover Jonah and shade him. Jonah was grateful.

You probably have stories when God favored you or brought you an awesome "coincidence" of His love. It may have been the parking space that opened when you were already late for an appointment. It may have been the check you needed to pay the rent, that arrived just in time. It may have even been a sense of peace as you prayed for your child. Those were God's ways of preparing a plant to shade you and protect your life.

God knows what you need, and He often provides unexpected pleasures. He wants you to know that He's there always. He favors you with His steadfast love and mercy.

Perhaps today, you could take time to praise Him for moments when He showed up, relieved the pressures of life, and let you know that you were not alone in any situation you faced. Give God the glory!

I was not born to be free. I was born to adore and to obey.

~ *C.S. Lewis*

Light Your Candle

You will tell those in darkness,
'Come into the light.' *Isa. 49:9, NCV*

After many gloomy days, you can forget what the sunrise looks like. Those who are imprisoned, physically or emotionally, or who have a spiritual blindness that keeps them wandering alone, never see the sun.

The sunrise happens every day though because God has ordained that if the earth exists, there will be day and night; sunrise and sunset. As a child of God, you are part of His sunrise service. You walk in His Light and are privileged to share that light. You are a voice that calls others out of the darkness.

If you're trying to imagine how that can even happen, just consider every person you meet as someone who needs your light. You put on your low beams and give them a chance to feel comfortable in your presence. You hold up a candle so they can see a bit more clearly.

When God is ready, He will light the candle of their hearts and make it possible for them to shine from that day on. It's exciting work. Today, the darkness prevails. With your help though, someone will come into the light. Hold up your candle! The sun is always rising somewhere.

We forgive a child who is afraid of the dark; but the tragedy of life is when an adult is afraid of the light. ~ *Plato*

Catching Kindness

May the LORD show you his kindness
and have mercy on you. *Num. 6:25, NCV*

Mother Teresa wrote, "Be the living expression of God's kindness." If you wanted to demonstrate those words, what do you think it would look like? How would you try to show kindness to those around you?

If you need a few ideas, try some of these. You can pay it forward. You can do something unexpectedly nice for a total stranger, just because you can and because God has blessed you enormously.

You can bring peace to a personal situation that has gone on too long. Allow your forgiving heart to come to the table, remembering any part you could have played in the controversy. Consider what God would have you do to show His mercy and grace.

Another option for kindness might be to keep a negative thought or opinion to yourself. Hold back on voicing things that won't inspire someone to do a better job. You can offer the hand of fellowship, with sound advice, and move on.

Finally, you can smile with love and encourage the heart of anyone you know who is suffering. Yes, you can be so kind that someone else may catch your goodness and strive to be a little kinder themselves.

Wherever there is a human being, there is an opportunity for kindness.
~ Author unknown

Let Go...Some More

In all your ways submit to him, and he will make your paths straight. *Prov. 3:6, NIV*

The little things may trip you up, more than the big things. You're pretty good at taking those bigger things to God because they simply feel out of your control.

God wants you to surrender everything though, both big and small because He wants you to be completely His. He wants you to give up the control you've convinced yourself is necessary. Does God really care if you smoke, or if you have other bad habits? Of course He cares! He cares about the guilt you feel when you smoke. He cares about the sense of loss you feel when your finances are out of control and you can't pay the bills. He's always concerned with your well-being.

So if you've tried before to give up a bad habit or a love for jelly donuts, then try again. Let it go! Let it go directly to God's ear and seek His help in overcoming what you can't take care of yourself. Submit your finances, your bad habits and your health to Him because then He can straighten things out. He wants only your good because He is your Father and your protector. He is the guardian of your soul.

Lord, help me to totally surrender those things that neither serve You well, nor benefit my life. I ask this in the name of Jesus.

~ Amen

Close to the Well

Yes, remember your Creator now while you are young, before the silver cord of life snaps and the golden bowl is broken. Don't wait until the water jar is smashed at the spring and the pulley is broken at the well. *Eccles. 12:6, NLT*

Solomon had water from the well and wine from the vineyard served to him with gold and silver goblets. He had wisdom beyond measure, even greater than his wealth. Solomon advises us to remember the things that God has done. As human beings our days are finite and so it's wise to speak to God while we have a chance.

Going on with the metaphor of the water and the well, imagine that God is the deep well, the life-giving water that causes you to thirst no more. When you go to the well and dip your jar into the water, God fills you up. The Spirit provides nourishment for your soul and helps you to live each day more fully.

Today, imagine the well is in your backyard. Draw the life-giving water supplied only by the Savior and offer your thanks and praise. Recount your blessings in His Presence and let Him know what pleasure you derive in serving Him. These are the things that will always keep you connected to your Savior and no matter what age you happen to be, they will fortify you.

We cannot find a worthy explanation of life eternal anywhere but in our Creator.

No Need to Beg

And we have received God's Spirit (not the world's spirit), so we can know the wonderful things God has freely given us. *1 Cor. 2:12, NLT*

Life is confusing. You witness vast differences in the way people treat each other. Some offer kindness and generosity. Others do not. Some sincerely lend a hand or volunteer their time. Others turn away.

What makes the difference for you? At your invitation, Jesus came into your life and you made room for Him in your heart. As you follow in His ways, you enjoy life with the kind of love and abundance He wants for you. He guides your actions and reactions to others. He gives you strength for your soul.

You open the door of your heart and God continues shaping your life. You don't have to beg for God to hear your prayers or comfort you through adversity because He's there. He wants you to enjoy His gifts of joy and peace and fulfillment. Don't look only to the confused world when you need help or a warm embrace; look for the One who loves you and redeemed you for all time.

True discrimination between right and wrong does not then depend on the acuteness of our intelligence, but on the wisdom of the Spirit. *~ John Calvin*

Prickly Hairs

That night the LORD appeared to him and said,
"I am the God of your father Abraham.
Do not be afraid, for I am with you." *Gen. 26:24, NIV*

Have you ever felt frightened enough that the hairs stood up on the back of your neck? You stood quietly and listened for a sound, or you quickly turned on the light, so you could see beyond the shadows. It was just a quick feeling of dread, but then all was well.

Imagine then, that you are visited by an angel of the Lord, or you hear an audible voice of God leading you, giving you information, even protecting you. When God's angels approached humans in the Scripture, they often said, "Fear not!" or "Don't be afraid."

We love God's Presence in little doses. We know how to handle that, but sometimes God comes even closer when we need help right away. Rather than embrace fear, move closer to God yourself. Walk with Him and talk with Him so often that you form the kind of relationship that makes His Presence a natural part of your life.

You never have to be afraid because God's comfort and love are truly with you.

Just as a lamp lights up a dark room, so the fear of God, when it penetrates the heart of man illuminates him, teaching him all the virtues and commandments of God. *~ Author unknown*

Mission Impossible

Jesus looked at them and said,
"With man this is impossible, but not with God;
all things are possible with God." *Mark 10:27, NIV*

Some days, nothing seems possible. Everywhere you turn bills are piling up, the kids are acting out, and nobody seems to really understand the stress you cope with each day. When will it change? When will things turn around and feel better?

The answer is, today! Today is the day you can sit down and have a heart to heart with God about every troubling thing on your list. Today is the beginning of things turning in your favor because you are no longer carrying them on your own. You are seeking God's face to receive His grace and guidance. You are no longer shouldering all the responsibilities. Stop everything and lay your burdens at the cross.

Will your debt mysteriously disappear, or your kids suddenly become charming and kind? Well, perhaps, but more likely you will have the support and patience you need to get through the chaos, imagine new opportunities, and bring hope back into your picture.

It's a good day to start again with the One who can make every mission possible.

Faith sees the invisible, believes the unbelievable, and receives the impossible. *~ Corrie ten Boom*

Phantoms

Do not hold against us the sins of past generations;
may your mercy come quickly to meet us,
for we are in desperate need. *Ps. 79:8, NIV*

It's not easy to shake off the ghosts of the past. They are the phantoms of regret, the embarrassing actions of days gone by. You've asked for and received God's forgiveness for them, but somehow, they keep showing up, making you feel unworthy of God's grace.

Even David prayed that God would forgive past sins; his own, and those of generations before him.

David had something that you may also want to consider. He knew God's mercy. He knew God's forgiveness and he received it. He received it despite the wrongs he committed. He simply tried to be a more devoted follower, a more intentional believer, and a greater lover of God from that point on. God considered David to be a man after His own heart.

God considers you to be a person after His own heart too. Every time you fail, and you come back to God with a contrite heart, He forgives you, raises you up and releases you from the demons of the past. Give Him thanks and praise for all He's done for you right now.

Never live in the past, just learn from it. *~ Author unknown*

Matters of Faith

Now faith is the substance of things hoped for, the evidence of things not seen. *Heb. 11:1, NKJV*

Your faith matters to God and He is continually drawing you closer to Him so that you can believe for even bigger things today than you did yesterday. Yesterday's faith was okay, but today's faith needs to be bigger yet.

How do you come to big faith? You come by seeking God's voice each time you pray. You come by looking for God's grace. You come by lifting your heart to God and seeking His comfort and blessing. In every matter of faith, God sees you and desires more for you than you even know to desire for yourself.

What areas of your life are stuck in a sinkhole of little faith? What could you do to help grow your small faith into big faith? Maybe you have to believe in yourself in ways that you've never tried to believe before. Maybe you must move away from people who have negative influences on your work or your beliefs. Maybe you simply must start again to grow those little faith seeds so that they are planted more firmly in God's mighty hand. When you do those things, nothing can keep you from moving forward and believing for bigger things. After all, in matters of faith, God is always with you.

Cling to your faith through every storm of life and God will hold you firmly in His hand.

What God Did for You

He is your praise, and He is your God,
who has done for you these great and awesome
things which your eyes have seen. *Deut. 10:21, NKJV*

Miracle moments, those sweet God moments occur far more frequently than you might even notice. God is in the details and He wants the best for you. He knows what you need and often provides for you before you even put in a request.

If you tried to write down all the things that your God of praise and glory has done for you, you'd be like the gospel writer who declared that if everything Jesus did were written down, all the books in the world could not contain the stories. You have stories. You have miracles and displays of utter kindness at the hand of God that cannot be explained in any other way.

You are beloved and sustained by the One who created the entire universe. What an amazing idea that is! It is difficult to even grasp all that God has done for you and for the people you love.

Open your eyes today to His Presence and give Him heartfelt thanks for the blessings He continues to give you.

We have short memories in magnifying God's grace. Every blessing that God confers upon us perishes through our carelessness, if we are not prompt and active in giving thanks.

~ John Calvin

MAY 25

What God Does

God thunders marvelously with His voice; He does great things which we cannot comprehend. *Job 37:5, NKJV*

David Livingstone, the Scottish medical missionary and explorer to Africa wrote, "Would you like me to tell you what supported me through all the years of exile among a people whose language I could not understand, and whose attitude to me was always uncertain and often hostile? It was this, 'Lo, I am with you always, even unto the end of the world'. On these words I staked everything, and they never failed.'"

You may not understand the world you live in much better than Livingstone understood his, but he put his life on the line every day, trusting that God would be there.

God does amazing things all around the world, every day. He's with you now and is prepared to be close to you and comfort you as you listen for His voice. If you need peace, then trust He knows your situation, your story, and is working even now to bring you relief.

You may not understand the ups and downs of your life, but nothing will happen to you that will surprise God. He goes before you today, guarding and guiding and protecting your heart.

Lord, thank You for always being with me. I know that even when I am not aware of Your presence, You are there beside me.

~ Amen

What God Doesn't Do

We will all die someday. We're like water spilled on the ground; no one can gather it back. But God doesn't take away life. Instead, he plans ways that those who have been sent away will not have to stay away from him! *2 Sam. 14:14, NCV*

Consider the things that God does, and then think about the things that God does not do. Culturally, we're inclined to give God credit or blame according to our own standards and our own imaginations. Giving God credit for nearly every good thing that happens to you is wise. Giving God blame is otherwise.

God respects the lives of His children. He breathed the breath of life into all His creation and He blessed it as good. He continues to pour out His Spirit into the hearts and minds of His children today. That's what God does.

What God does not do is cause evil to happen to any of us. He does not put obstacles in our way when we're about to achieve something He called us into doing. We often do that to ourselves. We build the walls and the obstacles and the doubt that persists when things go wrong.

When you take your concerns and your praise, and your life work to God, He blesses you. When you don't, He still blesses you, devising ways to bring you closer to Him with every step.

If God sends us on stony paths, He will provide us with strong shoes.

~ *Alexander MacLaren*

What You Do

The young man said, "I have obeyed all these things.
What else do I need to do?" *Matt. 19:20, NCV*

There's always a price of admission. The wealthy man who approached Jesus and wanted to know what else he could do to follow Him imagined it would be easy. He could follow Jesus because of all the good works he had already done. He was proud of his work and had a good heart. It seemed like that would be enough.

Of course, you know the story. There was only one thing left for the young man to do. He had to give it all up. Give up his pride, his title, his accomplishments and lay them all at Jesus' feet. Once he did all of that, he would be in the door. It appears that giving up everything was not in the man's plans, and as far as we know from the story, the man went sadly away.

We may ask for the price of admission. What else do I need to do to follow You, Lord? In our case, the answer is simple. The resurrected Jesus gives us an opportunity to accept His invitation and then He opens the door. We just have to walk in. What a relief that is!

What might you have to give up to make a firmer commitment to your faith? As always, it's up to you!

Oh, for a spirit that bows always before the sovereignty of God.
~ *C.H. Spurgeon*

Roller Coaster Life

They've put themselves on a fast downhill slide to destruction, but not before they recruit a crowd of mixed-up followers who can't tell right from wrong. *2 Pet. 2:2, MSG*

If you lived on a roller coaster, you'd probably get used to that startling quick descent and the whiplash feeling as you get jerked around the bend at high speeds. You'd adjust to the quiet moments, the lulls where you could look out at the peaceful landscape. After all, you'd get accustomed to the ups and downs of life.

Some people opt for a roller coaster life. They put themselves on the fast, downhill track to destruction. They love the momentary thrill of living life in reckless abandon. It's great, and they raise their hands in the air, screaming as loud as they can to make others believe they are having fun. The problem is, that the fun always stops, and then they are left to repeat the process on a track of life that simply goes nowhere.

God does not want you to live an up and down life. If any part of your life still exists on the roller coaster today, let it come to a stop, and get off. You have amazing things to do and God will put your feet on solid ground. Trust Him!

There are two kinds of people: those who say to God, "Thy will be done," and those to whom God says, "All right, then, have it your way."

~ *C.S. Lewis*

Time to Hope Again

Why am I so sad? Why am I so upset?
I should put my hope in God and keep praising him,
my Savior and my God. *Ps. 42:11, NCV*

Moments of sadness, loss, and anger happen to all of us. So what do you do when they happen to you?

Of course, you can keep on moping and crying and telling anyone who will listen how sad your life is. You can play the story in your head so many times, that the gloom around you becomes thicker and thicker. You can do that, but it may not be your best choice.

Perhaps you need to ask yourself, "Why am I so sad? Why am I so upset?" When you face those questions head on, you can usually see that part of the reason is that while you basked in the gloom, you had no sense of the light. You lost hope in all that could be, and all that God can do to comfort you and help you. You stopped trusting your Savior. If you find yourself in the place where you're allowing the darkness to prevail, step into the light. Come back to the Source of all good, the One who can bring you peace and hope for a brighter day tomorrow.

Turn on the light now!

We stand in life at midnight; we are always at the threshold of a new dawn.

~ *Martin Luther King, Jr.*

It's Not Magic

So the magicians told the king that the power of God had done this. But the king was stubborn and refused to listen to them, just as the LORD had said. *Exod. 8:19, NCV*

You may be a fan of science fiction and the magical world of Harry Potter, but as mysterious and fascinating as stories of magic can be, they pale in comparison to the real things that God can do. His work, His miracles, His continual Presence is making a difference in the world and in your life right now. It's not magic; it's God!

The king's magicians weren't powerful enough to go head to head with God. The king wanted to know he was able to control the outcome of things. He wanted to believe he already had the secrets of the universe. He was wrong.

Stubbornness has not died out. Centuries later, people still hope to be in control, to outwit, outsmart, outthink the God of the universe. Some try and for a time, God lets them think they are winning. For a season, God leaves them to live in their stubbornness.

The question is whether magical thinking ever gets you anywhere. How often does a stubborn heart serve you or God? Leave the fantasy to book writers and movie makers and give yourself to this one reality. God reigns and there's nothing magic about it, except perhaps His enormous gift of love.

Stubbornness should have been my middle name. ~ *Martin Luther*

Share Your Heart

The believers met together in the Temple every day. They ate together in their homes, happy to share their food with joyful hearts. *Acts 2:46, NCV*

God knows that like a single coal left outside the campfire, left on our own, we may simply burn out.

The good news about all those people you find in your church is that they are all just like you. They are sinners. They are people who recognize that God rules and they want to get it right from here no matter where they were before. They are forgiven, blessed, and loved and each one of them calls God, "Father."

The gift of churches and small groups and Bible studies is that they allow you to share your heart with people who will get who you are and where you want to go with your faith. You're surrounded by people on your same path, some further along for sure, and some just beginning, but still you're walking together.

Whatever you're going through, you have a family, organized and equipped by God to help you and love you when things are not going smoothly. Today, pray for your friends from church and give God thanks and praise for the joy they bring to your life.

The church is the gathering of God's children, where they can be fed and guided and brought to maturity in faith.

~ Adapted from John Calvin

June

JUNE 1

It's Not a Disaster!

Be strong and take heart,
all you who hope in the LORD. *Ps. 31:24, NIV*

A story about the explorer, Christopher Columbus, shares an incident in his life where nothing was going as planned. Columbus said, "I recognized that our Lord had caused me to run aground at this place so that I might establish a settlement here. And so many things came to hand here that the disaster was a blessing in disguise."

Of course, Columbus was about to begin a whole new world, even though that was not his intention when he sailed out of his home port. You may not be ready to begin a settlement in a new land, but you may well have had the experience where something that seemed like a disaster turned out to be a blessing in disguise. It may not have been something you understood immediately, but on hindsight you were able to realize the gift in your experience. You could see God's hand at work in your life.

When nothing seems to fit or come out smoothly or well, look around to see if God is at work. He may have a plan that is different than the one you are pursuing. He may want you to recognize that He has given you a blessing in disguise. Take heart, because God is with you to strengthen your soul.

We serve a gracious Master who knows how to overrule even our mistakes to His glory and our own advantage. ~ *John Newton*

Amazing You

For You formed my inward parts; You covered me in my mother's womb. I will praise You, for I am fearfully and wonderfully made; marvelous are Your works. *Ps 139:13-14,* NKJV

The fact is, you're amazing! You're unique and custom made. You're the spitting image of your Father and He's very proud of you.

Look at Psalm 139 and fill your heart and mind with the numerous images of what it was like when God formed you, and how intimately you are known. He marvels over you and He's given you the privilege of being His child.

The world does not often tell you how impressive you are. Perhaps on any given day, you don't have anyone working to put you on a pedestal so that they can honor you and share the delight they have in knowing you. If not, you're invited today to peek in the mirror and speak kindly to yourself. You can look at the person you see there and give God praise for making such a wonderful human being.

Sure, this idea is a bit over the top, but that's only because you so seldom hear how precious and valuable you are. Sometimes you must intentionally try to grasp the blessing that you are to others.

Now, all you must do in return as you go about your business today, is remember that everyone else is just as priceless as you are to their Father in Heaven.

May God bless you even more as you go through the day!

Let God In

Draw near to God and He will draw near to you. Cleanse your hands, you sinners; and purify your hearts, you double-minded. *James 4:8, NKJV*

Running on empty and overloaded with responsibilities? Do you imagine that if you just keep running, everything will be all right?

Here's the thing! If you're running, but you don't have any fuel in your tank, everything will come to a stop. You won't be able to navigate the twists and turns of the day. You'll fall flat on your face.

God wants to restore you with each sunrise. He prepares the path for you to walk. He takes note of what you'll be up against and inspires your heart and mind to manage the chaos. He guides you and guards you. He puts fuel in your tank. He does it best when you reach out to Him and ask Him to hold on to you wherever you must go. He's there for you and He wants to help you; He'll carry every burden that comes your way.

What will you do then? Will you suit up and walk on without Him, or will you stop everything else, seek His face and allow Him in. He won't come uninvited.

God is not far away from us. Rather He awaits us every instant in our action, in the work of the moment. There is a sense in which He is at the tip of my pen, my brush, and my needle.

~ Pierre Teilhard de Chardin

Puny Fists

Where were you when I created the earth?
Tell me, since you know so much! Who decided on its size?
Certainly you'll know that! Who came up with the blueprints
and measurements? How was its foundation poured,
and who set the cornerstone? *Job 38:3-4, MSG*

Sometimes we're tempted to shake our puny fists at God. We get worked up over an unanswered prayer or some unexpected chaos and so we question Him in somewhat unflattering ways. Sometimes though He answers back, as He did to Job in the Scripture above.

We quickly settle down, realizing that we are not the ones in control. We know that God often gives us a pass when we've done something foolish. He doesn't come back and remind us every time we made a wrong move. He just keeps loving and protecting and guiding us because He knows we'll do better tomorrow.

Perhaps when you're tempted to raise your fist to God, you might think about this. Think about opening your fist and simply raising your hands to God, thanking Him that you know He's working quickly to help you with your struggles. Praise Him for never looking the other way when you need Him most. It will bring you peace.

Don't be angry that you cannot make others as you wish them to be, since you cannot make yourself as you wish to be.

~ Thomas à Kempis

Glory to God

The righteous will rejoice in the LORD and take refuge in him; all the upright in heart will glory in him! *Ps. 64:10, NIV*

C. S. Lewis said, "The glory of God, and, as our only means to glorifying Him, the salvation of human souls, is the real business of life."

Perhaps we don't go around with words like "Glory to God!" on our lips with each sunrise, but maybe we should. After all, He is the only One who sustains life as we know it, choosing to bring a new day into the world. He answers our prayers and manages to orchestrate incredible things that we can't always explain.

Glory to God! One way we bring glory to God is by bringing His children back to the fold. When we help someone answer His call, then we have helped to facilitate their salvation. We have brought glory to God!

Your heart may lead you to truth and understanding, strengthening your spirit when things are not going well. Open your heart then to praise God and give Him thanks for your work and your family and the things you do that bring joy to your life. Give God the glory each time you have reason to rejoice in something He clearly has done to show His love for you. When you do, a certain peace and contentment will fill your soul!

Lord, I give You the glory for the amazing things You continue to do in my life. I praise You and thank You. *~ Amen*

JUNE 6

Don't Panic

He [God] says, "Don't be afraid, because I have saved you. I have called you by name, and you are mine." *Isa. 43:1, NCV*

Most of us walk around carrying a heavy load. We are weighed down by anxiety, fears of the craziness of the world, and worries about things that may never happen, but keep us confused. We simply need a break from it all. We must let go of the burdens, both imagined and real.

If any of this describes you, then pay attention to this Scripture from Isaiah. It is a great reminder of the One who is really in control. God controls the entire planet, the universe around us, and yes, even your life. He knows you and He sees you. You are never off His radar.

You don't have to be afraid when the greatest force in any galaxy draws near to you and calls you by name. He holds you in His powerful hands and He will not let anything separate you from Him.

Today, as you look out at the world and as you say your prayers, unshackle yourself from the weights you're carrying. Rest your worries on the shoulders of Jesus who will carry them for you. There's no need to panic, no need to feel alone. God is with you now and He will be with you wherever you happen to go. After all, He told you, "You are mine!"

Pray, and let God worry. ~ *Martin Luther*

Blessed Unrest

So what do people get in this life for all their hard work and anxiety? Their days of labor are filled with pain and grief; even at night their minds cannot rest. *Eccles. 2:22-23, NLT*

You probably know people who remind you of the writer of Ecclesiastes. They always have to see the gloomy side of life. It may be their reality, but it doesn't have to be yours.

God wants you to get amazing things out of this life. He created you perfectly and designed you for the work you do. He filled you with a variety of talents and speaks to your spirit through prayer and blessing.

Yes, your life is not all roses. There are times of grief and sorrow, and times of joy and celebration. God brings sun and rain into everyone's life, the good and the evil alike. He wants us to live fully and completely and you can't always appreciate the sunshine, if you haven't had a few rainy days.

Rest easy today. Surrender your anxieties, your troubles, and those things that cause your heart to worry and let them all go. You're in good hands, and they are loving and powerful hands. Give God credit and praise for every good thing He has done for you. That should keep you busy for the next week or so.

Anxiety is the rust of life, destroying its brightness and weakening its power. A childlike and abiding trust in Providence is its best preventive and remedy. *~ Author unknown*

Two A.M. Blues

What you decide on will be done, and light will shine on your ways. When people are brought low and you say, "Lift them up!" then he will save the downcast. *Job 22:28-29, NIV*

We all need a 2 A.M. friend. You know, the person you can call to ease your weary mind. Some days, your mind continues to tell stories late into the night. You need someone to come along beside you and listen to the things that trouble you!

It turns out that God is ready to have a chat any hour of the day. He's able to lift you up again and strengthen and renew you. He's a great 2 A.M. friend!

Step away from the noise that won't settle down and simply call God's name. Let Him know your troubles. Share your frustrations and your anger and your uncertainty. Once you've gotten all of that out, stop! Stop everything and listen. Give the Spirit of God a chance to help you.

Nothing about your life is a surprise to God. Nothing can be hidden from His view. The dark of night is just as bright as noontime for Him, so He already knows and already sees the things that trouble you. Seek His face, and if need be, His forgiveness and let Him speak to your heart and mind.

It won't be long until you fall into blissful sleep, ready to serve Him another day.

Lord, thank You for being my friend and listening to my heart. You mean everything to me! ~ *Amen*

Credit Check

If you love those who love you, what credit is that to you? Even sinners love those who love them. And if you do good to those who are good to you, what credit is that to you? Even sinners do that. *Luke 6:32-33, NIV*

You may have never considered your credit rating based on this passage from Luke, but it's a good one to think about. After all, the better your credit is, the more opportunities can come your way. God credits you for everything you do for Him or for any of His children.

The catch is, that you must expand your territory. You must widen your net and do all you can for people that are outside of your comfort zone. You're good at loving those you've already embraced, but what about those people that aren't on your friendship list? What about the people you pass by all the time; those that don't fit into your idea of "lovable."

If you want to raise your credit score, you might look at ways that you can minister to those who need your help, regardless of their economic or spiritual level. You're a generous and kind person and somebody out there needs your special attention today. You get extra points if you don't have to even think twice about helping them. Let your heart guide you forward.

We have a call to do good, as often as we have the power and the occasion. ~ *William Penn*

JUNE 10

Singing Lessons

Sing to the LORD a new song; sing to the LORD, all the earth. Sing to the LORD, praise his name; proclaim his salvation day after day. Declare his glory among the nations, his marvelous deeds among all peoples. *Ps. 96:1-3, NIV*

It's your day to sing your heart out! That's right! Lift your voice up to Heaven and give God an attitude of joyful praise. You may not be a singer, but there's not one thing in this Scripture that says only the good singers need apply. In fact, you don't even have to audition. No one cares about the quality of your singing.

You may not be in a place where you can suddenly belt out a song. Maybe you're at work or you're at the grocery store. Somehow it doesn't seem quite right to suddenly look for a karaoke microphone. Okay, you're off the hook... for the singing part that is.

You're still on the hook to tell of the marvelous deeds that God has done in your life. You're still poised to share God's love for those around you. You're in the perfect place to give God the glory for the ways He provides for you and your family. Yes, it's okay if you need a few singing lessons, but don't wait until you get them to share God's stories. He always loves to hear you sing!

Lord, I honor You and offer my heartfelt praise today. It always lifts my spirits to think of You and share Your stories. ~ *Amen*

Friendship Matters

I wish for the days when I was strong, when God's close friendship blessed my house. *Job 29:4, NCV*

If you're not feeling God's favor in your life, what can you do right now to turn things around? Perhaps the first step is to let God know how you feel. Be honest. Be sincere and offer Him a contrite heart if you were the one who walked away.

Even though God never walks away from you, He won't come into your life without an invitation. He might nudge you from time to time to see how you respond, but He waits patiently to hear from you.

Your friendship with God matters. It's a two-way street though and He likes you to give Him a call now and then. He loves to hear stories of what is going on in your life so He can offer you advice and encouragement. He wants you to win at all that you're doing and so He works to strengthen you and renew your spirit. All you must do is let Him know you're interested.

Perhaps this is a good day to renew, recharge, or build your relationship with the One who longs to talk to you. Give Him a call!

May God bless you and your household from this day forward.

You have made us for Yourself and our hearts are restless until in You they find their rest. ~ *Augustine of Hippo*

Live Boldly

[Boldly Face the Future] Invest what you have, because after a while you will get a return. *Eccles. 11:1, NCV*

When was the last time you made a bold move? Maybe you went after a dream nobody else supported, or maybe you adopted a baby after your other kids were grown. It took a bold move to get things going.

Boldness requires you to be proactive. You do what you can do, and you ask God to help you do the things you can't. You move forward bravely because you've got a mission to complete and you won't let anything get in the way of doing it. After all, your mission was given to you by your Creator and so it's a job that simply must be done.

Time is your friend, but it won't go on forever. The future is coming quickly and so your job is to stay the course. Be so connected to God and to His direction for your life that you won't miss a step.

You may seem brave or bold or even brazen to others, but you can be sure God is cheering you on as you step out in faith and invest in your future. Live purposefully and boldly today. You're not alone!

Leave nothing to chance and leave everything to God.

~ Author unknown

God's Favor

For he says, "In the time of my favor I heard you, and in the day of salvation I helped you." I tell you, now is the time of God's favor, now is the day of salvation. 2 Cor. 6:2, NIV

Today is going to be extraordinary! Today you are walking with God and He wants to bless you beyond measure. How do you know that is true?

You know because you have been in God's favor since the first day you asked Jesus to make His home in your heart. You have been on God's list of redeemed, loved, and amazing people ever since. The question is whether you truly recognize God's hand at work in your heart and mind.

God gives you a sense of peace and happiness. He wants you to feel secure in His love and His provision for your welfare and for your spirit. He's with you from the moment you see the first rays of morning light, to when you snuggle down into your warm blankets at night.

God knows your life purpose. He knows the mistakes you've made and the struggles that distract you and grieve your spirit. He knows those things because He watches over you as His beloved child. You're in His favor.

Thank Him for the blessing of His love and salvation; thank Him for knowing you so well!

Everything comes from love, all is ordained for the salvation of human beings. God does nothing without this goal in mind.

~ *Catherine of Siena*

Angels and Other Helpers

For He shall give His angels charge over you; to keep you in all your ways. In their hands they shall bear you up, lest you dash your foot against a stone. *Ps. 91:11-12, NKJV*

Did you know that your angels are always near, watching over your life and doing what they can to protect you and comfort you? God has assigned the angels to pay attention to His children and help however they can. It's a comforting thought and one to hold on to when your life feels somewhat uncertain.

You may remember the angels that begged Lot to hurry and leave Sodom and Gomorrah, or the angels that Jacob saw in his dream that were going up and down a ladder from earth to Heaven. Moses talked about thousands of angels who protected God's people, and the shepherds witnessed angels too numerous to count in the starry night sky when Christ was born.

As you go about your work today, be mindful of those who guard you wherever you go. God is with you and angels draw near to you. Be at peace in your mind and heart and give God thanks for all He does to show you how much you're loved. Take heart and know that God has not forgotten you in any way. He knows everything you need and watches over you with love.

Beside each believer stands an angel as protector and shepherd leading him to life.
~ *Basil the Great*

Let's Be Clear

"But those who follow the true way come to the light, and it shows that the things they do were done through God." *John 3:21, NCV*

When you're going through a rough patch, it's hard to remain clear about your direction. If your goal is to please God with the things you do and to shine your light for Him, then you have to strive to make a difference to others even when your own life feels a bit off kilter.

When your day does not go well, you could spend time in your misery, or you could stop everything and invite God in to clear the path. You could focus on Him and not on yourself.

It's not easy, but it's helpful. It's helpful because focusing on what God wants and what others need, lets you forget about your own troubles for a while. It even strengthens and renews your spirit as you see people responding to your kindness.

God sees your light shining and works to provide for your needs. As you help others, He helps you, not because you must do something for Him before He'll help you, but because He knows that you feel better and happier as you give to those around you. God is clearing the way for a better day for you. That's a promise!

May God bless you and keep you and make His face to shine upon you today.

Managing Expectations

Listen to my voice in the morning, LORD. Each morning I bring my requests to you and wait expectantly. *Ps. 5:3, NLT*

Sometimes we whisper quick prayers all through the day as we go about our routines, sending up a prayer for a homeless person we see on the street corner, remembering a friend who is ill while we're heading to the grocery store. It's all good and God hears every prayer that is spoken from the heart.

Other times though, we become more intentional because we are praying over something that is highly important to us. We're praying for the outcome of a surgery, or for a teenager to get clean after abusing drugs.

When we offer very intentional prayers, we repeat them morning, noon, and night. We beseech God, sometimes even pleading with God to hear our prayers and answer us in a timely manner. We feel the pressure of a deadline or the helpless sense of worry that simply won't stop making noise in our heads.

If you're going through any kind of crisis, then seek God's face early in the morning and all through the day, expecting Him to answer. Trust Him and wait patiently for His reply. He knows your every need and He will provide strength for your soul.

Don't pray for tasks equal to your strength. Pray for strength that is equal to your tasks. *~ Author unknown*

Upside Down Day

May the LORD answer you in times of trouble.
May the God of Jacob protect you. *Ps. 20:1, NCV*

This Psalm reads like a greeting card that you might send a friend who is going through difficult times. It's not only a sentiment to be shared, but one to be taken to heart.

Whenever life simply turns upside down, the first place to go is to God. The God of Jacob is the living, eternal, only god of the universe. He calls Himself "I Am!" which basically means that He is now, and He always was, and He always will be. You can't appeal to a greater force anywhere in Heaven or on earth.

When you pray about your troubled times, you want an answer to your problems. You want to know you're not carrying a burden alone and that help is on the way. You want the spiritual equivalent of the cavalry to show up in the nick of time. You are desperate for the Lord to answer.

Today, may the Lord hear your heart and answer your immediate prayers, releasing you from worry and stress. May the Living God show you His favor today.

What a spirit—what a confidence was in his very expression! With such a reverence he petitioned, as one begging of God, and yet with such hope and assurance, as if he spoke with a loving father or friend. ~ *(Overhearing Martin Luther pray)*

JUNE 18

What You Achieved

May he give you the desire of your heart
and make all your plans succeed. *Ps. 20:4, NIV*

You work hard to develop a brilliant idea or a dream you hope to accomplish. You don't know every step you need to take, but you are willing to risk failure because the project is so important.

When you're aiming for something you feel called to do, you work to achieve it with everything you've got. You give it your best shot, follow through when things get sticky, working through the difficult parts and then trust God to help you with all the details.

Today, step back for a moment and remember the blessings that came because you had a mission and you went after it, unwilling to stop until it was done. Use that same energy as you commit to a new goal today, something that is doomed to fail unless you and God do it together. Once you've figured out what you want to accomplish, submit it all to God in prayer, surrendering the outcome and leaving the results in His hand.

Your job is to answer the call and to do so with your whole heart. You want to do more than talk about your goal. You want to accomplish it!

After all is said and done, there is usually more said, than done!

~ Author unknown

JUNE 19

When God Speaks

For God speaks again and again, though people do not recognize it. He speaks in dreams, in visions of the night, when deep sleep falls on people as they lie in their beds. *Job 33:14-15, NLT*

You may not always be aware of God's attempts to speak to you. Of course, He may speak to you through the voices of others. You may resonate with the Sunday sermon or the advice you heard from a radio station on your way to work. You may sense God's Presence as you humble yourself in prayer.

In Job, we see that God even attempts to speak to you in your dreams, giving you visions and opportunities to discover His plans.

The question is how available are you to receiving His messages? Sometimes, you may wonder whether a thought you have, came from God. You feel the nudge of the Holy Spirit, but still aren't sure how to complete the task you've been given. The main thing is to listen. Be open to any way that God might try to speak to you. When you are intentional about hearing God's voice, you'll be surprised at just how much He has to tell you. Let the One who guides your life, speak into your heart and mind today.

God is our true Friend, who always gives us the counsel and comfort we need. Our danger lies in resisting Him; so it is essential that we acquire the habit of hearkening to His voice.

~ *F. Fénelon*

Duck, Duck, Goose

Then he said, "I tell you the truth, unless you turn from your sins and become like little children, you will never get into the Kingdom of Heaven." *Matt. 18:3, NLT*

The Kingdom of Heaven is available to people who surrender their lives to God, living like little children who trust Him for their every need and embrace His ways; holding Him close to their hearts all the time.

God has opened the door to the Kingdom of Heaven and He invites you in right now. He knows that all it takes is your willingness to believe that He's there for you, that He has your best interests at heart, and that He loves you more than you can imagine. He wants to be embraced as the loving parent that He is.

There are wonderful things about having childlike faith, gently and generously giving your heart to God, believing His promises and accepting His invitation to spend eternity with Him.

Of course, you don't have to play "Duck, Duck, Goose," but you can't be so adult that you miss the chance to come to His party. It's a great day to remember how beloved you are and to show God how happy you are to be His child.

A simple, childlike faith in a Divine Friend solves all the problems that come to us by land or sea. ~ *Helen Keller*

JUNE 21

Coming Up Empty

For you know that God paid a ransom to save you from the empty life you inherited from your ancestors. And it was not paid with mere gold or silver, which lose their value. *1 Pet. 1:18, NLT*

You are strong and capable and have been designed for a particular purpose. As good as you are, there are limits to what you can do. For example, when it comes to salvation, you come up empty. You cannot save yourself.

That's good news because that means you can't screw it up and miss your ticket back to Heaven. God made it easy. He chose to give you a place in eternity. All you must do is accept His invitation, receive His Son, and He can put you on the train to Heaven someday. Of course, your choices after that are up to you. You're back in the driver's seat unless you surrender the wheel and give it to God. The fact is, it's a lot better to go along for the ride than it is to have to map out the route.

You may come up empty on earthly matters as you create a plan for a new project, but you'll figure things out. On Heavenly matters though, God has filled your heart with His Presence, and you will never be empty again. His Spirit goes before you and watches out for you. After all, He paid a very dear price for you.

Salvation is the work of God for people; it is not the work of people for God. *~ Lewis Sperry-Chafer*

JUNE 22

Here Am I

"I revealed myself to those who did not ask for me; I was found by those who did not seek me. To a nation that did not call on my name, I said, 'Here am I, here am I.'" *Isa. 65:1, NIV*

Sometimes you look for God to show up, but you miss seeing Him. This scripture from Isaiah is a reminder that this problem may well be a two-way street. There may be plenty of times where God has looked for you and waited patiently for you to notice Him, only to have you walk in the opposite direction.

God says that He reveals Himself to people who do not even ask for Him. He draws near and whispers His name to them, hoping someone will hear and recognize their need for Him.

God wants you to find Him. He wants you to pray and seek His guidance and counsel. He wants to walk before you and with you and draw near any time you need Him. Don't be baffled when there is silence. Don't stop praying because you don't get a sense of His nearness. Instead, persist. Trust that He is near.

When you need His help or His comfort or His forgiveness, stay close. Keep praying! It won't be long before you'll hear Him approach saying, "Here am I, here am I!"

Whenever you walk in God's direction, He sees you coming and runs to embrace you.

Rubber Souls

Stand firm then, with the belt of truth buckled around your waist, with the breastplate of righteousness in place, and with your feet fitted with the readiness that comes from the gospel of peace. *Eph. 6:14-15, NIV*

No matter what kind of shoes you wear, God is prepared to keep your feet fitted with readiness. He makes you ready to walk further, or ready to walk beside Him. He keeps you alert so that each step you take brings you closer to the place He would have you go.

Like a runner sporting your favorite brand of rubber soles, you're off to do God's bidding. You have been fully equipped and you know how to make your way around the track of His choice. He has provided wisdom and knowledge and truth and outfitted you with everything needed to bring souls to Christ.

Perhaps as you go for a job or a walk around your neighborhood today, you could imagine for just a moment that you're moving closer to someone who needs to know about God's saving love and grace. Open your heart to sharing the Good News any chance you get. Who knows, you may help someone prepare to walk right into Heaven. As a runner, it will do your heart good each time you pass the torch of God's love and let someone else's life shine.

The will of God will never take you where the grace of God cannot keep you.
~ *Author unknown*

JUNE 24

The Great Deceiver

Jesus, full of the Holy Spirit, left the Jordan and was led by the Spirit into the wilderness, where for forty days he was tempted by the devil. *Luke 4:1-2, NIV*

The devil likes it better when we act like he doesn't exist. The truth is, his whole job is to do everything he can to get you to cut your ties with God. He wants to whisper in your ear any time it pleases him. He wants to beguile you in the same way he deceived Eve in the garden. He simply looks for that one spot where you're weak or worried, the place where you're apt to listen.

Luke reminds us here of how Jesus was tempted in the wilderness at the beginning of His ministry. It's interesting because we see how Satan even tried to keep Jesus from listening to God. Satan wants to keep us from doing God's work. He does not want you to spread the Good Word. He does not want you to speak God's name in public. The more you do those things, the more he will try to draw you away.

When you sense the deceiver is coming around you, it may be that you're becoming more ministry minded. As your heart becomes more dedicated to God Satan simply can't stand it. Whatever it is, don't let him tempt you even for a moment. Resist him and he will flee from you. Stand firm in your faith!

The devil loves to fish in troubled waters. ~ *John Trapp*

Two Steps Forward

Isaiah answered, "This is the LORD's sign to you that the LORD will do what he has promised: Shall the shadow go forward ten steps, or shall it go back ten steps?" *2 Kings 20:9, NIV*

Whether or not we witness any signs and wonders, we know that God keeps His promises. Sometimes in Scripture, we note that God was willing to give a sign of His promise to those who walked with Him. For Hezekiah, He promised to move the sundial either forward or back, whichever the king would choose.

Of course, moving the sundial meant moving the earth as well. Such an enormous feat would be beyond our imagination, but God was willing to do so to show His servant that He was with him.

Most of us make choices every day that move us a few steps forward or a few steps back. We adjust to the new direction each time, not always realizing what those steps meant for our lives. We're better off when we seek God first and look for His promises. We want to keep going forward in a good way and please Him by the things we do.

God is willing to move Heaven and earth to reveal His love. He is willing to establish His promises in ways that we will never forget. Take two steps forward toward God's steadfast love and mercy today.

God's promises are like the stars; the darker the night, the brighter they shine. *~ Author unknown*

From Darkness to Light

For God, who said, "Let light shine out of darkness, "made his light shine in our hearts to give us the light of the knowledge of God's glory displayed in the face of Christ. 2 Cor. 4:6, NIV

When God let His light shine into our hearts, He did so to keep us illuminated, aware, knowledgeable of His Presence all the time. He did not want us to ever have to face the darkness without Him.

The light of God's love always shines in the faces of His children, letting others know that Christ lives within them. It seems like a simple concept and yet it is significant. It means that we do not have to slip into the darkness and wander aimlessly ever again. We do not have to search for the path because we're already on it.

The psalmist said that "God's word was a lamp unto his feet," and so it is with us. As we plug into the Source of light and seek to shine more brightly, He continues to teach us and help us stay free of the darkness.

Give God thanks today that He has placed a portion of Himself inside your heart so that you can radiate His love and kindness to those around you without even having to say another word. May others be drawn to your light today, as they move closer to the Lord Himself.

If you have knowledge, let others light their candles at it.

~ Thomas Fuller

Course Correction

Understanding is a wellspring of life to him who has it.
But the correction of fools is folly. *Prov. 16:22, NKJV*

Most of us linger somewhere between the brilliant and the foolish. Sometimes we listen to reason as we navigate the waters of life. Other times, we simply can't hear the advice others offer us and so we foolishly go our own way and create our own chaos.

Our spiritual life is like that too. Some days, we're committed to prayer and reading the Word. We listen for God's voice and put our concerns before Him, asking for guidance and His perfect will. This approach serves us well.

Other days, we make our own decisions and plans. This seldom takes us where we want to go. It isn't long before we need a course correction. We need to turn around or turn back to God and ask for His input into the things we do. We must give up the controls and hand them over to the One who can see everything and the One who knows everything about us. He's equipped with the Godhead, the Spirit of the three-in-One, ready to come to our aid.

Confess your foolishness and your stubbornness, and let God guide you into His perfect will for you today.

A heart is right when it wills what God wills. ~ *Thomas Aquinas*

When in Doubt

And He said to them, "Why are you troubled? And why do doubts arise in your hearts? Behold My hands and My feet, that it is I Myself. Handle Me and see, for a spirit does not have flesh and bones as you see I have." *Luke 24:37-39, NKJV*

Can you imagine what it was like to encounter Christ for the first time after the resurrection? His followers could not believe their eyes. They were seeing Him, but their minds did not think it was possible. There He was in full bodily form, flesh and bones, able to be touched and hugged and seen and heard. It was incredible!

Sometimes we doubt our own eyes and our own experiences. You may have felt something like that when you first encountered the living Christ for yourself. You may not have been able to touch Him, but in your heart, you saw Him, and you knew He was real. You felt different in His Presence and you understood things that never made sense to you before.

If you're having any doubts today about whether you've experienced the gift of Jesus' love, ask Him to draw near to you. Ask Him to show you who He is as you read Scripture and pray. Look for His handiwork as you go about your business so that you return to the place of truth and understanding. It's always a good day for a fresh encounter with your Lord and Savior.

Faith lives in honest doubt. ~ *Alfred Tennyson*

Oil of Gladness

Anyone who is sick should call the church's elders. They should pray for and pour oil on the person in the name of the Lord. *James 5:14, NCV*

Throughout the Old Testament, we discover that God often had the prophets anoint His chosen leaders with oil. He also had the priests use oil to anoint the altars and consecrate the places where they would serve. The oil was a symbolic way of setting them apart for their service to God.

The New Testament church often used oil to heal the sick. The idea was that the person would be blessed by God as they were prayed over, bringing them into the light of God's healing power. In this case, it was not the sick person who had to believe God for a healing, but more so, the ones who prayed. Anointing people with oil isn't generally the custom today, but perhaps it is still a way to remind ourselves that we can obediently set ourselves apart and be made whole and holy by the One who hears our prayers. No matter what concerns us, whether it is illness or spiritual depression, or some other affliction of the body and soul, then come to God for a fresh anointing so that He can renew you with the oil of gladness and nourish your spirit in every way.

John's words "unction" or "anointing" are just a very graphic way of describing the influence and the effect of the Holy Spirit upon the believer.

~ Martyn Lloyd-Jones

Light Your Fire

Be like a fire that burns a forest or like flames that blaze through the hills. *Ps. 83:14, NCV*

If you measured the flame that first burned within you in your love of Christ, would you find that it has been reduced to a flicker, at least in comparison to when you first believed? Would you find that it glows with a steady sort of ember that simply is, but doesn't seem to fuel the rest of your life in any significant way?

Perhaps your flame has gone out and you've had to pray that God would reignite it. It's nice to have a steady, quiet flame that shows your love for the Lord, but what if you got out the bellows of the Holy Spirit and really fanned it to life? What if you took it from the embers and made it a rip-roaring fire?

Perhaps you would find that you are always aware of God's Spirit and truth. You are always ready to share His love with others.

Make this be the day that you take your ember of love for Christ and fan it into flames of passionate fire. When you do, you'll spread the news to everyone you meet. You won't be able to stop yourself!

Lord, light me up again so that people are warmed by the glow of Your love every time they draw near to me. *~ Amen*

July

Proof Positive

Then Gideon said to the LORD, "If you are pleased with me, give me proof that it is really you talking with me." *Judg. 6:17, NCV*

Conversations with God can feel complicated and confusing. We're simply not sure if we're hearing what God is saying correctly.

Gideon was a warrior and though he came from the tribe that was considered the least among the Israelites, the angel of the Lord came to him. God spoke to Gideon and as you discover in the book of Judges, allowed him to seek proof that God was indeed directing Gideon's steps.

Some days we long for a Gideon moment. We want to know if we're on the right track, or if we are hearing what the Lord is asking us to do correctly. With all the other noises and spiritual forces in the world, it feels hard to be certain.

Sit quietly today and lean in to the voice of the Lord. He has much to tell you and loves to spend time with you. You may not get a literal sign of His Presence and direction as Gideon did, but the more you listen, the more you will be sure that the steps you take are guided by His love for you.

May the God of signs and wonders bring peace to your heart today!

In order to come to union with the wisdom of God, the soul has to proceed rather by unknowing, than by knowing.

~ *St. John of the Cross*

JULY 2

Heart and Soul

Love the Lord your God with all your heart and with all your soul and with all your strength. *Deut. 6:5, NIV*

One measure of your love for someone or something is to look at the ways you think about them. To love with your whole heart means you are committed to them through the ups and downs, and the good and the bad. It means you trust them without question, and you can't imagine life without them. You would do anything for the recipient of your affection to be sure they were happy, cared for and loved.

Loving with your whole heart and mind and soul then is a big thing. It's not something you do lightly, and it's not the kind of love you have for every person you meet.

You're probably still learning about what it really means to love God with all your strength; to hold on to Him when everything else explodes into chaos. God is worthy of your love simply because He has loved you from your first breath and He will never leave you. He is the Rock, the One you can count on no matter what else happens. God nurtures your heart, strengthens your mind, and rescues your soul.

He will be with you always. Love Him with all your might! Think about Him and serve Him with your whole heart and you will have strength to do wonders.

Our only business is to love and delight ourselves in God.

~Brother Lawrence

JULY 3

Steadfast Trust

Some trust in chariots and some in horses,
but we trust in the name of the LORD our God. *Ps. 20:7, NIV*

The psalmist is considering what he believes to be worthy of his trust. If he trusts in his chariots, then he would believe he had the best ones in the land. If he trusts in his horses, he would believe them to be the fastest and the strongest horses anywhere. If he trusts in his material possessions, he would imagine that they were without limitations.

Sometimes we do that too. We trust in our jobs and then we are suddenly laid off. We trust in our spouse, only to have them undermine our relationship with a harsh word or an act that is disappointing. We trust in our finances and then our stocks go belly up and we have nothing to save us.

If we trust in God then, what does that mean? It means we go to Him for every circumstance in our lives, believing He will provide for our needs, grant us forgiveness, or guide us when we need direction. It means we know we can count on Him, not just once, but for every day of our lives. It means He does not change His love for us, but that He is forever with us. Trust in the Lord and all things will work together for your good.

Dear Lord, although I am sure of my position, I am unable to sustain it without you. Help me or I am lost. ~ *Martin Luther*

Lookout and Outlook

Late in the afternoon, since it was the Day of Preparation (that is, Sabbath eve), Joseph of Arimathea, a highly respected member of the Jewish Council, came. He was one who lived expectantly, on the lookout for the kingdom of God. Mark 15:42-45, MSG

Joseph of Arimathea was on the lookout for the Kingdom of God. He trusted and believed in who Jesus was. His outlook was based on his knowledge of the Scriptures and what he heard and observed about Jesus Himself. He was the one who lovingly wrapped the Lord's body and placed it in a tomb that had never been used before.

If we are on the lookout for the Kingdom of God, we must have an outlook that motivates us toward believing we will find it. The more we embrace the Kingdom of God, the more we see it all around us. God has not hidden Himself from us. When we search for Him, we find Him easily.

What are you on the lookout for in your life? Are you on the lookout for a new car, or a new job, or a life partner? Those are all good things, but when you search for God, He can guide you into discoveries you never imagined. Be on the lookout for the Kingdom of God. It will change your outlook about the world you live in and bring peace to your soul.

There can be no kingdom of God in the world without the kingdom of God in our hearts. ~ *Albert Schweitzer*

Truth Within

Send me your light and truth to guide me. Let them lead me to your holy mountain, to where you live. *Ps. 43:3, NCV*

One writer noted, "If you don't learn and know your truths, you cannot speak them, you will know a prison within. Tell your truths to yourself, and then to others. The truth really will set you free."

All of us receive certain truths, values, and guidelines for living based on the culture where we were raised. These truths may serve us well for a time, or we may learn that we were wrong in our thinking and that we need to look for the truth that does not change with time or culture. We need eternal truths.

When Jesus came to earth He shared eternal truths, some that had never been considered before. People who had been raised in the culture of the day had to decide whether they would listen to Him and leave their family wisdom behind, or whether they would reject Him.

We must make that same choice, not just once, but every day of our lives. When we seek to know Him and to determine His will, then we are free in ways we've never been before. We are truly free to be who we are in Christ Jesus.

May this truth radiate within your heart and mind and give you peace today.

The things in the Bible aren't true because they're in the Bible. They're in the Bible because they're true. *~ Author unknown*

Above and Beyond

With God's power working in us, God can do much, much more than anything we can ask or imagine. *Eph. 3:20, NCV*

When everything you do feels like an effort, it might be time to plug back into your power Source. After all, you can only go so many miles on your own without getting recharged. Your energy may be drained from simply not getting enough sleep, to stressing over the bills, to wondering what to do next in your current situation. It can be very troubling, and your heart and mind can grow weary trying to drum up another answer to keep you going.

The fact is you've already got the one, most important, answer. Take it all to God and get as close to Him as you can so that you can draw on His power. Stay there until you feel a resurgence of faith and possibility. Then plug into the Word and prayer until you know without a doubt that He is with you.

Give God a chance to change your attitude, raise your spirits and help you feel His Presence. When you do, He'll work above and beyond all the issues you have. God knows your heart and what you need, and He's able and willing to help you right now.

Just say "Amen" and "Thank You, Jesus!"

God has two thrones: one in the highest Heaven; the other in the lowliest heart.

~ *Author unknown*

In Your Distress

But while in deep distress, Manasseh sought the LORD his God and sincerely humbled himself before the God of his ancestors. And when he prayed, the LORD listened to him and was moved by his request. So the LORD brought Manasseh back to Jerusalem and to his kingdom. Then Manasseh finally realized that the LORD alone is God! *2 Chron. 33:12-13, NLT*

Manasseh was a king in Israel from the time he was twelve years old until he died over fifty years later. He worshiped other gods and got into witchcraft and things that did not please God. However, eventually he remembered the way his father Hezekiah had worshiped the one true God. He called out to God in his distress and God had pity on him. Manasseh learned who God really was.

God still hears our cries of distress. He has pity on our circumstances and reaches out to help us. He does those things because He is good and because He knows that we need Him desperately.

If you're in distress today, don't look to any other source for help. Go only to your Father in Heaven who will come immediately to your aid. Even if you have not been faithful to Him most recently, He is still faithful to you. He is still eager to help you and answer your call. Let Him know that you understand that He alone is God.

If God was small enough for us to understand, He wouldn't be big enough for us to worship. *~ Author unknown*

Stress Signals

Your justice is eternal, and your instructions are perfectly true. As pressure and stress bear down on me, I find joy in your commands. *Ps. 119:142-143, NLT*

The psalmist says that pressure and stress make him feel the joy of God's commands. Hmmm...what could that really mean?

Theologians may give you a variety of answers, but let's consider this one. Maybe knowing that God is in control and that He rules is a good starting point. After all, He is above the authorities that are causing you stress and even though they have a certain amount of power, they don't have His power.

Perhaps too, we might be grateful that God has established boundaries and guidelines that everybody must adhere to. That means they can't sidestep the law or the eternal truths that prevail.

If you're getting stress signals today, don't pull out the white flag and surrender to the issues at hand. Surrender instead to your Father in Heaven who has every side of your situation in His hand. He's there with you and that is a reason to find joy.

It is not the armor as armor, but as armor of God, that makes the soul impregnable. *~ William Gurnall*

Love the Unlovable

"But I tell you, love your enemies and pray for those who persecute you, that you may be children of your Father in heaven. He causes his sun to rise on the evil and the good, and sends rain on the righteous and the unrighteous." *Matt. 5:44-45, NIV*

Have you ever been around someone who doesn't seem to have any common sense, or they don't appear to adhere to the values you hold dear?

The people who are emotionally and spiritually outside your circle are the ones who need you the most. You may recall that Jesus said He didn't come to save those who were already on the right path, He came to save the sinners. He came to save those who were not yet in His circle.

God wants you to pray for those who might be in your sphere of influence, but who are not yet aware of the power of God. He wants to save them because He loves them every bit as much as He loves you.

It's not easy to be around people who are vastly different than you are, and it's not your job to try to rescue them all, but God does want you to pray for those who are still in the enemy camps. He wants to rescue them as soon as possible. He's counting on you.

Lord, help me to bless those who irritate me and love them into loving You. Amen.

In Jesus and for Him, enemies and friends alike are to be loved.

~ Thomas à Kempis

Blue Light Special

The buyer haggles over the price, saying, "It's worthless," then brags about getting a bargain! *Prov. 20:14, NLT*

It's easy to be attracted to the blue light specials. These are the deals that seem too good to be true, and usually are. The deals are just amazing and so you fall right into the trap that was set so well. You end up with something that doesn't do the job, but you have no one to blame but yourself.

In this Proverb, we have the other side of the coin. The sales person is trying to make an offer, but the buyer keeps pretending the merchandise is faulty or worthless. They say it enough times that they manage to get an amazing price. Walking away with their treasure, they are pleased with how well they duped the salesman into doing what they wanted. They got something valuable for very little money.

Neither of these stories has a happy ending because they both rely on deceit to make the deal. In any case, you always must be wary and wise. When you're making a choice, or any kind of business deal, cover yourself in God's protective armor. Listen attentively until you can discern the truth of the situation. Ask God to help you see clearly what you should do. May God watch over you today, protecting you in all that you do.

What we have in us of the image of God is the love of truth and justice.

~ Author unknown

Power Outage

He [the Lord] protects those who are loyal to him,
but evil people will be silenced in darkness.
Power is not the key to success. *1 Sam. 2: 9-10, NCV*

Many people imagine that power, whether by wealth or authority or position, is indeed the key to success. Whether they have a dominant personality that works to keep those around them walking on egg shells, or they run a corporation, or even a country, they have not learned how God wants power to be used in this world. The reason for that is God is the power Source and He wants us to only plug into Him.

When we align ourselves with Him, He turns on the power so that we can do the things He planned for us to do. He gave Jesus enormous power to heal the sick and raise the dead, and Jesus said that when we stay connected to God, we can do those things too. In fact, He offered through the Holy Spirit to give us even more power. Our Source never loses strength or diminishes.

Your relationship with God matters. When you turn to Him in prayer and choose to walk with Him each day, He gives you the power to fulfill His desires and to succeed in His ways. After all, He designed you for a purpose and He gave you all the power you need to accomplish His tasks.

The measure of a person is what that person does with power.

~ Author unknown

Restore Button

See what this sorrow—the sorrow God wanted you to have—has done to you: It has made you very serious. It made you want to restore yourselves. It made you angry and afraid. It made you want to see me. It made you care. It made you want to do the right thing. In every way you have regained your innocence. 2 Cor. 7:11, NCV

When your computer goes haywire, you may have to shut it down. If it doesn't come back ready to do the right thing once you reboot, you may have to hit the restore button and go back to an earlier time before the mess happened.

For most of us, a restore button would be a good thing. Simply press a button, go to an earlier time, and get ourselves out of the mess we've made. If only life worked that way!

Perhaps it does. With God's gift of forgiveness, we get another chance to start again with a clean slate. He puts our mistakes as far away from Himself as the east is from the west. Yes, God does have a "restore" button. He restores us to Himself when we come before Him in our utter shame, seeking His forgiveness.

God's restore button is even better than the one on your computer. God freely gives you Jesus and then He makes you brand new. You're His baby once again.

Lord, thank You for restoring my heart and mind to serve You today.

~ Amen

Trembling Faith

Keep on working to complete your salvation with fear and trembling, because God is working in you to help you want to do and be able to do what pleases him. *Phil. 2:12-13, NCV*

Isn't it wonderful to know that you are not working on your salvation all by yourself? Your efforts are amazing, but the truth is that God is doing the work within you so you can become more like Jesus.

What causes you to view the work of faith with fear and trembling? Chances are good that you're so aware of your shortcomings that you can hardly imagine a way to sustain the goodness that wells up in you sometimes. You love those moments when your spirit and God's Spirit feel perfectly aligned.

You are a human being working hard to become a child of God. Of course, Jesus did the work that gives you the opportunity to create your relationship with God, but you must take it from there. You must show up every day ready to please God. He wants you to trust Him with the good and the bad of all you are.

He loves you just as you are and every day He works to help you become a better version of yourself. If you are trembling, don't let it be about your faith, let it be about the awe you feel at receiving the incredible gifts of God.

See that your faith brings forth obedience, and God in due time will cause it to bring forth peace. ~ *John Owen*

Shivering Spines

Hezekiah rallied the people, saying, "Be strong! Take courage! Don't be intimidated by the king of Assyria and his troops—there are more on our side than on their side. He only has a bunch of mere men; we have our GOD to help us and fight for us!" Morale surged. Hezekiah's words put steel in their spines. *2 Chron. 32:6-8, MSG*

Do you believe that God is on your side? If you don't find it easy to step aside from your fears and call on the name of God to protect you, you may need some steel in your spine.

Yes, you're a simple human being, but when you are closely connected to God, you are packed with power.

The shepherd boy, David, told King Saul that he did not need armor to go out and fight the giant, Goliath. David told the king that God was his armor and he could fight the giant because God was at his side. Of course, Goliath never knew what hit him, and David won the day.

When you have a shivering spine, just remember that you're not alone. The Creator of the entire universe is with you and there is no obstacle in His path.

The Holy Spirit is no skeptic. He has written neither doubt nor mere opinion into our hearts, but rather solid assurances, which are more sure and solid than all experience and even life itself.

~ *Martin Luther*

Get Up and Walk

"Which is easier: to say to this paralyzed man, 'Your sins are forgiven,' or to say, 'Get up, take your mat and walk'?" *Mark 2:9, NIV*

We know there is great power in the words we speak to either wound or to heal those around us. When we listen with kindness and respond in love, we make a big difference in the way someone receives our words. God wants us to always be aware of the ways we choose to speak to others.

Mark gives us another view of the way our words have power. Sometimes the power is in the words themselves. Sometimes power is in the way that we speak, or our heartfelt motivation behind the words we say.

When Jesus spoke to the paralyzed man, He knew that the man was ready to be healed. He knew this because the man was a sinner and needed forgiveness. Jesus had the power to heal and, also to forgive sins. Both things imply a broken relationship and Jesus was there to heal those things.

As you weigh the words you speak today, measure the intention behind what you say. Are your words meant to heal someone's heart, encourage them to walk on and keep shining their light? We can each do something to help those we meet to "get up and walk." We can inspire them to move closer to Jesus.

Words which do not give the light of Christ, increase the darkness.

~ *Mother Teresa*

JULY 16

Follow Me

Still another said, "I will follow you, Lord; but first let me go back and say goodbye to my family." *Luke 9:61, NIV*

Sometimes our faith just isn't convenient. We want to follow the plan that God has for us and demonstrate the love of Jesus wherever we go, but we've got other things to do.

What if we didn't have a "Yes, but," attitude in our daily walk with God? What if we listened intently for His voice and no matter what we're doing, we simply responded, "Yes"? It appears that many of the disciples simply dropped their nets and followed Jesus. They didn't try to explain what they were doing to people around them and they didn't try to go back and take care of unfinished business. They just left everything and followed Him. Of course, they had heard about Him and already believed in Him.

What God wants from you is a surrendered heart. He wants to know that you will not give Him an excuse when He calls you to do a task. When He comes for you He wants you to say "yes" right away.

What gets in the way of your total surrender? What gets in the way of you simply saying, "Yes, Lord, here I am?" You can be sure that Jesus is "all in" for you. He gave His all, so you could be in your Father's Kingdom.

Lord, help me to simply say "Yes" to You today. ~ *Amen*

Weather Watch

The Pharisees and Sadducees came to Jesus and tested him by asking him to show them a sign from heaven. He replied, "When evening comes, you say, 'It will be fair weather, for the sky is red,' and in the morning, 'Today it will be stormy, for the sky is red and overcast.' You know how to interpret the appearance of the sky, but you cannot interpret the signs of the times." *Matt. 16:1-3,* NIV

The apps on our phones alert us when the weather changes. They show us the storms that are brewing and advise us to "seek shelter immediately."

Jesus warned the people of His day to read the signs of the times. It appears that they were somewhat blind to what was happening.

What about us? If we can't trust a sign from the weather station that all is well, how will we interpret the things that really matter? How will we read the signs that help us understand what God would have us know right now?

Perhaps we don't need to see signs and wonders. We simply need to stay close to the One who reigns. We need to watch for Him and stay alert to His coming. He's given us a lot of information, taught us what to do to be ready, all we need to do is trust Him. No surprise there.

To see God is the promised goal of all our actions and the promised height of all our joys. *~ Augustine of Hippo*

No Answer Yet

I call on the LORD in my distress,
and he answers me. *Ps. 120:1, NIV*

When you've been praying with your whole heart and nothing has changed, it gets more difficult to believe that God will answer. After all, when you've prayed for weeks or years you can't help wondering if the answer is, "No!" or if you need to put in your request in a different way. You try to avoid that downward spiral that suggests no answer is coming. You try, but it's hard, especially when your prayer is passionate and heartfelt.

What should you do? Maybe the first thing to do is to give up. That doesn't mean giving up on your prayer request, but it may mean giving up on what you imagine to be best. It may mean simply surrendering your prayer to God to answer in whatever way He deems to be the best. Surrender simply means you're not trying to get your way; you're trying to get God's way.

God is in the business of answering prayers. He loves you and He knows exactly what you need. Trust Him with your prayers, with your life, and with your loved ones. Sometime soon, you'll recognize His answer. Though you may not understand it, you can still trust He has your interests at heart.

Do not lose heart then in pursuing your spiritual life.

~Thomas à Kempis

Change Is Ahead

Do the things that show you really have changed your hearts and lives. *Luke 3:8, NCV*

Change is either something you have come to dread, or it's something you embrace. Some of us like consistency so much we don't handle even the smallest of changes very well. Others of us are off and running with just a little boost from this thing called change.

Perhaps what we need is not to resist the inevitability of change, but to recognize it as a philosopher, a teacher, an employer giving us a full-time job. Change is trying to make us better, give us new perspective and keep us on our toes.

The writer of Luke reminds us that when we accepted Christ into our hearts, we were asking for a change. We were asking Him to save us from ourselves and to help us become better people.

Look at the difference that being a Christ-follower has made in you. If that difference is not yet apparent, then maybe there's work for you to do.

One thing is sure, just up ahead change is walking toward you and something is going to happen to cause you to seek God's direction. He's there and He knows you're coming. With the help of Jesus, you have a heart for God that embraces any change He wants you to make.

Remember change and change for the better are often two different things. *~ Author unknown*

Blowing in the Wind

"The wind blows where it wants to and you hear the sound of it, but you don't know where the wind comes from or where it is going. It is the same with every person who is born from the Spirit." *John 3:8, NCV*

When the believers in the upper room waited for the Spirit of God, it began by making a mighty noise. They heard something like a great wind blowing through the upper rooms where they had all gathered. The noise persisted and was deafening.

The Spirit of God is often likened to a mighty wind, blowing wherever it will, and no one knows where it comes from or where it goes. You may be aware at times of feeling the breath of God as it draws near to awaken your heart. Being born in this way gives you eyes to see and ears to hear what God wants you to know.

We may be blowing in the wind as we walk through life, but if that breeze comes from the Spirit of God, we can trust that wherever we go, He is with us.

Today, be thankful for the amazing Spirit that blows around you, giving you insight into the nature of God and granting you peace.

Spirit-filled souls are ablaze for God. They love with a love that glows. They serve with a faith that kindles. ~ *Samuel Chadwick*

Tipping the Scales

The LORD hates dishonest scales, but he is pleased with honest weights. Pride leads only to shame; it is wise to be humble. *Prov. 11:1-2, NCV*

To "tip the scales" means we want to influence the outcome to be more in our favor. We want to win. This kind of winning may involve deceit of some sort, whether we're simply exaggerating as we tell a story, or we're literally using a dishonest weight when we charge a customer for a slice of ham.

We know that God is 100% about integrity. He does not deceive us, and He does not want us to deceive each other. He knows what we're up against because the master deceiver is working his way around every part of the globe.

We know what it's like to be caught in a lie...embarrassing, humbling, sad. Those are not things that make any day feel better. Perhaps the best way to tip the scales in your favor then is to be humble and honest. Those two attributes will never trip you up or cause you to apologize.

If a little white lie, or a foolish deceit has caught you in its web, get out of it by confessing it to God and if need be, by making amends to anyone involved. You will suddenly feel a lot lighter and your scales will be perfectly balanced in God's sight.

Nothing weighs you down like self-deception.

JULY 22

Can You Take a Pill for This?

"Heal the sick, raise the dead to life again, heal those who have skin diseases, and force demons out of people. I give you these powers freely, so help other people freely." *Matt. 10:8, NCV*

If you watch any nightly TV channels and you wade through the commercials, it can feel like there must be a pill for everything. Miracle cures and supplemental antidotes abound, along with the side effects that are almost worse than whatever ails you. Are we missing something?

It may be that we need the kind of healing that can't come from a pill bottle but is much more powerful than that. We need to turn our diseases over to God and seek His help. We need to be more discerning about when to pop another pill, or when to pop another prayer. Sometimes we need both to make whatever is messing with our bodies or our minds go away.

The Holy Spirit is alive and well. He can heal and bring change into our lives. He has power that goes beyond our imaginations. See your doctor if you are ill and take your prescribed medicine. Then surround yourself with prayer warriors and turn your illness over to God. God is still in the miracle business and He'll always do what He can to heal your heart and mind.

Lord, bless all those who need Your healing touch today, that they may surrender their hearts and minds and bodies to Your care.

~ *Amen*

For Crying Out Loud

I'm caught in a maze and can't find my way out,
blinded by tears of pain and frustration. *Ps. 88:9, MSG*

You've probably been there. Life has taken some unexpected turns, and you find yourself in a mess you helped to create. You didn't do it intentionally, but somehow you feel like crying. You may even be tempted to shake your puny fist at God and ask Him what is going on or even inquire as to why He has abandoned you.

When you're in one of those places where you just feel like shouting, "For crying out loud…enough already!", then it's time to stop looking around and look up. This mess calls for Divine effort.

Once you've begun to look up, you might be able to breathe more easily, pray more intentionally and seek the guidance you need. Put the whole crazy mess at the foot of the cross and let Jesus work with you to straighten things out. Of course, He could do it without you, but if He does it with you, you'll experience His love and forgiveness. You'll be better prepared to do the right thing the next time before you would get into a jam.

Take heart! God sees you and even now is preparing the way out for you. He will rescue you. Dry your tears and seek His face. He'll make the way clear as He goes before you.

When you're between a rock and a hard place, head toward the Rock!

JULY 24

I Got It!

Give me understanding and I will obey your instructions;
I will put them into practice with all my heart. *Ps. 119:34, NLT*

Don't you wish you could truly understand the things of God? You've been embracing learning about God for a long time now. The thing is, there's so much more to understand. Every time you finally get the lesson, you move right on to the next lesson.

How can you learn faster with all your heart and mind and soul? One of the best ways is to simply be quiet. That means resting in the Lord's Presence and asking Him to teach you what you need to know right now. Like Solomon, you can pray for wisdom.

God knows what you can handle. He knows how much you love Him. Keep walking with Him and embrace His Word. Listen for His voice wherever you may be, and He will increase your understanding. He wants your faith to grow and He wants you to be confident in knowing Him.

Like most important things, you won't get through the process quickly. You didn't get to graduation by skipping all the requirements to get there. You're a lifelong student, but if you keep studying and being intentional about learning more about God, you'll move to the head of the class.

God wants Divine truth to enter the understanding through the heart.
~ *Author unknown*

Think Twice

Think twice about bringing evil against your people! Think of Abraham, Isaac, and Israel, your servants to whom you gave your word, telling them 'I will give you many children, as many as the stars in the sky, and I'll give this land to your children as their land forever.'" And God did think twice. He decided not to do the evil he had threatened against his people. *Exod. 32:13-14, MSG*

God's discipline is not something we can always understand. Part of the reason is that we don't have the whole picture. At best, we learn through hindsight. This passage from Exodus though helps us see that sometimes God will think twice about the actions He plans to take. After all, He has all the power.

No doubt He restrains His power to discipline us even today. If He did not, none of us would stand. Why does He do so? He loves us, and He wants us to draw near to Him. He wants to be a good Father to His children.

Perhaps today, you might think twice about how you choose to show God that you love Him and that you want to walk more faithfully with Him. Ask Him what you need to do to be more consistent in your prayer life, and in the good deeds you do for others. Ask Him to think twice about you and bless you with greater understanding and love.

The goal of God's discipline is restoration—never condemnation.

~ Author unknown

Don't Throw in the Towel

"Master," said David, "don't give up hope.
I'm ready to go and fight this Philistine." *1 Sam. 17:32, MSG*

There may come a point when you feel like throwing in the towel, but it's not today. Today you have hope. Today you have every reason to believe that with God all things are possible.

It can feel like some sort of Goliath is just waiting for you around every corner. Most of the giants, the obstacles in your path are probably ones you put there yourself. You may have allowed worry to take over and push your faith into the background. The problem is that the world is muddy, and it's hard to see your way clear if you're listening to any voice but the One voice that can help you.

Whatever you're going through may be big. God is bigger! He's bigger than the obstacles you see around you. He's overcome the world and He knows what you need to do. If you're feeling even remotely like throwing in the towel, then remember the words of young David as he spoke to King Saul about the giant Goliath. He said, "Don't give up hope. I'm ready to go and fight."

That's what God says to you now. He's right there with you, ready to slay the giants in your life. Together, you're unstoppable!

Lord, please walk with me today and help me move past any obstacles in the path. *~ Amen*

JULY 27

Keep Going

God guards you from every evil, he guards your very life.
He guards you when you leave and when you return,
he guards you now, he guards you always. Ps. 121:8, MSG

Imagine that one of the greatest point guards of all time is with you as you play the game of life. Every place you turn, he's there! He's got the drive and the skill of Magic Johnson, impressive beyond belief, and He can block anyone from scoring. The other team trembles just seeing him come onto the court.

That's a picture of what it's like to have God guard your life. He is there at every turn, steps in just when you think someone else will win the day, changing the view to make it harder for you to be attacked. He protects you from head to toe and no one can separate you from His long, protective arms. He guards you as you work and as you make plans with your family.

You may not be able to see all that's happening around you. You may not know which way to turn so that you're still safe. If that's true for you, then remember the One who guards you. He's steadfast and consistent and your enemy is shaken when He comes out on your court. He guards you so you both win!

Lord, thank You for being ever at my side; ahead of me, behind me, and close to me always. ~ *Amen*

The Finish Line

A life frittered away disgusts GOD; he loves those who run straight for the finish line. *Prov. 15:9, MSG*

You've been in the game for some time; the game of life, that is. When you chose to follow Jesus, you became part of His team and you started running toward some new goals. He changed your heart and your direction. It's been quite an adventure and you're probably doing a great job staying the course and keeping up with those who are running right along with you.

However, some days you unconsciously fritter time away because your heart is troubled. You slow down almost to a halt and nothing gets done; at least, nothing that helps move you or the Kingdom of God forward.

Sometimes it's good to stop and let the world go by. Move away from your work, your schedule that seems overwhelming, and the things that cause you to get off track. Just sit quietly with the Coach and ask Him to help you find your way again.

If you get out of step now and then, let the Holy Spirit provide a fresh wind and give you a resurgence of energy so that you can continue the race. May God energize your opportunities to bless others with the victory you've already won through Christ.

Keep running! The race is well worth the effort!

If you aim at nothing, you'll hit it every time. ~ *Author unknown*

A Bout with Doubt

He said to them, "Why are you troubled,
and why do doubts rise in your minds?" *Luke 24:38, NIV*

Most of us would erase the dark cloud of doubt right out of our lives if we could. Of course, putting the condition of "if we could," means that we don't believe we can help ourselves. Doubt has a place in your life, but it doesn't need to have a place in your spiritual life.

Perhaps the best thing to say about doubt, hesitation, misgiving, is that it causes you to keep thinking so you don't act too quickly. However, when you doubt God, then it means you're uncertain about who God is, or what God's character might be. It means you haven't spent enough time with God to really know Him and trust that He watches protectively over you. When you hesitate to believe that your prayers matter or that God cares, it means you've confused the truth and the promises you find in Scripture.

When you're troubled, wondering if prayer works, or if God is there for you, surrender first any hidden doubts that may linger in your mind. Sweep them away and go to God with your whole heart, confessing your doubts, seeking His grace, and centered on His love and mercy.

You'll quickly get over your bout with doubt.

Where do you live? Many a believer lives in the "cottage of doubt," when he might live in the "mansion of faith."

~ C.H. Spurgeon

JULY 30

Keep Your Powder Dry

Be alert and of sober mind. Your enemy the devil prowls around like a roaring lion looking for someone to devour. *1 Pet. 5:8, NIV*

Heading into battle in the 1830s caused Oliver Cromwell to direct his soldiers with this comment. "Trust in God and keep your powder dry." Of course, the idea was two-fold. Trust in God was the first part and be ready to take action was the second part. Get ready for the imminent battle.

This adage applies to our daily lives as well. After all, the current climate in the world makes us strive to trust God for everything. We want to know that He's on our side, fighting with us to keep us from temptation or evil. We go to Him for help any time or any place, because there's no light anywhere else.

Peter suggests we are still in a continual battle. We need to be aware of the ways the enemy lures us into difficulties and tempts us to deceive ourselves. He is relentless. We must keep our powder dry so we're ready to go into a skirmish at any time. We must trust God that He is always close and that He is our shield.

Today, stay alert. Be ready to deflect the wiles of the devil, because he will take any part of you that you allow him to have. Stand guard! Trust God! Keep your powder dry!

Lord, grant that the FIRE in my heart will melt the lead in my feet.

~ Author unknown

Faith in Action

Some men brought to him a paralyzed man, lying on a mat. When Jesus saw their faith, he said to the man, "Take heart, son; your sins are forgiven." Matt. 9:2, NIV

Faith is what brought a paralyzed man to Jesus. We don't know whether the man asked his friends for their help. We don't know if the paralyzed man had faith at all. We only know that the men who brought the man on a stretcher believed that Jesus could heal him. They believed if they just got their friend close to Jesus, he would be able to walk again.

Well, you know what happened. Jesus was pleased to see that the four men had such faith and that they trusted in His help. He immediately restored the man's health and so the man got up, took the stretcher and walked home.

It's important to understand that your faith, your willingness to take someone to Jesus could bring healing to their lives as well. You could be the catalyst, the opportunity for someone else to begin to walk with the Lord.

Take heart as you pray for others and believe that the faith God has given you can also be a light that changes the lives of those around you. You are the hands and feet of Christ.

Lord, thank You for the people of faith who help me to walk with You. May I put my faith in action to help those around me today.

~ *Amen*

August

The Way of Love

"But love your enemies, do good to them, and lend to them without expecting to get anything back. Then your reward will be great, and you will be children of the Most High, because he is kind to the ungrateful and wicked." *Luke 6:35, NIV*

If you are to love your enemies, you must define who they are. Perhaps you don't have people you would put in your enemy camp. You may have a few strained relationships or friendships that have wasted away but labeling them as enemies seems a stretch.

Perhaps if it said, "Love your critics, or love your arrogant boss, or love your ill-tempered brother-in-law," you could get closer to the feeling of this Scripture. The idea is that your life is probably going to have more than a few people in it, who are not necessarily your friends. For whatever reason, they just remain outside of the list of those you want to invite into your world. The reminder here is that you still must treat them well. In fact, you must love them.

Why? Because you're trying to be more like Jesus. You want to be the person God called you to be and Christ's example is that He's kind, forbearing, helpful, and generous to even His enemies. That's a tough act to follow, but you can do it. You may even turn those relationships into friends, and better yet, friends of God.

In Jesus, and for Him, enemies and friends alike are to be loved.

~ Thomas à Kempis

More Rain than Rainbow

See! The winter is past; the rains are over and gone. Flowers appear on the earth; the season of singing has come. *Song of Songs 2:11-12, NIV*

When life feels like you're getting more rain than rainbows, move away from those low-hanging black clouds. The gloominess around you may break into sunshine any minute and you want to be ready to receive it.

Finding the sunny side of the street and staying positive is not easy. It takes courage to bravely step out into the world when your spirits are sagging. Before you do that, it may help to make a list of those things that are the biggest weights on your heart and mind.

Make the list, then make your way to the Scriptures and comfort yourself with some good Psalms. David went through periods of uncertainty, but he always came back to trusting God. God knew that no matter what, David would lay his troubles at God's feet...and leave them there. You can do that too.

Breathe in the Spirit of God's love. Call a friend, pray, and adjust your attitude and it won't be long before hope returns. The rain may still come down through the rays of the sun, but God's promise stands. He watches over you and He will always help you find a rainbow. Keep looking up!

My heart leaps up when I behold a rainbow in the sky.

~ *William Wordsworth*

When God Is Right

God will always give what is right to his people who cry to him night and day, and he will not be slow to answer them. *Luke 18:7, NCV*

Why does it take us so long to learn God's lessons? We struggle through an experience once or twice or more times than that, only to come back and realize that God was right all along. Why couldn't we just listen to Him the first time?

When God tries to show you the right path, but you don't embrace it, you may regret your actions. You may begin to wonder if God will forgive your stubbornness and your stupidity.

The good news is that God waits for you to acknowledge His teaching. He waits until you demonstrate your love for Him by your willingness to change. He knows your heart. He forgives your mistakes as soon as you ask Him to do so. For your sake, He prefers you not make those same mistakes again. After all, once you know the right thing to do, there's no need to repeat the old blunders.

Let go of yesterday. Let go of your past sins and let them be buried beneath the cross of your Savior. He loves you so much, He wants to set your heart free...right now. What a glorious day for you both!

Lord Jesus, thank You for setting me free, and for offering me forgiveness for my sins.

~ *Amen*

AUGUST 4

Is Someone to Blame?

Jesus said, "You're asking the wrong question. You're looking for someone to blame. There is no such cause-effect here. Look instead for what God can do." *John 9:3-5,* MSG

It's only natural when we're suffering through some tangled mess that we try to find someone to blame. After all, it's not usually obvious to us that we played a part in the chaos we're experiencing. Adam moved quickly to blame Eve when the Lord confronted them about eating the forbidden fruit. Of course, Eve quickly moved to blame the snake. The snake knew who was at fault and simply enjoyed his own cleverness. Evil loves to create chaos, looking for any vulnerable target it can find.

So, if you're going through something difficult and you're feeling a need to blame someone or some thing for the circumstances, give it up. Give the whole thing over to God. Ask your Creator what you can do to make amends or fix the mess.

When you stare at difficulty long enough, it begins to look impossible. Even Adam and Eve realized the mess they made would not end there for God would deal with it. God found a way to bring His children back to Himself. That's what He does for you! Thank God for cleaning up your messes with love and kindness.

The reason people blame things on previous generations is that there's only one other choice. ~ *Doug Larson*

Unplug from Fear

Where God's love is, there is no fear,
because God's perfect love drives out fear.
It is punishment that makes a person fear,
so love is not made perfect in the
person who fears. *1 John 4:18, NCV*

Fear is just worry on steroids. It comes along and quickens your pulse, makes your heart race, and fills your head with noise. You need help and the best help is to step up, face the fear, and put on the full armor of God.

Only God can fully take on the heartache and the chaos fear wants to manifest in your life. Only God can love you through the worry and the anxiety that is topping the charts of your weary mind. God sees you. He hears your prayers and He is working quickly to bring you relief.

While He's working on things, you might choose to give yourself a break. Hand the weight of fear over to God and don't take it back again. Jot down the things that make you fearful and pray about each one of them. Do something that makes you feel good. Talk to a friend. Eat dessert. Volunteer somewhere. Unplug from your fear and head toward God's warm embrace. He's waiting for you and He already left the Light on for you.

You have nothing to fear!

Fear knocked on the door. Faith answered, and no one was there.

~ *Author unknown*

AUGUST 6

Cope or Hope

For in this hope we were saved. But hope that is seen is no hope at all. Who hopes for what they already have? *Rom. 8:24, NIV*

The answers to some prayers don't come immediately and it can be helpful to simply let a coping mechanism take over. The problem is that coping, instead of hoping, may mean you've given up before God had a chance to act.

As the Scripture from Romans declares, "Who hopes for what they already have?" If what you are hoping for still matters to you, then it's a good idea to put your hope in front of God and seek His counsel. He may give you an insight you had never considered. God is listening to your heart and your prayers and He is not ignoring the things you hope will happen.

Samuel Johnson said that the natural flight of the human mind is not from pleasure to pleasure, but from hope to hope. It's good to have things you hope for and dream about. It's good to share your heart's desires with God. Let God answer your hope in a way that satisfies your spirit. Don't give up on it or imagine that it just can't be.

Keep trusting God and His infinite wisdom for the best possibilities for your life.

Do not look to your hope, but to Christ, the source of your hope.

~ C.H. Spurgeon

Where Love Leads

Be devoted to one another in love.
Honor one another above yourselves. Rom. 12:10, NIV

Think of the things you've done in your life just because love was leading the way. You may recall the detailed plans you made for your wedding day. You may imagine the birthday cake you made for your child that made you both smile.

Love is Divinely inspired. It drives us to want to make someone else happy. It seeks ways to express itself clearly. Love is always focused on the good and the well-being of others. God planned for you to come into the world. He knows you personally and calls you by name. He knows everything about you, and He loves you because of all you do, and despite all you do. He loves you unconditionally and eternally. His love will never end and there is nothing you can do to separate yourself from His love.

Devoted love goes past the moment, past the disappointment, past the unexpected behavior. Devoted love is so real and so intentional that it reflects something Divine. Being devoted to someone is a calling on your heart. This is the kind of love that truly never fails. This is the kind of love your Father in Heaven has for you. This is the kind of love you deserve to give and receive.

Love is all we have, the only way that each can help the other.

~ *Author unknown*

Resolute Reboot

As you know, we count as blessed those who have persevered. You have heard of Job's perseverance and have seen what the Lord finally brought about. The Lord is full of compassion and mercy. *James 5:11, NIV*

Job was resolute. He did not yield to the logic of his so-called friends. He did not bend to their criticism or their desire to bring him down. Instead, he held firm to his belief. His belief was that God is sovereign and God has the right to do as He pleases.

With one tragic event after another, Job stubbornly stayed true to God. He didn't understand God, but even that did not matter to him. Job persevered and ultimately God did a reboot. He restored to Job everything he had before and then some.

Satan is looking to prove to God that human beings cannot be loyal. So, what does that mean? What would we do to show God that we believe He has all authority over us no matter what happens? How loyal and persistent are we when one trouble after the other occurs?

God's compassion reigns supreme. As we persevere in our willingness to listen to Him and obey Him, He renews our spirits until we feel whole again. Stay close to your Savior today. He is close to you.

When the heart weeps for what it has lost, the spirit laughs for what it has found. *~ Author unknown*

Imperfectly You

But when perfection comes, the things that
are not perfect will end. *1 Cor. 13:10, NCV*

You know your shortcomings. You don't need critics or continual reminders from others about what you do and don't do well. You know you're not perfect and you're not trying to be.

The first thing to know is where to set the bar. What is perfect? One standard is simply to look at Jesus. He lived the way God would have us live as well. He told people about His Father with excitement and love. He healed those who were depressed and oppressed and unhealthy. He spoke kindness into the hearts of orphans and widows. He never gave up on His mission, even to the point of death.

We are His heirs and imperfect as we are, we can try harder to follow our Lord. We can listen with compassion to the needs of others. We can pray with all our might for friends and strangers alike. Why? Because we want to be more like Jesus and grow toward perfection.

As one adage says, "God loves you as you are, but He loves you too much to leave you that way." God wants to inspire your heart toward holiness, toward becoming more of what He called you to be.

Perfection is achieved, not when there is nothing more to add, but when there is nothing left to take away.

~ Antoine de Saint-Exupéry

AUGUST 10

Spinning Your Wheels

The lazy will not get what they want,
but those who work hard will. *Prov. 13:4, NCV*

God's plan for you is one of continual growth. He doesn't want days to go by without drawing you closer to Himself. He wants to nurture your thoughts and actions. He leads you to accept life's challenges and as you overcome them, you learn to trust His personal guidance plan.

Growing is hard work. Growing requires adaptation and patience. It requires learning new things and failing and starting over and trying again. A growth spurt will take you forward to another level of possibility and understanding.

Your job then is to be willing to grow, not to be stuck, and not to simply waste away. You are uniquely gifted by the Lord with talents that others need you to share. If you're simply spinning your wheels today, then shift into higher gear.

Lift your head toward Heaven and praise the God of the universe with your whole heart. He has amazing places that He wants you to go. He wants you to keep your engine running, fueled with His grace and mercy, and keep going. Get out there! You've got a lot to do!

Spiritual growth consists most in the growth of the root, which is out of sight. ~ *Matthew Henry*

Faith Works

"If you do not stand firm in your faith,
you will not stand at all." *Isa. 7:9, NIV*

We all need a firm foundation, a place to stand, that defines us and holds us up. For some of us, it's our faith. Jesus is our Rock and when everything goes haywire, we run back to Him for safety and stability. We depend on Him every day of our lives. He is our Cornerstone.

You probably have people in your life though who don't recognize Jesus as the Cornerstone, the weight-bearing wall, the One they can count on when the going gets tough. So what do they do? Where do they stand when things are falling apart all around them?

Some of us have been seduced into thinking we are smart enough or good enough or wealthy enough, that we can handle anything. We are enchanted by our "followers" on various social media sights, somehow imagining that our validation is there, that our friends are there.

Perhaps a foundation of faith is not what everyone is looking for, but God gave you a Faith Book, a way to be His follower. You have a place to go when the darkness prevails and chaos rules. You are on a firm foundation built on the gift of Jesus Christ. May He bless you and keep you close to His side today.

Lord, thank You for giving me a strong foundation in You. ~ *Amen*

AUGUST 12

Cool Your Jets

"Slow down. Take a deep breath. What's the hurry? Why wear yourself out? Just what are you after anyway?" *Jer. 2:25, MSG*

Pace yourself! You are just one person and you weren't built to have to do it all. Racing from one task to the next usually means that something either falls through the cracks, must be done over, or that nothing gets done well. God created the world in six days, but He rested on the seventh and He'd like you to follow His example.

If you set goals, complete with deadlines and expected results in mind, you might find it difficult to delegate, but delegate you must. You must pace yourself!

Now that you've slowed down, pull out your Bible and look for some Psalms that might bless your spirit and give you peace. Read through each one with the intention to strengthen your soul. Once you've done that, breathe in the Spirit of God as you say your prayers and surrender your to-do list. Ask for His help in creating priorities according to His plan and purpose for you today. Walk, don't run, to get things done!

If you go through life at a slower pace, chances are good, you'll have much better days. Promise!

Oh, Lord, You know how busy I must be today. If I forget You, do not forget me. Thank You, Father! Amen

~ *Adapted from Sir Jacob Astley*

Look Around or Look Up

It is necessary for the Son of Man to be lifted up—
and everyone who looks up to him, trusting and expectant,
will gain a real life, eternal life. *John 3:14-15, MSG*

Most things in life are about getting a good perspective. When you look around, you'll get one point of view. You may see the world as fast-paced and difficult to understand. You may see it as beautiful and generous. Much of your vision depends on the attitude of your heart.

God wants you to look up. Look up and see the vastness of the sky, the blueness that covers the planet, sprinkled with sunshine and clouds that dot the horizon, things that can help you feel better. It's okay that you are not the one in control. Looking up reminds you that God still reigns and when you look up to seek Him, He looks back at you.

Remember what He has already done for you. Consider your special moments of crisis and the times of celebration and remember how you knew God was in the midst of those things.

If you look up and then look around, you should see yourself and everyone else as living, and moving and having their being in Christ Jesus. When you see things that way, everywhere you look, becomes beautiful.

If better were within, better would come out. ~ *Thomas Fuller*

AUGUST 14

Good Deed Doers

"In the same way, let your light shine before others,
that they may see your good deeds and
glorify your Father in heaven." *Matt. 5:16, NIV*

The person who has the resources to donate thousands of dollars to charitable causes, is not necessarily doing more than the person who fills bags with Christmas candy for orphans. Both are giving what they can and the only difference in the works themselves has to do with how much love was shared as part of the process. It's a difference of attitude and gratitude.

Your light can shine for one person or for hundreds of people. Your good deeds are counted as blessings when they are done in love. Little things always make a difference. Your smile might change the way someone feels today.

Sharing a moment of quiet conversation or offering to help someone do a menial task, can be a Godsend. A text with a note of encouragement, gives someone a sense that they are known and loved. Whatever you do, start with love and your good deeds will radiate, all the way up to Heaven.

Lord, help me to do the little things that brighten the lives of others today. Amen.

The love of God is the principle and end of all our good works.

~ *John Wesley*

No Worries

"Therefore I tell you, do not worry about your life, what you will eat or drink; or about your body, what you will wear. Is not life more than food, and the body more than clothes?" *Matt. 6:25, NIV*

You seldom have to worry about whether you'll be able to have another meal or have clean clothes to wear. You've been blessed with the means to take care of those things every day.

More often, we worry about people we love, or having sufficient income, or how to better manage finances. These kinds of things change on any given day, because illness and accident and other unforeseen events challenge our lives.

You have your own list of worries and you may consult it regularly, but the question here is this. Isn't life more than any worry you may have? Of course it is, so then what?

Jesus wants you to realize that life, your life, is more valuable than anything else and how you live your life matters to Him. Worry will never make a difference, but prayer will.

Every prayer that takes the place of worry moves you forward. If you can turn your life over to God's grace and mercy, and trust Him, He will be there for you. He always will say, "No worries."

With God all things are possible and there is no room for worry.

~ Author unknown

AUGUST 16

Worry Lines

"You cannot add any time to your life by worrying about it." *Matt. 6:27, NCV*

One thing you've learned by now is that you can't add one minute to your time line unless God changes your calendar. He created the dates for your entry and exit on Earth before you even arrived. Nothing you can do will change that.

Worry's agenda is not intended to make your life better or longer or happier. It doesn't bring more food to your table, fix the car when it breaks down or find the money for your child to go to college. Worry doesn't have one positive trait. It's a parasite, feeding off your mind and leaving you with nothing at all.

How do you reduce its impact on your life? You focus on what you can do yourself and then surrender the rest to God. You look to Him and pray, and you don't stop until worry has left the building. You always have a choice.

You can spend days on the dead-end path of worry, or you can take that time and add to the growth of your spirit. Turn worry over to God as soon as you're aware of its presence. You don't have to give it control. You can give God the control. It's your choice. What will it be?

You can't change the past, but you can ruin the present by worrying about the future. *~ Author unknown*

No Shoes

"And why do you worry about clothes?
Look at how the lilies in the field grow. They don't
work or make clothes for themselves." *Matt. 6:28, NCV*

Jesus knew people were concerned about everyday provisions and so He made a point to help them rethink things. He looked at the way God adorned the lilies of the fields and the birds of the air and reminded His listeners that God dressed them beautifully, so they could flourish. He does even more than that for you.

The most exquisite part of your outfit any day of the week is your smile. Your smile radiates with the love of Christ to everyone around you. It makes the most stunning gown pale in comparison to your Heavenly glow.

God knows what you need, and He provides for you when you need a new piece of clothing. However, He provides for you every day by blessing you with a spirit of joy to share with those around you. You light up the room any time you enter it no matter what you wear. Kick up your heels and rejoice!

The world always looks brighter from behind a smile.

~ *Author unknown*

What's Going on Tomorrow?

"Don't worry about tomorrow, for tomorrow will bring its own worries. Today's trouble is enough for today." *Matt. 6:34, NLT*

Some of us are savers. We save coupons and cereal box tops. We save old family pictures and mementos from childhood. These are things we can't throw away and so each time we move we cart them to our new location.

It's good to save fond memories, but it's not so good to pack up the troubles of yesterday and take them with you in to tomorrow. Before you know it, you've got a heavy load and you can barely manage to sling it over your shoulder.

Jesus reminds you that you don't need to carry those weights yourself. You don't need to haul yesterday's worries and yesterday's mistakes into today. You can set them down at His feet and He will gladly carry them. Not only that, but He will offer forgiveness and opportunity for you to lighten the load immediately. He will throw out those old sins with His power of forgiveness.

If you've got a lot to get done today, shed the weight of yesterday and give yourself the freedom to walk in joy. When you choose to let go of the burdens, you have more room to create loving memories with those around you. Treasures are always worth keeping. Tomorrow already looks brighter!

Lord, thank You for helping to lighten the load of worry and concern. You are the gift of my heart and soul each day. *~ Amen*

Troubled Hearts

"Don't let your hearts be troubled.
Trust in God, and trust also in me." *John 14:1, NLT*

The biggest problem with having a troubled heart is that it takes up all your time. It takes you away from having a trusting heart. You can't trust the chair to hold you up, if you're also not willing to sit in the chair because it might break. Your actions speak louder than your words.

Trust requires action. You can choose to not let your heart be troubled because you know that God is with you. You know that with God all things are possible, and you can put your trust in Him. Of course, it's easier to trust God when you don't have anything you're trying to trust Him for.

When you're troubled, put your concerns in God's hands and truly leave them there. Give God time to work things out.

Thank God for being with you. Go on with your daily work because you are free to apply your heart and mind to other things. Enjoy your day and smile because you trust that all things will work together for your good. Choose today to give up your troubled heart and embrace God's strength and love and mercy. Trust in Him today, tomorrow, and always!

He who trusts in himself is lost. He who trusts in God can do all things. ~ *Alphonsus Liguori*

AUGUST 20

A Little More Courage

Be strong and brave. Don't be afraid of them and don't be frightened, because the LORD your God will go with you. He will not leave you or forget you. *Deut. 31:6, NCV*

Sometimes without even seeing a shadow, we find ourselves troubled and uncertain. We're afraid that we can't handle an upcoming event, or a much-needed conversation with a loved one. We feel vulnerable and defenseless on our own. Our lack of courage means we've taken our eyes off God and put them on the object of our fear or simply on ourselves.

So, how can you overcome the tentacles of fear that wrap themselves around your heart and mind? You can release the grasp of fear when you remember that you are not alone, not now and not ever! God has given His angels to watch over you and He guards your heart and protects your spirit. He holds you firmly in His powerful hand.

God will never forget about you. He can't. You are connected to Him and you are precious in His sight. He knows each thing you face and all He needs is for you to surrender your weakness. Call on His strength and His power to sustain you. Look for Him to show up and help you. When you do, you will live in His peace, ready to take on whatever is ahead. Have courage and rest in His love today.

Courage is the strength or choice to begin a change. Determination is the persistence to continue in that change. ~ *Author unknown*

Courage Wakes You Up

Be alert. Continue strong in the faith.
Have courage, and be strong. *1 Cor. 16:13, NCV*

What kinds of things require your courage? Would you think about the courage it takes to stand up and speak in front of a group? Would you note the courage you need when your financial picture is sagging? Perhaps you'd list the courage it takes for you to just get out of bed to face a new day.

Things that cause you to be brave strengthen your resolve, build your character and help you grow spiritually and emotionally. The gift of needing courage to speak in front of a group is that it motivates you to prepare your presentation and learn how to speak from your heart. The fact that your finances are suffering may cause you to have to make better choices or do something new to supplement your income. Those kinds of choices require change and change of any sort requires courage.

The thing God gave you early on to help you be brave and strong is faith. Your faith will serve as a guide and a guard, shielding you and reminding you that you can handle whatever is up ahead. Wake up your senses and put your faith in God. Together you can do whatever needs to be done!

Have courage and be strong!

One person with courage becomes a majority. ~ *Author unknown*

Be Calm Today

When Jesus woke up, he rebuked the wind and said to the waves, "Silence! Be still!" Suddenly the wind stopped, and there was a great calm. *Mark 4:39, NLT*

You've dealt with the winds and the waves of life that toss you from one fear to the next. You've experienced what it means to see chaos reign when all you wanted was for things to calm down and be at peace.

Since you know what chaos feels like, perhaps this word from Scripture can serve to remind you that Jesus is in control. God the Father and God the Son have power over all elements of your life. You only need to surrender to their loving grace and mercy.

When Jesus spoke to the wind and to the waves as the boat rocked over the waters, they heard His voice and surrendered to Him. He was the Creator, the One who caused them to be in the first place. It is the same with you. God is your Creator and He is in control. Surrender to His desire to bring you peace today. Let Him get into the boat with you and challenge the chaos to be still. With Him, you can be at peace.

It looks like the sun is coming out after all. Enjoy your day in His light!

Let nothing good or bad upset the balance of your life.

~ Thomas à Kempis

Hold on to the Promise

God's way is perfect. All the LORD's promises prove true. He is a shield for all who look to him for protection. *2 Sam. 22:31, NLT*

Science fiction movies may depict a force field that surrounds a space craft. It's dramatic and protective! It's not so far-fetched to think of God as your force field, the One who shields you and protects you when you reach out to Him. He knows when you are vulnerable, and He promises to be right there with you.

God has been making promises to His children since the beginning. He placed a part of Himself within us so we could recognize Him and learn to know Him better.

Knowing that God has not changed and does not change helps us realize that His ways are perfect and that He always keeps His promises. No matter how many times human beings have stepped over the line or how many times we've sinned against God, He continues to be faithful. Jesus promised He would always be with us and that He would take us back to the place He prepared for us when we go home again.

As you consider His promises today, take heart. Those promises will be fulfilled in God's own timing and they will keep you safely within His grasp.

There is a living God; He has spoken in the Bible. He means what He says and will do all that He has promised! ~ *Hudson Taylor*

AUGUST 24

Be Encouraged

Therefore comfort each other and edify one another, just as you also are doing. *1 Thess. 5:11, NKJV*

Some people instantly put you at ease, so you feel better just being around them. You may not completely understand the calming effect they have on you, but their peaceful presence makes a difference. Those people have that sweet countenance and personality just naturally.

Others have to work at doing what they can to comfort those who need a good word or a kind thought. Whichever way it is for you, the message is to be an encourager, a motivator, a sustainer of possibility to the people around you. You may encourage them simply by giving them information that strengthens or renews their path. However, you offer encouragement, you make a difference.

You can no doubt remember many times when others have lifted your spirits. Today, God calls you to be more aware of your neighbors and your co-workers and even family members who simply need to know they have a place to go when their hearts are heavy, or their load is too much to bear. Comfort them. Renew them and help them find their way. Let them see the love of Christ through the things you do.

To ease another's heartache is to forget one's own.

~ Abraham Lincoln

Don't Pet Your Pet Peeves!

And do not grieve the Holy Spirit of God,
by whom you were sealed for the day of redemption.
Let all bitterness, wrath, anger, clamor, and evil speaking
be put away from you, with all malice. *Eph. 4:30-31, NKJV*

It's okay to let off steam in positive ways like getting some exercise or sharing your frustrations with a friend. The thing you don't want is to pet your pet peeves so much that they become bigger than they are.

Ever since the day you were filled with the Holy Spirit, God has been working with you to remove all bitterness and envy. He's been teaching you how to love your enemies and how to bring good out of negative situations. It sounds like a big job and it is.

Angry words, evil deeds, those things that separate people from each other and from God are not the way to go. God has a better plan and it all starts with you. You can bring the light of kindness, gentle speech and the gift of humor to your circumstances. You can make a difference and keep everyone and everything around you in peace.

Your pet peeves may still frustrate you, but they don't have to dominate you.

Let go of your attachment to being right, and suddenly your mind is more open. You're able to benefit from the unique viewpoints of others, without being crippled by your own judgement.

~ *Ralph Marston*

Rocking Chair Worries

"And which of you by worrying can add one cubit to his stature? If you then are not able to do the least, why are you anxious for the rest?" *Luke 12:25-26, NKJV*

Wishing has a place in your life, but when it comes to things you absolutely have no control over, it's a waste of time. After all, you probably have not made yourself grow taller, thinner, or extraordinarily talented simply by wishing it would be so. These things are rocking chair worries. You rock and rock, and wish and wish, and worry and worry, but you will not move from your spot. Nothing will change!

God wants you to stop worrying because He knows it will never get you anywhere. You can mount that rocking horse as many times as you want, but it will never leave the room. It won't get you where you want to go.

What can you do instead? You can stop rocking and get down on your knees. You can put your worries into God's hands and leave them there. He will come to your side, bringing guidance and comfort and direction.

God is with you. He will always want to hear about the things that concern you. When you stay close to Him, you can leave your worries behind and simply ride like the wind.

Worry is like a rocking chair. It will give you something to do, but it will never get you anywhere. *~ Author unknown*

Freedom from Fear

"Do not fear, nor be afraid; Have I not told you from that time, and declared it? You are My witnesses. Is there a God besides Me? Indeed there is no other Rock; I know not one." *Isa. 44:8, NKJV*

The prophet Isaiah worked hard to share the things of God with the people of his day. He tried to inspire their hearts to leave the man-made gods behind and worship the only God of the universe.

God suggested to Isaiah that He had looked around and could find no other gods besides Himself. He is the Rock, the foundation of our lives.

If we believe there is only one God, then we can also believe that God can be trusted. We are witnesses to the fact of His existence, partly by the words we speak, and partly by the confidence we share that He is with us. Our willingness to trust in Him, letting go of fear and worry and those things that are totally beyond our control, shows the people around us, that we are free. We are free to offer praise and worship because we know that God reigns.

Imagine how you would feel if you truly let go of fear and worry. How many hours could you reclaim in a day because you didn't spend them steeped in anxiety? How many years would you redeem of your life? Will you let go of fear today?

As we are liberated from our fears, our presence automatically liberates others. ~ *Nelson Mandela*

AUGUST 28

Stronger than You Know

But God chose the foolish things of the world to shame the wise; God chose the weak things of the world to shame the strong. *1 Cor. 1:27,* NIV

C.S. Lewis wrote, "According to Christian teachers, the essential vice, the utmost evil, is Pride. Unchastity, anger, greed, drunkenness, and all that, are mere fleabites in comparison: it was through Pride that the devil became the devil: Pride leads to every other vice: it is the complete anti-God state of mind."

Pride is one of the worst demons to overcome. It works to make those with wisdom, forget that God made them wise. It causes those in authority to forget that God reigns. It shames us before God because we are each prey to its temptations. Arrogance, pettiness, judgment, disrespect, all are in league with pride to cause you to sin.

God demonstrated how foolish pride is by showing us the direct opposites. The wise can be brought down by the foolish. The strong can be overpowered by the weak.

Resist pride and seek God's loving direction. See each person in your path today as one who is redeemed and loved by God and therefore worthy of your respect and kindness. When you do, you shine a light on all that God meant for your good.

Learn to break your own will. Be zealous against yourself. Allow no pride to dwell in you. ~ *Thomas à Kempis*

It's No Trouble

In Joppa there was a disciple named Tabitha (in Greek her name is Dorcas); she was always doing good and helping the poor. *Acts 9:36, NIV*

Wouldn't it be wonderful to come to the end of your life and have someone write your story? Perhaps, like Dorcas, they would write, "you were always doing good and helping those who were in need."

You are writing your life story every day and what you do for others is a big part of your tale. It is the part that creates warm memories and builds a legacy with your family and friends.

People who are always doing kind things for those around them do it with whole-hearted joy and say something like, "It's no trouble!" even though they had to go out of their way to help.

The things we do for each other make a difference in the Kingdom of God. He knows your heart and He applauds all that you do for any of His children.

Lord, keep me mindful of those who might need my help today. Amen.

Even if it's a little thing, do something for those who have need of help, something for which you get no pay but the privilege of doing it. *~ Albert Schweitzer*

Calm Balm

"You are battered from head to foot— covered with bruises, welts, and infected wounds— without any soothing ointments or bandages." *Isa. 1:6, NLT*

If you feel battered and bruised by life, there is only one thing to do. Don't let the bruises work through your heart and mind. Instead, turn them over to the Holy Spirit who will comfort you with His healing balm and wrap you in His calming embrace.

When Jesus offered to send the Comforter, the Holy Spirit to earth after His resurrection, He did so because He knew His people would need help to revive their spirits and to find peace in their lives.

The Holy Spirit draws near to you to pamper you with God's grace and mercy. He knows what you need and seeks your good.

You can only do a simple band-aid fix. The Holy Spirit can do everything. He can bring healing to your heart, uplift your soul, and protect your life. If you're walking around wounded today, stop everything and ask for God's soothing ointments of grace and peace. Wrap yourself in the comfort of the Holy Spirit who cares about your life and wants you to be healed.

Every time we say, "I believe in the Holy Spirit," we mean that we believe that there is a living God able and willing to enter human personality and change it. *~ J.B. Phillips*

Worry Never Paid a Bill

Worry weighs a person down; an encouraging word cheers a person up. *Prov. 12:25, NLT*

Worry is a dead weight. It causes your body to feel lifeless. It interrupts your thoughts and keeps you from focusing on more important things. It manipulates your day and prevents you from moving forward.

If all that is true, and it is, then why do we continue to give worry so much space in our heads? What if you replaced its nagging noise and memorized a Bible verse about God's desires for your life, or about how to embrace peace. Maybe you could squash worry in its tracks. Wouldn't that be better for you?

Once you decide, and it is up to you, to throw the weight of worry off your shoulders, you may be surprised at how quickly you feel more energetic and hopeful. You may discover that you can hear God's voice as you pray and that you are at peace because you've turned everything over to the One who loves you more than anything.

Once worry leaves, you'll be ready to step out into the world and offer words of encouragement to everyone you meet. Imagine the good cheer you'll be bringing to those who desperately need you...because they are still worrying themselves.

Lord, I place all my worries at the foot of the cross, and I embrace all the goodness You have for me today. *~ Amen*

September

The Rescue Team

The men designated by name took the prisoners, and from the plunder they clothed all who were naked. They provided them with clothes and sandals, food and drink, and healing balm. All those who were weak they put on donkeys. *2 Chron. 28:15, NIV*

The rescue team in Chronicles was pre-selected, chosen for the job to treat the prisoners well. They would relieve their sufferings. Compassionate rescuers, today, called First Responders, have been a part of every generation and God calls those people specifically to the task. He sees their hearts and knows what they can do.

Mother Teresa worked tirelessly to relieve suffering in the world and will always serve as an example to us. God calls each of us to have a heart of compassion, one that reaches out to a neighbor, or a teenager, or an aging family member. Each of us can bring peace to the hearts and minds of others by doing simple things like listening to their concerns and offering a meal.

Even you may need a compassionate rescue team sometime. You may be a prisoner of your own doubts, or past mistakes, or poor choices. You may need to know that someone else sees you, cares for you and wants your life to be better. Jesus came to rescue all who are lost and we each can follow His example.

Lord, help us to reach out to others in need in any way that we can today. *~ Amen*

SEPTEMBER 2

I'm Having a Pity Party

If anyone has material possessions and sees
a brother or sister in need but has no pity on them,
how can the love of God be in that person? *1 John 3:17, NIV*

Have you ever held a pity party? You focused on the craziness of life, and all the things that are simply unfair. You deserved to pout! Does that sound familiar?

The sad part is that the pity party can only take you to an even deeper level of depression and disappointment.

God does not want you to beat yourself up over every poor choice, and every unkindness you can recall. What He wants is for you to remember that you're a human being who needs to love yourself. God loves you and though He may be waiting for you to seek His help with your troubles, He has not given up on you, and He never will. He sees all that is good about you.

The same thing is true for people you know. Your friends who have heavy hearts need one thing. They need you to reach out to them with the gift of compassion and love and remind them who they are in the eyes of God. God has pity on them and wants them to come to Him for healing and grace. Once they do, they can have a real party to celebrate their joy.

Lord, help all of us know that we can come to You no matter what is going on in our lives. *~ Amen*

Fix the Broken

The sacrifice God wants is a broken spirit. God, you will not reject a heart that is broken and sorry for sin. Ps. 51:17, NCV

The fastest way for God to "fix" us is if we come to Him "broken." If you don't have any broken parts of your life, then God has blessed you enormously, but if you're like most people, you have a few broken pieces.

When you take your broken pieces to the Potter, He can heal you and make you whole again. He can redesign you so that you are free to move beyond them. You don't have to drag your past brokenness around with you anymore. What good news!

So, what's the secret? How do you prepare your heart so that you can go before Him and seek His grace and healing? You simply need to have a heart that is sorry for your sins, sorry for the mistakes you've made, the crazy choices you've allowed, and even the pride that may have gotten in the way. Surrender everything you are, and God will hold you close. He will see your sorrow and embrace you and make you even more beautiful.

If anything in your life is broken today, then gather up every piece of brokenness and surrender it to God. His forgiveness will create new opportunities to feel His love.

God can do wonders with a broken heart; if we give Him all the pieces. ~ *Author unknown*

Anxious for Nothing

God, examine me and know my heart;
test me and know my anxious thoughts. *Ps. 139:23, NCV*

We may not know exactly what relief the psalmist was looking for as he invited God into his heart and asked Him to know his anxious thoughts. We don't need to know because we often have anxious thoughts ourselves.

You may worry because it's the end of the month and you aren't sure if you'll have money for all the bills. You may have anxiety about your teenager or your spouse and you're not sure how things will work out.

Anxiety is an equal opportunity intruder. It doesn't matter where you are or who you are, it will push its way into your mind and do everything possible to keep you stirred up. Prayer alleviates anxiety.

Prayer gives you a chance to tell God everything that is bothering you. It gives you the opportunity to share your heart. You can tell God how you feel about the situation at hand and confess any part you might have played in your current difficulty. Then prayer does one more thing. It gives you the chance to hand it all over to God, seeking His counsel, and trusting that He has your back. He knows your heart, and He knows what you need. Pack up those anxious thoughts and send them away. You don't need them.

Lord, help me to let go of any anxious thoughts. I leave them all at Your feet. *~ Amen*

The Spirit of Truth

When the Spirit of truth comes, he will guide you into all truth. He will not speak on his own but will tell you what he has heard. He will tell you about the future. *John 16:13, NLT*

The Holy Spirit is sometimes called, the Spirit of Truth. Since we know that God is offended by lies and deceit, truth deserves to be connected to holiness.

Truth asks us to stand firm in our beliefs. It wants us to live in righteousness and not bend the rules. It wants us to set our egos aside and move humbly toward the throne of God. Truth wants the best of us. Truth is a shining beacon that can guide all we do and help others to see God's ways more clearly.

It's funny how often we avoid truth. We don't want to confess that we had two donuts for breakfast, when all we've talked about for weeks is losing weight. We don't want to admit we shared a bit of gossip. We have a thousand and one ways to disguise truth and yet, we want to be honest people.

Today, remember that the Holy Spirit walks in truth. He wants us to reexamine our own behaviors. With His help, more light pours into our hearts and we feel better and more at ease. As Jesus said, "The truth will set you free!"

The Spirit of Truth and the Spirit of Freedom...these are pillars that build a strong foundation. *~ Author unknown*

Take a Day Off

He told them, "This is what the LORD commanded:
Tomorrow will be a day of complete rest,
a holy Sabbath day set apart for the LORD." *Exod. 16:23, NLT*

Some people can scarcely remember the last time they took a day off. They simply keep going, marching to the beat of the to-do list they created.

They may succeed at their work, but they might lose sight of the importance of taking time to rest. Even God took a day off. He worked hard creating the universe and He rested on the seventh day, pleased that all was well.

What happens when you rest? For one thing, your mind and your body are set at ease. They don't have to race from one place to the next. They don't have to be anxious about the things that are not getting done.

Rest gives you quiet time to spend with God. You can focus on your prayers and on your reading of Scripture. You can focus on the needs of those around you. You can treat yourself to doing things that give you joy.

The best part is that you can rest in the embrace of your Savior. You can spend time with Him in ways that help energize you for everything else you will do tomorrow. Take a day off! It will do you good.

How beautiful it is to do nothing, and then rest afterward.

~ *Author unknown*

When God Shows Up

Increase the days of the king's life, his years for many generations. May he be enthroned in God's presence forever; appoint your love and faithfulness to protect him. *Ps. 61:6-7, NIV*

Prayer gives us the opportunity to thank God for all He has done in the past, praise Him for His awesomeness, and then put in our requests for those things that affect life today. When we ask God for help, the deep desire of our hearts is that He will show up and that our issues will be resolved immediately.

The thing we know is that we have no control over the outcome. We trust God to be our Source for good in all things. We need Him to come to our aid, be at our side, and simply help us sort out our difficulties.

When we pray, God not only hears our requests, but He's been working on the solutions to our needs before we ever came to Him for help. He leans in to hear our hearts.

When your heart speaks, God shows up every time. He is the only One who can make a difference. Pray and then reflect on all the previous times God has shown up just for you. When you finish praying, go back to Him with a heart of gratitude. He loves to know you appreciate all He has done.

Lord, thank You for the many times and the many ways You have shown up in my life. I give You thanks and praise! ~ *Amen*

SEPTEMBER 8

It's a God Thing!

Then the Lord said, "I am making this agreement with you.
I will do miracles in front of all your people—things
that have never before been done for any other nation
on earth—and the people with you will see my work.
I, the Lord, will do wonderful things for you." *Exod. 34:10, NCV*

Have you ever had a miraculous moment? Maybe you received an unexpected bonus. Whatever it was, it just seemed to happen. You might say, "It's a God thing!"

It's great to remember the things God does to bless our lives because we often are willing to give God the blame, but not the credit.

In Exodus, God is offering to do something special, something He's never done before simply to show the people of the earth what He can do. He promises to do wonderful things in front of everyone. He wants all of them to understand that this is "a God thing!"

God still keeps the earth in its orbit and allows the sun to come up each day. He sets all things in motion and He protects those He loves. Wherever you go today, look around you, and look up. Discover for yourself something that God is doing right now, right in front of you. Give Him the glory for doing only what He can do because He's doing a God thing!

Lord, I can't count all the ways You bless my life. Thank You for each new day.
~ Amen

Be the Light

"In the same way, you should be a light for other people. Live so that they will see the good things you do and will praise your Father in heaven." Matt. 5:16, NCV

One reason for shining your light is simply that Jesus asked you to do so. He said that it wasn't much help to have you put your light under a bushel because if you did that, the room would still be dark. You put your light on a stand for everyone to be able to see what is going on.

Another reason is that each time you shine your light, you simply glow. That's right! Your face becomes brighter, your heart is lighter and those around you notice a discernable difference in your voice and your mannerisms. The light of God's love has made you a warmer and happier person.

Perhaps another reason is the fact that your light draws others to the Lord. When someone stands in that light, they feel better, more at peace and more loved. They may not know the reason why, but you will have caused them to want to know more...to know more about Jesus.

Your light makes a difference and God gave you that light as a blessing. All He asks of you is that you will just "be" the light!

I want my light to shine, even if only in a small way, like a match struck in the dark. Perhaps then it will illumine the way for someone else.

~ *Author unknown*

Zapped and Sapped

God will speak to this people, to whom he said, "This is the resting place, let the weary rest"; and, "This is the place of repose." *Isa. 28:11-12, NIV*

That's it! You're done! You've given every ounce of strength you have, and you simply can't do any more. You are zapped and sapped, and you need to rest.

You've come to the end of your proverbial rope and all you need to do now is listen to God. He invites you to a resting place, a place of recovery and renewal. He may not take you to a little cottage on the beach or to a quiet spot up in the mountains, but He takes you to a place you can get to instantly. He asks you to come close to Him, sit at His feet, and simply listen to His voice.

Rest! Take time apart from all that you have been charged to do and give yourself permission to simply be quiet. Read some Scripture, meditate on the Psalms, imagine that there's no one in the world, but you and God. Feel His Presence in such a way that your whole body becomes engulfed in peace.

It's okay for you to take a break! God offers you renewal and the blessing of the One who loves you unconditionally and always.

Rest is a matter of wisdom, not law. ~ *Woodrow Kroll*

The Cost of Deceit

But he said, "Your brother came with deceit and has taken away your blessing." *Gen. 27:35, NKJV*

Most of the time deceit is a negative and ugly form of behavior. It's usually motivated by greed or some other self-serving opportunity. Certainly, Jacob deceived his father Isaac into thinking he was Esau out of selfishness. He was not the first born, even though he was a twin, so he would not have received the blessing given to a first-born child. Isaac's blessing was tantamount to receiving God's blessing and Jacob wanted that. He got it, but by deceit.

Sometimes deceit is obvious. We can clearly see it at work as we recognize the ways human beings fool each other, deceiving each other with promises that can never be kept.

The thing to be clear about here is that God hates deceit. He hates lies in any form and so when we find ourselves being tempted to deceive someone, or if we've been the victim of someone else's deceit, the first thing to do is seek God's help. Open your heart to Him and listen for His wisdom. He will guide you back into truth and possibility. He will make sure that you receive the blessing that He had meant for you.

Nothing is so easy as to deceive oneself; for what we wish, we readily believe.

~ *Author unknown*

Mountains and Molehills

They talk big, lie through their teeth, make deals.
But their high-sounding words turn out to be
empty words, litter in the gutters. *Hos. 10:4, MSG*

It isn't good to make mountains out of molehills. In other words, it's important to look at the reality of a situation and not become so involved in worrying about it that you make it bigger than it is. You can deal with molehills much more effectively than those mountain peaks.

Sometimes you are enticed into trusting someone who offers you a mountain of possibility when all they have is a molehill to sell. The problem is that they package their lies in such a beautiful way you lose sight of the truth. They tempt you to eat the forbidden fruit and you take a bite.

It's important to be mindful of the ways you can be deceived either by the stories in your head, or by the smooth salesmanship others use to get you to trust them. If someone paints a picture for you that seems too good to be true, it probably is. Intellectually, you already know this, but emotionally, you might buy in even when you know better.

Ask God to guide you into all truth so that you only buy into the things He wants for you. With His guidance, you will experience peace and hope. Trust Him!

Lord, I know that I can be easily drawn off the path or deceived by others. Please keep me close to You and lead me in truth.

~ Amen

From Suffering to Hope

We also rejoice in our sufferings, because we know that suffering produces perseverance; perseverance, character; and character, hope. *Rom. 5:3-4, NIV*

Most of us are not cheering when we go through misery. The fact is that we want the misery to be over as quickly as possible.

Difficult times help build our own character and help us understand the Divine character of God. We learn to trust Him more fully as He walks with us through the misery and He leads us into hope.

God wants us to understand that we may be going through a rough patch, but when we do, He helps us persevere, trust, believe, and ultimately stay on the path He directs. When we do that, it appears there's an even greater gift to receive. God can work out the suffering and produce something good, something safe and sustainable. God can strengthen us to such a degree that when we look back on the suffering we can easily see His hand at work. We can understand why even those tough times were worthy of praise.

Hope sustains you through the hardest parts of your life. Now that is indeed a reason to give God thanks and praise. May You feel His Presence in all you do today.

If it were not for hopes, the heart would break. ~ *Thomas Fuller*

Do it Right!

But be sure that everything is done properly and in order. *1 Cor. 14:40, NLT*

Part of your lifelong training has been about process and procedure. There is an order to getting things done. When you buy a product requiring assembly, you may ignore the instructions that come with it, assuming you're smart enough to figure it out. It's a bit annoying when you have to finally go and read the directions.

Doing things right means that we are willing to surrender our way to get something done and go to the rule book, look up the steps to take and then follow the process outlined. As Christians, our rule book is the Word of God. It's the best place for us to begin any process and the only place where we can seek God's direction for our lives.

When we begin anything without God's guidance, somewhere along the way, we'll have to backtrack or begin again. Our efforts will not produce the outcome we had hoped for, or the one God had intended, because we didn't do it right. Doing something right may reflect a moral choice, but often it reflects a spiritual choice. Did we start with God?

Whatever you're trying to accomplish today, do things in proper order. Pray, seek God's help, and then move toward your goal.

Lord, help me to read your instruction book, before I start anything today.

~ Amen

Raise Your Praise

Praise the LORD! Praise God in His sanctuary; Praise Him in His mighty firmament! Praise Him for His mighty acts; Praise Him according to His excellent greatness! Praise Him with the sound of the trumpet; Praise Him with the lute and harp! *Ps. 150:1-3, NKJV*

Imagine a parade to honor God that goes all around the world. It would have every kind of instrument possible, people clapping their hands and singing out loud to share in the joy of God's love and majesty. That parade would go on for days because every heart that is turned toward God would want to march to the sounds of the trumpets and the big bass drums to share God's glory.

It's an awesome parade because every person, every float, every musical note has only one intention, and that is to praise the Lord! You may not see this parade coming to your town any time soon, but maybe today you could lean in and listen for the sound of joy as the birds sing above you and the breezes blow through the trees. Maybe today, you could see the parade going on in nature as it fills the Heavens with the blessings that God created.

Open your heart and mind to simply give God the glory for all that you have and all that you are in Him.

Praising God is one of the highest and purest acts of religion. In prayer, we act like men; in praise we act like angels.

~ *Thomas Watson*

Yield

But the wisdom that is from above is first pure, then peaceable, gentle, willing to yield, full of mercy and good fruits, without partiality and without hypocrisy. *James 3:17, NKJV*

What happens when you pray for wisdom? God's wisdom is right, righteous, pure in the sense that it is the best insight you can receive. As you take it in, you feel at peace, knowing you can trust your senses and your thoughts about what you should do to please God in the situations you face.

You also know that God is not forcing His ideas on you. He's not trying to control you. He's simply giving you gentle guidance and direction. He's willing to continue the conversation with you about what might be done, even willing to consider your thoughts as well.

Because God is full of mercy, He will then work all things out for your good, knowing that you've come to Him with a surrendered heart and a willing mind to do as He suggests. Yielding then to what God wants you to do becomes easy because He has shown you that He is with you and will continue to walk with you in all that is ahead of you.

It's a good thing to pray for wisdom. The wiser you are, the more you will follow in His steps, trusting Him all the way. From that, you will yield only joy!

~ Author unknown

How Can You Help Yourself?

Study to be quiet. *1 Thess. 4:11, KJV*

When you're going through troubling events, one of the hardest things to do is let your mind simply be quiet. After all, you're looking for answers and you need something to happen right away. Everything inside your head is noisy. So how can you help yourself?

To quiet your mind, pull out the Word of God and study what it says. Look for Scriptures that bring you peace or seek Psalms that bring comfort. Whatever you do, sit quietly with the Lord so that He can speak to you, above the noise and chatter. Something about getting into a search mode, a study posture helps to restore you and let you be still.

Think back to when you were in school and had to study for a test. You had to focus on the material, memorize portions of it, and reflect on it. You wanted to be sure you understood it so that you would have the answers you needed to pass the test. Studying then helped you to concentrate and do a better job.

Whatever circumstance you face, imagine that you're preparing for a test. You're getting ready to make choices, move forward and do your best. Give God the opportunity to teach you, to help you, and to quiet your soul. He's ready any time to read along with you as you study His Word.

The more you study, the more steady you become in God's merciful hand.

Signs of the Times

"And in the morning you say that it will be a rainy day, because the sky is dark and red. You see these signs in the sky and know what they mean. In the same way, you see the things that I am doing now, but you don't know their meaning." *Matt. 16:3, NCV*

Jesus' followers, primarily fisherman, were able to understand the weather patterns because they lived long enough in that area, witnessed enough storms, to have the experience of knowing what was ahead when gray clouds gathered.

Jesus reminded them that they could use that same kind of thinking to recognize Him and what He was striving to do among them. Of course, they still lacked spiritual eyes and Divine discernment to understand Him. Over time, many of them came to know the living Christ and witnessed to people around them about His Kingdom and His salvation.

Do we understand the signs of the times? Do we recognize who Jesus is so that we can witness about Him? Are we willing to interpret the signs of His love that He has truly displayed in front of us and go out and tell the world?

The Lord put a portion of Himself within your heart and mind so that you would recognize His hand at work in your life and then share the Good News with those around you. You are a sign of His love!

Detachment from visible things is to open your eyes to the invisible.
~ John Climacus

Rewrite Your Story

The person who tells one side of a story seems right, until someone else comes and asks questions. *Prov. 18:17, NCV*

One of the beauties of Scripture is that it serves as a Divine story book. We are often presented with one side of a story and then later given the other side of the story, until we finally can unravel the mystery of the tale. We learn about the amazing things that God did through the obedience of the Patriarchs like Abraham and Moses and David, but we also learn that they had very human stories as well.

We each have a story and part of our work is to keep writing down the truths we have learned. As we write, we can move away from those things that do not serve God well and renew ourselves in God's love and forgiveness. We can rewrite our stories because there's more to us than one incident or one situation can depict. In fact, we are much more than our stories. We are God's stories, playing out the details as He helps us learn who He is and who we are and what we can be.

Whatever your story was is not nearly as important as what your story can be. With God's help your story is sure to be inspiring and wonderful!

In the book of life, the answers aren't in the back.

~ Charles Schultz

Your Time to Win

Depend on the LORD in whatever you do,
and your plans will succeed. *Prov. 16:3, NCV*

Your friends and family depend on you, but you can't always be there. You may not be available to help when your friend moves away. Or you can't attend when your child is starring in the school play, as you've suddenly been called out of town. It's disappointing to all of you. Life goes on and it can't always depend on you.

The good news is that you can always depend on God. He's there in your relationships with friends or family. You can seek His help with the big project at work and He'll show up. You can take all your plans to Him and He will be with you and help you to succeed. You can depend on Him.

Of course, depending on God means you have a solid relationship with Him. You are used to going to Him and He knows you well. He knows instantly what you need. If you take your plans to the Lord, He will act to accomplish His will and purpose for you and help your plans to succeed. You can depend on Him!

Trust the past to God's mercy, the present to God's love and the future to God's providence. *~ Augustine of Hippo*

Think Big, No, Bigger!

Jesus looked hard at them and said, "No chance at all if you think you can pull it off yourself. Every chance in the world if you trust God to do it." Matt 19:26, MSG

Have you ever had big plans? Your plans are big because you're doing something new, something you've never even imagined before. Are you willing to attempt something so big that you simply can't do it alone? Without God, your plans will fail!

You're used to trusting yourself. If you want to get something done, you do it. Without you, a lot of things won't change. That's all good, but it's not enough.

Jesus reminded His followers that when they had big plans, they needed to realize those plans had no chance of succeeding if they tried to do them without God's help. They couldn't build a ministry, they couldn't heal the sick, they couldn't make a difference in the lives of other people all on their own. They needed God's guidance to succeed.

We might have a great idea, an awesome talent to accomplish it and very lofty goals, but we cannot move forward on our own. We need to take our plans to the only Source of possibility that exists. We need to be fully connected to God for our dreams to come true. Think bigger right now and invite God into your plans.

Lord, please bless my plans according to Your will and purpose.
~ Amen

Benefits of Loving Others

Above all, love each other deeply, because
love covers over a multitude of sins. *1 Pet. 4:8, NIV*

One of the sweetest Scriptures to embroider on a pillow is this one from 1 Peter. Motivated by love, we give each other room to make mistakes, to disappoint us and yet be forgiven. We know that there is nothing like the grace of a loved one, drawing us back into the inner circle and healing our wounds.

This analogy also works for your relationship with God. Because of His great love for you, He is willing to forgive your mistakes, even when He is greatly disappointed. He hears your cry and draws you back to Himself by His grace and mercy. Love covers a multitude of sins.

Remind yourself what it means to love others deeply. You love them past their craziness, past their poor choices and beyond the ways they disappoint you. You love them more than they love themselves. You see all that they can be, all that God designed them to be, and you do your best to love them into being better people. Love each other deeply is not a simple statement.

May God continue to teach you what it means to love Him and others deeply.

We can do no great things; only small things with great love.

~ *Mother Teresa*

SEPTEMBER 23

Keep On Growing

As newborn babies want milk, you should want the pure and simple teaching. By it you can mature in your salvation, because you have already examined and seen how good the Lord is. *1 Pet. 2:2-3, NCV*

You've probably experienced a few "growing pains". You went through an awkward phase, but it helped you grasp what it might mean to be an adult. You were striving to grow up and take on more responsibilities.

The same thing happens in your spiritual growth. You can be nurtured for some time on the simple teachings of faith, but eventually, you must embrace it in such a personal way that you can grow within it. The more you understand what God has done for you by the death and resurrection of Jesus, the more you grow as His child.

When you're mature in your faith, you can go through difficulties and know that you will also grow through struggle. You come out on the other side of your trials with a stronger sense of all that God does to provide for you and what it truly means to have a heart for God.

You'll continue to grow in your faith until God calls you home again. Imagine the wonders of His grace and love that are still before you and give Him thanks and praise.

Mere change is not growth. Growth is the synthesis of change and continuity, and where there is no continuity, there is no growth.

~ *C.S. Lewis*

Positive Thoughts

Brothers and sisters, think about the things that are good and worthy of praise. Think about the things that are true and honorable and right and pure and beautiful and respected. *Phil. 4:8, NCV*

Negative thoughts never do you any good. You can toss those thoughts around, shake them up, look at them several times, and still not get one good thing out of them. You let your inner critic jump in and destroy your day simply on a whim.

So, what if you change things around today? What if you tie those negative thoughts up in a bag and throw them out, trash them, send them somewhere far away from you and replace them with those that are worthy of your time?

Christ redeemed you and that means you are now part of God's family, blessed and loved beyond measure. Focus on all that God has done in your life that is good and wholesome and worthy of praise. Spend time thinking about the things that delight your soul and cause your spirit to rejoice. Those positive thoughts that are pure and right and beautiful and respected are about you. You simply have to choose to bring those to the surface.

Cancel out every negative thought with this one phrase, "Jesus loves me today and always."

Every thought is a seed. If you plant crab apples, you can't harvest Golden Delicious. *~ Author unknown*

Just Say You're Sorry

If my people, who are called by my name, will humble themselves and pray and seek my face and turn from their wicked ways, then I will hear from heaven, and I will forgive their sin and will heal their land. *2 Chron. 7:14, NIV*

You can carry the baggage of all your sin if you want. You can declare each day to be full of tumult and chaos and uproar, never getting ahead, never feeling truly loved or saved. You can do all that, but why would you? After all, your Lord and Savior already has provided relief from the weights you have on your shoulders.

He wants you to surrender whole-heartedly, and once-and-for-all, put the baggage down and ask forgiveness. Tell God that you're sorry for being stubborn, or prideful or just plain blind about His desires for your life.

Once you do, all the forces of Heaven will lighten your load and bring you into the possibilities that were meant for you all along. Seek the face of the One who waits patiently for you to come back to Him and He will do all the rest. He's ready to lift you up and help you become more than you ever dreamed possible.

God knows everything about you and He loves you more than you can even imagine. Lift up your heart to Him today and be filled with His joy and peace.

Lord, please know how sorry I am any time I offend You. Forgive my stubborn heart. *~ Amen*

Crazy Days

Chaos calls to chaos, to the tune of whitewater rapids. Your breaking surf, your thundering breakers crash and crush me. Then God promises to love me all day, sing songs all through the night! Ps. 42:7-8, MSG

Sometimes you feel like you're just moving from one struggle to the next, and you wonder what to do. The answer is that God calls out to you in the chaos, and He says, "I'm here!" Not only is God close to you, but He promises that no matter what you're going through, He will love you forever.

God's promise suggests that you don't need to focus on the chaos. You don't have to worry about being forsaken or forgotten because God sees you and He is there with you. He loves you every moment of the day.

As nighttime approaches, you can continue to wrestle with the wind and the waves of worry, or you can set them adrift and listen for the voice of God. He will be humming softly to let you know that He is with you all through the night as well. He brings you comfort and peace as you rest in Him.

Crazy days can feel overwhelming, but all you have to keep in mind, is that they are not bigger than the God who loves you and offers you His peace.

Afflictions are but the shadows of God's wings.

~ George McDonald

Who Serves?

"Who is greater, the one who is at the table or the one who serves? Is it not the one who is at the table? But I am among you as one who serves." *Luke 22:27, NIV*

One writer said, "What you must decide is how you are valuable, rather than how valuable you are." In other words, do you hope to serve others, or do you hope to have others serve you?

Jesus tried to help His followers see the difference when He asked them to consider the person who sat at the table and the person who came and served the one sitting at the table. "Which one is greater?"

Jesus remarked, "Is it not the one who is at the table?" He wanted them to consider who the person was that would be sitting at the table, perhaps a dignitary or a Pharisee, or a theologian. Clearly the one seated must be the greater of the two.

However, Jesus quickly gave them another view. He reminded them that He was there, teaching them, working with them, changing their lives, not as a king, but as a servant. He was willing to make sure that they had what they needed. They sat at the table, and He served them.

The message here is to serve others to the glory of God and He will reward the work of your hands.

Lord, help me to serve You with my whole heart and serve others with grace and love. *~ Amen*

Unconditionally Loved

But even with all these things, if I do not have love,
then I am nothing. I may give away everything I have,
and I may even give my body as an offering to be burned.
But I gain nothing if I do not have love. *1 Cor. 13:2-3, NCV*

Catherine of Siena wrote, "For I created your soul with a capacity for loving—so much so that you cannot live without love. Indeed, love is your food." Catherine received these words in a vision.

God speaks to all of us. He wants to remind us that love is the story we're here to tell. Love is what feeds our hearts and minds.

The writer of Corinthians understood the necessity, the power, the opportunity that love creates in every situation. He could understand that love was everything, a thing that we each must strive to receive and to give.

As a believer, you are unconditionally loved meaning that nothing on this earth, above or below the earth or anything at all can separate you from God's love. You are loved from here to Heaven and you always will be.

Love is a creative power. It mends hearts so they are free to give and receive; so love with all you've got. Love God, love others and love that person reflected in your mirror. Love makes all the difference.

We learn to love by loving. ~ *Francis de Sales*

SEPTEMBER 29

Divine Joy

You will teach me how to live a holy life.
Being with you will fill me with joy; at your right
hand I will find pleasure forever. *Ps. 16:11,* NCV

As a student of God, anxious to learn all you can about how to love others and become more holy, you realize your lessons will continue forever. You'll never graduate because God has more to teach than you have time on Earth to learn. The beautiful part is He'll make sure you understand each lesson.

Your education in Divine matters started the day you embraced Christ as your Savior. When you come to God in prayer, seeking greater understanding through His Word, or listening for His voice, He is there.

Your lessons were uniquely designed by God because His purpose for you is different than it is for someone else. He brings you closer to Himself and inspires your life direction.

God will sustain your heart and soul from now through eternity with His love and generous Spirit. If your lessons have slowed down a bit, or you haven't learned anything new lately, then ask God to teach you something special that will honor Him and benefit His Kingdom. He will enlarge your heart, fill it with His Divine joy and give you many ways to tell His stories.

You're such a good student!

One filled with joy, preaches without preaching. ~ *Mother Teresa*

SEPTEMBER 30

Be Tenderhearted

And be kind to one another, tenderhearted, forgiving one another, even as God in Christ forgave you. *Eph. 4:32,* NKJV

Imagine that you've been called to God's throne for a conversation. You've never actually been there before so you're somewhat nervous. Perhaps this Scripture shares your hope. You hope God will be kind to you, tenderhearted, and willing to forgive you for all the times you offended Him. You want Him to surround you with grace and love.

When God forgave you through Jesus Christ, that is exactly what happened. He showed you His kindness, His tender mercy, and His ultimate forgiveness. He gave you more than you could ever earn or deserve.

Taking that idea out into the world where you work and play and live then, means that you must have this same attitude toward others. You must speak kindly, embrace others with compassion and be willing to forgive those who offend you deeply. These are behaviors that God has demonstrated toward those He loves, and they are ones He wants His children to demonstrate toward each other.

Offering the hand of forgiveness may not be easy, but keep in mind that by His grace, God does this for you every day, no matter how you are treating Him at that moment.

Offer your best self to others every chance you get.

You don't live in a world all alone. Your brothers and sisters are here too. ~ *Albert Schweitzer*

October

Lost and Found

Don't worry about the donkeys you lost three days ago, because they have been found. Soon all the wealth of Israel will belong to you and your family. *1 Sam. 9:20, NCV*

Sometimes we lose valuable things. We lose them and worry we won't recover them. However, if we look at the story of our relationship with God, we know that there is indeed a happier ending. We were lost. We did not have any sense of purpose or direction and yet the Lord would not let us go. He found us and He moved us toward the light of His love. We have been found for eternity.

So far in this life, you've won and lost, and known great joy and great sorrow. Through every event, you know God is with you to help you grow or change or grasp more of what He has for you.

If you're uncertain of your path today, then don't head off to the nearest Lost and Found. Head in the direction of your Savior, the One who waits to embrace you and lead you forward. Reach up to Him and He will take your hand. You will never be lost again because He will continue to restore you.

Give God thanks and praise for finding you and claiming you as His own. You're sure to have an amazing and purposeful day.

There is no one so far lost that Jesus cannot find him and cannot save him.
~ Andrew Murray

No More Masks

We use no trickery, and we do not change the teaching of God. We teach the truth plainly, showing everyone who we are. Then they can know in their hearts what kind of people we are in God's sight. *2 Cor. 4:2, NCV*

Sometimes we go through life wearing masks. We put the masks on because we're not sure that we'll be accepted by others. We might pretend to be less than we are or more than we are, because we know it serves the situation better. Any mask keeps us from being who we are and from being loved as the people we are.

Your faith in God changed all that. You never need a mask. You can present yourself before the God of Heaven and share your grief or your joy, your intentions or your passions and He will receive you in love and bless you in spirit. You are beloved just as you are.

Of course, God sees you as being more awesome than you might ever see yourself. God reveals Himself to you in truth and love every time you approach His throne. He wants you to come as you are, any time and in any place. You're always free to be uniquely you. You have absolutely nothing to hide.

Lord, thank You for loving me just as I am, and for working with me so that I can do more to please You. *~ Amen*

Don't Be Fainthearted

Now we exhort you, brethren, warn those
who are unruly, comfort the fainthearted,
uphold the weak, be patient with all. *1 Thess. 5:14, NKJV*

Spurgeon wrote, "It will do us good to be very empty, to be very weak, to be very distrustful of self, and so to go about our Master's work."

No matter what you do for a living, you feel strong when you're on top of your game. You trust your thoughts and ideas and you trust God has equipped you for the work at hand. What do you say though, when you've had serious set-backs or you wonder if God still hears your prayers?

God must always become bigger, filling all the spaces of your life so He can equip you to do new things. His work is perfected in you when you are weak, and He is strong. He alone sees the whole picture.

If you are fainthearted, then give God the glory. Give Him the glory because He is perfecting the course of your life and when the time is right, He will strengthen you to deliver His message to those around you.

Be patient with yourself because God uplifts you and He knows what He wants you to accomplish. Surrender your skills and talents, hopes and dreams, and even your weak and faint heart to Him, and He will renew your strength.

The way to grow strong in Christ, is to become weak in yourself.

~ C.H. Spurgeon

OCTOBER 4

Another Blue Day

But Hannah answered and said, "No, my lord, I am a woman of sorrowful spirit. I have drunk neither wine nor intoxicating drink, but have poured out my soul before the LORD." *1 Sam. 1:15*, NKJV

Hannah was having a *blue* day as she poured out her heart before the Lord. She was completely overcome with sorrow.

Blue days happen when we are disappointed by our life circumstances. The more we focus on our feelings of discontent, the faster we slide into a state that we may have difficulty overcoming. You may have good reasons, as Hannah did, for your sense of melancholy about your life, but your story doesn't need to end there.

Ask yourself whether you believe that God is aware of your situation. Do you think He knows what is going on in your life? Do you think your trouble is beyond God's ability to fix it?

If you recognize that God knows your troubles and that He can fix it, then you already have a reason to feel better. Take your blues and seek His help, trusting that He has a plan to help you starting right now. You're not alone. You have the Creator of the Universe on your side. Let His light shine upon you and change your blues to brighter days.

No matter how low you feel, if you count your blessings, you'll always feel better. *~ Author unknown*

OCTOBER 5

The Spirit of Christ

For this reason I bow my knees to the Father of our Lord Jesus Christ, from whom the whole family in heaven and earth is named, that He would grant you, according to the riches of His glory, to be strengthened with might through His Spirit in the inner man, that Christ may dwell in your hearts through faith; that you, being rooted and grounded in love … *Eph. 3:14-17, NKJV*

Though Christ has strengthened you on many occasions, you still feel like a learner. You've learned that to be strong, you have to present your weakness to the Lord. You've learned that as good as you are at what you do, you cannot do it alone. You've learned you must nourish your spirit, with God's Spirit every bit as much as you fortify your body with food.

Your thoughts are no longer able to naturally coincide with the thoughts of the world. Your mannerisms are being softened toward those that would more normally offend you. You are being changed from the inside out and this is God's enormous gift to you. Why? Because God is shaping you to live a life of love. He is helping you to take up the Cross, open the door to the Light, and show others the resurrected Jesus.

God knows that you are beautiful because all He sees in you is the blessed Spirit of His Son.

If there is light in the soul, there will be beauty in the person.

~ Author unknown

Already Clean

"You are already clean because of the word which I have spoken to you. Abide in Me, and I in you." *John 15:3, NKJV*

If we had to earn our salvation, most of us would be playing catch-up all the time. We'd do a few good things, earn a few stripes, and then, "Bam!" we'd do something crazy and have to start all over again. Part of God's astounding brilliance is that He did not leave it up to us to do enough good things that one day we'd get into the gates of Heaven. No, He made it simple. He asked us to invite His Son to live in our hearts and minds and souls. Basically, all we did to "earn" salvation was say, "Yes!"

The story only starts there though. You may not have to earn salvation, but you might be a witness to it. You might be the person God uses to bring someone else into the Kingdom. You might be the example of faith that inspires the hearts of neighbors and friends.

Since you are already made clean by Jesus, you might want to stop going back over those past sins. You are forgiven. You are loved. You are in Christ and He is in you and that means your spirit can live again, thrive in the present, and have great hope for the future.

What in me is dark, illumine. What in me is low, raise and support.

~ *John Milton*

Renewable Resource

Do not conform to the pattern of this world,
but be transformed by the renewing of your mind.
Then you will be able to test and approve what God's
will is—his good, pleasing and perfect will. *Rom. 12:2, NIV*

Most of us don't want to live in a neighborhood of "cookie-cutter" houses. We don't want our style to be dictated by the current magazine trends and we don't want to drive the same SUV that everyone else drives. Yet, we are still tempted to conform to the thinking of the world.

We don't have to think like everybody else does. In fact, it's best if we don't conform to the world, because the world just doesn't get it right most of the time. The world refuses to recognize the God of Heaven and it refuses to be transformed by His Spirit into a more loving, grateful, and amazing place.

You can leave the world behind and move closer to God. He will transform your life in ways that you would never believe possible. Through His will He will help you understand your unique design.

The world is a great place to visit, but you don't want to live there. You want your home to be in eternity!

You never think a "right" thought, never do a right act, you never make any advance heavenward except by grace.

~ *C.H. Spurgeon*

A Blown Out Light Bulb

The light shines in the darkness, and the darkness has not overcome it. *John 1:5, NIV*

As comfortable as we are in the light, there is one problem. If we only shine among all the other lights, we won't change the darkness.

You are called to be the light and that means you may sometimes find yourself in some awkward and dark places. The first thing to know is that God won't send you out into the darkness with a blown-out bulb. He won't ask you to do anything you're not truly ready to do. He wants you to be bathed in His Light so much that you can't help letting others see His hand at work no matter where you are.

God has many people waiting in the darkness too. They are His children, but they have not yet awakened to the light of His love and mercy. All they need is for someone to touch their hearts and minds and help them to see Him more clearly. With a little light, God can build a flood of new possibility and brilliant opportunity for them to know Him better.

Your little light is meant to make a difference and it will. When you are ready to shine, God will clear the path for you to do so. Keep standing in His light for now.

Father in Heaven, I stand before You as Your humble light, ready to pierce the darkness at Your beckoning call. ~ *Amen*

Good Plans

"I say this because I know what I am planning for you," says the LORD. "I have good plans for you, not plans to hurt you. I will give you hope and a good future." *Jer. 29:11, NCV*

Have you ever planned a surprise party? Maybe you orchestrated a big party to celebrate a birthday or anniversary, or you headed up the group who welcomed soldiers home from foreign lands. You were excited about the plans because you knew the joy they would bring.

God does the same thing for you. He loves to plan little surprises that only He can orchestrate. Only He can find the perfect house when you decide to move. He knows the people you need to meet and the church you need to attend. He knows how to bless your future.

No matter how many ideas you have about your present life or your future, you are not the only one making plans. You are being nudged to move, to grow, and to change so that you are ready to embrace those things God is already designing for your good. He goes ahead of you, setting up the right opportunities, bringing together the people He knows will bless you, and attending to every detail. Why?

Because He wants you to realize that He loves you so much that He plans nothing but the best for you.

Dear Lord, help me to follow where You would lead me for I rejoice in all that You are planning for me. ~ *Amen*

OCTOBER 10

You Are God's Child

For in him we live and move and have our being. As some of your own poets have said, "We are his offspring." *Acts 17:28, NIV*

Don't you love celebrating a baptism? It might be a baptism for a baby, carried to the altar on the hope of faithful parents. It might be an older child or an adult ready now to commit their life to Christ. The person being baptized, the officiant, and you, the person observing the event, all understand the same thing. You each know that God has received one more child into His Kingdom.

As believers, we may not reflect on what it means to be the "offspring" of God, but perhaps we should. Some of us lose the innocence of childhood, becoming too much adult. We put away childhood things, and even box up our childlike hearts, resisting the temptation to ever look back.

God does not want you to remain a child in thought and deed. However, He does want you to remain His child, forever trusting Him without reservation, coming to Him to share your joys and concerns and expressing your love for Him. You were not made a child of God only once. You were born into God's family through faith and baptism, once and for all.

Your Father's door is always open to you. Share your heart any time you choose.

The responsible person seeks to make his or her whole life a response to the question and call of God. ~ *Dietrich Bonhoeffer*

A Force for Good

God "will repay each person according to what they have done." To those who by persistence in doing good seek glory, honor and immortality, he will give eternal life. Rom. 2:6-7, NIV

Most of us have heroes. Heroes have accomplished great things, or they've shown incredible courage, or they've simply done good things over and over again. Whether your personal heroes are real or animated red-caped super figures who always arrive in the nick of time, they are important. They serve as examples of goodness and make a difference in what you believe is possible.

According to Scripture, God takes note of your good deeds. He looks for your attitude toward giving, and for your persistence in doing good. He sees your heart and knows what motivates you. One day, He will honor you for your good work. He will give you praise and reward you with the opportunity to live with Him forever. What you do now with your earthly family makes all the difference.

Say a prayer for each of your personal heroes, living or not, because they have influenced your life and have caused you to want to step up and do more yourself. Who knows, you may be someone else's hero without even knowing it. It's okay if you aren't aware of that though, because God is and He's preparing your celebration even now.

Lord, help me to bravely and intentionally do all I can for the good of others. ~ *Amen*

God's Favor

For he says, "In the time of my favor I heard you, and in the day of salvation I helped you." I tell you, now is the time of God's favor, now is the day of salvation. *2 Cor. 6:2, NIV*

Sometimes we pray for God's favor. We hope and pray that He will show up right when we need Him, or guide our steps, or simply grant us His Providential good will. We are right to seek God's favor, but He is more inclined to hear our pleas if we have already established our relationship with Him. The better our friendship is with Him, the more we can clearly express what we need and desire.

The writer of Corinthians says that we are already living in God's favor because He has provided for our salvation. That means we have a way to get back home again after we leave the earth. We have already established and experienced His forgiveness and His love and so we can continually live in His favor.

When you consider asking a friend for a favor, or seeking God for His favor, think a bit more about the relationship you share. Is there more that you can do to create a deeper and more abiding friendship or more that you can do for God? Your heart will help you with the answer.

Rejoice in God's love and favor today.

No one is useless in this world who lightens the burdens of another.

~ *Charles Dickens*

OCTOBER 13

The Greatest

At that time the disciples came to Jesus and asked, "Who, then, is the greatest in the kingdom of heaven?" He called a little child to him, and placed the child among them. And he said: "Truly I tell you, unless you change and become like little children, you will never enter the kingdom of heaven." *Matt. 18:1-3,* NIV

We don't know exactly what took place in the minds of the disciples as they posed the "Who is the greatest?" question to Jesus, but most likely they were more earthly minded than they were Heavenly minded.

Jesus reminded them that something in them needed to change. He suggested that they become like children.

Would they have thought a child to even be important? They certainly would not say a child would be the greatest. Perhaps what Jesus wanted them to see is that children accept authority and they think with their hearts, sharing what they have. A childlike heart inspires greater understandings of Heavenly things.

It won't matter who is the greatest in Heaven because we will all be blessed to be with our Lord and Savior. We will be awed that the Creator of the universe has allowed us to sit at His table. We will be present with the greatest supernatural force that will ever be.

Heaven will be the perfection we have always longed for. All the things that made Earth unlovely and tragic will be absent in Heaven. *~ Billy Graham*

OCTOBER 14

Into the Woods

The LORD is my shepherd, I lack nothing. He makes me lie down in green pastures, he leads me beside quiet waters, he refreshes my soul. *Ps. 23:1, NIV*

It's amazing how easy it is to see God's hand at work when you stroll through the woods and remove the noise of your daily routine. You can feel yourself breathing in the freshness of plants and moss and trees, the habitat for countless critters who find refuge there.

One of the reasons the Shepherd in David's psalm takes His sheep to green pastures and quiet waters is to give them comfort and rest. He nourishes their bodies and spirits and watches over them, bringing refreshment to their souls.

The same Shepherd wants to do that for you too. He leads you to places where you can experience exquisite sounds of nature. He restores your soul. He will never leave you or forsake you.

If you can't get to a wooded glen, then do yourself a favor. Lean back in your chair and imagine yourself with the Shepherd, being refreshed in His Presence near the cool waters and the rich green grasses. He's there for you, ready to anoint your head with oil and bring you His peace.

What peace and inward quiet should he have who would cut away from himself all busyness of mind, and think only on heavenly things.

~ Thomas à Kempis

Clear Paths

Your word is a lamp to my feet
and a light to my path. *Ps. 119:105, NKJV*

As a believer, you need a guide because it is so easy to get off the track, to start hearing the voices of the world and neglect the nudging of the Spirit.

God helps you stay on the path and gives you the opportunity to see things more clearly. He gives you His Word on all things and on every step you will take.

His Word is a rich volume of stories from history, giving you glimpses of miracles and examples of how those who have gone before you lived. He gave you poetry and role models, shepherds and kings, light and darkness.

God provided the Holy Bible because He wanted you to understand how to walk with Him. The Holy Spirit inspired every word of the text so that by thoughtful reading you would feel the light of God's Presence. That light would lead you through every step you would ever take because God would go before you to help you see the way.

When you turn your heart and mind over to the Word of God, He helps you see Him more clearly. May His Word enrich your spirit and keep you close to Him every day of your life.

The Bible is not only a book that I can understand. It's a book that understands me. *~ Author unknown*

Show Me the Way

Show me Your ways, O LORD;
teach me Your paths. *Ps. 25:4, NKJV*

The words, "Show me the way" sound like you've made a choice to follow someone to get where you want to go. As you get in line though, you may discover the path is not easy, perhaps more like hiking a mountain trail. You even wonder if you made the right choice at all.

As a follower of Jesus, you say, "Show me the way." Sometimes your path is straight, easy, and understandable. You feel like you're making good progress. You're happy you chose to get in behind Him.

Then to your surprise, He takes you somewhere you've never been and it's a bit scary. If you take your eyes off Him for even a moment, you won't feel certain of your direction. Every step is hard and each one causes you to wonder what might yet be up ahead. At last on the horizon, you see the difficult path was the most rewarding. You learn to trust Him for each step you take, and the path gets smoother.

When you ask Jesus to show you the way, be prepared to venture into some new terrain, knowing He is with you every step of the way.

Dear Lord, help me to follow You through this life, seeking to do all I can to please You. *~ Amen*

God's Peace

God's peace, which is so great we cannot understand it, will keep your hearts and minds in Christ Jesus. *Phil. 4:7, NCV*

All right, this is it! This is the moment when you are going to stop all the noise and head for someplace serene and calm. You're going on a personal mission to find peace...God's peace.

You may look for solitude or an opportunity to simply let the world vanish before your eyes. You look for those moments, but they are hard to discover.

In Jesus' day, it was no different. People were suffering, going off to wars, wondering how to make ends meet, and so caught up with the web of life, they could scarcely breathe. The concept of peace eluded them.

Perhaps shepherds felt that kind of peace on the hillsides, or those who spent hours in prayer. Lonely pursuits are not the same as those that intentionally unite your heart with the Spirit of God. God's peace connects you with His Presence and you are transported to a place that is simply Divine.

You can have that kind of peace. All you must do is decide that today's the day and seek the peace that only God can give you. Be still and know the One who loves you beyond measure.

Desire only God, and your heart will be satisfied.

~ Augustine of Hippo

Talking in Your Sleep

The saying is true: Bad dreams come from too much worrying, and too many words come from foolish people. *Eccles. 5:3, NCV*

You've probably had occasions where you tossed and turned through the night. You had trouble finding a relaxing position to sleep, or your pillow just wasn't giving you the right support. You drift in and out of sleep, but never quite slip into quiet rest.

Worry is the culprit. It turns up the volume at night, poking you until you're too awake to drift off to dreamland. Worry brings its friends, those voices of people who have tried to give you advice or who have attempted to put their spin on your situation. You wonder whether to listen to them, but like it or not, you're listening to them as you try to sleep.

Your adversary on this planet also jumps in, dredging up old news, old sins that God has forgiven long ago. He likes to post them like a billboard on a highway to cause you misery and despair.

Call on the name of Jesus. Ask Him to be near you and to comfort your mind. Seek His advice about what you can do to calm your nerves and the situation you face. Together you will come to a solution and before you know it, you'll be sound asleep. Pleasant dreams!

I worry until midnight and from then on, I let God worry.

~ *Louis Guanella*

Renew Your Spirit

As God's grace reaches more and more people, there will be great thanksgiving, and God will receive more and more glory. That is why we never give up. Though our bodies are dying, our spirits are being renewed every day. 2 Cor. 4:15-16, NLT

Samuel Chadwick, a Wesleyan minister who had a personal encounter with God, talked about what it means to have a renewed spirit. He wrote, "Spirit-filled souls are ablaze for God. They love with a love that glows. They serve with a faith that kindles. They serve with a devotion that consumes. They hate sin with fierceness that burns. They rejoice with a joy that radiates. Love is perfected in the fire of God."

The best part of us has nothing to do with our physical body or our life work. God's Spirit connected to our own sets us on fire for Him and takes us places we might never anticipate.

Your spiritual self stays young and enthusiastic. It goes into the world with gusto, shining its light for all to see. When you're not in good health, rest. As you pray for renewed health, pray also for the renewing of your spirit. The little flame inside of you will help you to glow and you will delight to give God the glory. You will feel His warmth and love for you as He holds you close to His heart.

Lord, I pray that You would heal my body, and bless my spirit to be fully renewed, recharged, and on fire for You! ~ *Amen*

Keep the Door Open

Here I am! I stand at the door and knock. If you hear my voice and open the door, I will come in and eat with you, and you will eat with me. *Rev. 3:20, NCV*

We love to dine with good friends and catch up on each other's news. Those special times bond our relationship and help us create a greater understanding of one another.

This invitation from Jesus is one of the most well-known Scriptures in the Bible. It is a simple request to open the door when Jesus comes to call. If you do, He will be delighted to come in and eat lunch with you, just like a good friend.

Even if you opened the door a long time ago, wouldn't it be wonderful to open the door again, to see Jesus standing there with a big smile on His face, a basket of fried grouper and potato salad in hand, and ready to share a meal?

Make your faith more personal. Invite Jesus to your table once again and share your stories, your joys and sorrows, and throw in a few brownies. It's sure to be a special day for you both. You can do this any time you choose, because it was offered to you as a standing invitation.

Just keep the door of your heart open to Him!

We are called to an everlasting preoccupation with God.

~ A.W. Tozer

Get Some Fresh Air

Do everything readily and cheerfully—no bickering, no second-guessing allowed! Go out into the world uncorrupted, a breath of fresh air in this squalid and polluted society. Provide people with a glimpse of good living and of the living God. *Phil. 2:14-15, MSG*

You make a difference to a lot of people. You have something they can't quite verbalize that always makes them glad to see you.

That undefinable something is the gift of God's Spirit that radiates through you. Your light is on all the time and it glows. You are a breath of fresh air because you encourage others, offer them hope, and remind them they are loved. You remind them of the living God because you provide a glimpse of Him.

Some like to stand in your shadow because their hearts are stirred. Others will come closer to you because they are drawn to Christ within you. A few will shy away, wondering what makes you different, but uncertain about whether they are ready to discover what it is.

You are a breath of fresh air because you are not afraid to let God show Himself through you. You are a lamp in the darkness, and a candle that can never be blown out. God sustains your light because He holds your heart.

Lord, thank You for Your generous and loving Spirit. Help me to honor Your presence in my life with each thing I do. ~ *Amen*

OCTOBER 22

Down, But not Out

Even though good people may be bothered by trouble seven times, they are never defeated, but the wicked are overwhelmed by trouble. *Prov. 24:16, NCV*

Troubles don't claim the victory; they don't win the day.

They may cause you to feel sad, but you are not defeated because you rely on God to help you. You know you are not alone and that one day soon the troubles will pass.

One writer wrote, "Be not dismayed at the troubles of the earth. Tremble not at the convulsions of empires. Only, fear God; only believe in His promises; only love and serve Him; and all things shall work together for your good, as they assuredly will for His glory."

You'll experience troubles, but those troubles are only temporary. They can never shake you out of God's hand.

Whatever you or a loved one may go through, remember that God is with you and that He alone sees the big picture. He alone knows how the story will unfold and what you need. Because you are His child, He works all things together for your good, creating new opportunities for brighter days ahead. If you're feeling down, then look up and pray until your heart is at rest in your Heavenly Father.

Instead of allowing yourself to be so unhappy, just let your love grow as God wants it to grow, seeking goodness in others.

~ Henry Drummond

Regarding Miracles

Then Jesus criticized the cities where he did most of his miracles, because the people did not change their lives and stop sinning. *Matt. 11:20, NCV*

Jesus did miraculous things. Would you have been awed by His works and changed by His example?

It seems reasonable to think that most of us would have been transformed, or at least transfixed by this amazing man. He could do things in ways that no one else had ever done. His demonstration of God's power would have been enough to cause us to drop everything and follow Him. It seems that way, but apparently, that was not the case.

Jesus did miracles, healings and exorcisms and even raised people from the dead, and though the crowds were awed and surprised and maybe even momentarily captivated, many were not changed. They did not understand the miracles or the message. Jesus was no doubt disappointed and frustrated by them. He may feel the same way about us.

Today, we have the Bible and the Holy Spirit and yet we still resist Him. We still walk past the miraculous truth of His life and go our own way.

He loves it when we change our behavior, dedicate our lives to serving Him, and seek forgiveness for our sins. Follow Him with your heart, mind and soul.

Lord, help me to desire more of You so that I follow You with my heart always. *~ Amen*

Blessing Button

Praise be to the God and Father of our Lord Jesus Christ,
who has blessed us in the heavenly realms
with every spiritual blessing in Christ. *Eph. 1:3, NIV*

Advertisers create slogans and buttons and other devices that will bring attention to their products. One company created an "easy" button. They wanted you to press the button and remember how easy it was to use their service.

Perhaps if God were to try to get your attention, He might give you a "Blessing Button". He would want you to give Him thanks for His generosity. Together, you could recount stories of His love.

If you had a "Blessing Button", would you press the button when you got out of your comfy bed after a good night's sleep? Would you press the button for that steaming cup of coffee? Would you press it again for a warm shower and clean towels? You've only been awake about ten minutes, and you've been pressing the button every minute.

You get the point. God continually blesses your life. Today, go to Him before you even have that first cup of coffee and thank Him for every little blessing you can count. Somewhere in there, a bell should go off in your head that says, "God blesses me all the time." Give God the glory!

God is more anxious to bestow His blessings on us than we are to receive them. *~ Augustine of Hippo*

OCTOBER 25

When You're Smiling

"The LORD bless you and keep you; the LORD make his face shine on you and be gracious to you; the LORD turn his face toward you and give you peace." *Num. 6:24-26, NIV*

This is a powerful prayer. The first phrase, "The Lord bless you and keep you," should bring a tear to your eye because it reminds you that God invited you in to His life. He chose to give you good things right from the start of your relationship.

He blesses you and He keeps you, which means that He has saved you, protected you, sustained you and watched over you your whole life. He holds you close, and He will not let you go because you are His eternal love-child.

When God's face shines on you, it means He gives you His favor. It means He sees you right where you are and that He delights in you. It means that He radiates His loving Spirit toward you to bring you joy.

The Lord then looks on you with His Spirit of Divine mercy reminding you that you cannot earn His love. By His grace and His desire to be in a relationship with you, He offers you His blessing each day.

Finally, the Lord turns toward you and offers you His peace so that your heart will not be troubled. You have every reason to smile then, because the Lord is with you.

Lord, I praise You and thank You for Your great love and mercy!

~ Amen

Try, Try Again

Brothers and sisters, I know that I have not yet reached that goal, but there is one thing I always do. Forgetting the past and straining toward what is ahead, I keep trying to reach the goal and get the prize for which God called me through Christ to the life above. *Phil. 3:13-15, NCV*

Your life goal is to carry out the purpose God planned for you right from the beginning. How do you begin to accomplish it?

Memories and past sins can make you feel unworthy or cause you to lose heart. However, since the day you asked God to forgive those sins, He did so. Your past does not need to hold you hostage.

The present is the best place to be as you "strain" toward the goal. Straining requires effort and persistence and strength. It means that you have to focus on where you're headed and if you fail, you have to try, try again.

God has called you to be the person you are. He knows everything about you and He loves you into being a better person each day.

Don't let anything past, present, or future get in the way of moving ahead. Give God the glory of a life well-lived in humble service.

'Tis a lesson you should heed, try, try again.
If at first you don't succeed, try, try again.

~ *William Edward Hickson*

Overwhelmed

Nothing will hold you back; you will not be overwhelmed. *Prov. 4:12, NCV*

Some days nothing can stop you. You know what you want to accomplish, and everything comes together smoothly. You may even hit your goal the first time out; it's stunning. You sit back and wonder why it happened this time because it seldom has happened before.

Other days, you can't even imagine the finish line. You wonder if God has forgotten you. No matter what direction you take, the way is blocked.

In either case, the winning or the losing requires one thing. You have to start with God. You don't need to be overwhelmed by the circumstance. In fact, the more incredible it seems in a good way or a difficult way, then the faster you might want to get on your knees. God is always with you and there are times when He knows you need answers and you need to complete your work without interruption. Other times, He simply wants you to trust Him to handle the details.

Nothing needs to hold you back today because you have God's mercy and grace and peace on your side. He will help you with each step if you seek His counsel and let Him go before you. You've got this! God has your back today!

You give God your will, and He gives you His power!

~ Author unknown

Soul Search

My soul wants to be with you at night, and my spirit wants to be with you at the dawn of every day. *Isa. 26:9, NCV*

Some of us are seekers, soul searchers, waiting to discover the truth of God's love and the path to His salvation. We may go about for years, unaware of who God is or what kind of difference His Spirit brings to human life. We may get a glimpse of Him, only to imagine that we must have been mistaken as we wander away slightly confused and give the world advantage.

It's a process that can take a lifetime, but God is unwilling to lose any of His children and so He consistently and persistently positions Himself to be discovered. He does it in the most unexpected ways. He may speak to us through a song we hear on the radio, or through a message from a friend. We may start to search for Him when we are entangled in grief or a life crisis or fear of what is ahead. He waits patiently, lovingly, knowing that once we know Him, we will love Him and want to serve Him always.

Your soul may still be searching. If so, be assured that it will one day rest in the arms of your loving and everlasting Father. He will be ready at your call to come into your heart and live with you eternally.

The soul is in itself a most lovely and perfect image of God.

~ John of the Cross

Tomorrow's Sun

You who say, "Today or tomorrow we will go to this or that city, spend a year there, carry on business and make money." Why, you do not even know what will happen tomorrow. *James 4:13-14, NIV*

If you've set your five-year plan or you just wander from day to day, take heed of this Scripture from James. He reminds us that we can make all the plans we want for the future, but what we have is now...today. Tomorrow is not a promise or a guarantee because only God is in control.

God wants us to focus directly on today. What would you be doing right now if this was to be your last day, your only day to complete some things that are important to you? Would you be sure to make that call to your parents or your children or your best friend? Would you want to be sure that you told everyone you know how much you love them?

Perhaps it's a good idea from time to time to simply stop looking for tomorrow's sun and peek through the window of today. There's a lot to be done and you have a purpose to fulfill. The key is to live this day as fully as possible and leave tomorrow in God's hands.

He has blessing after blessing meant just for you right where you are.

Lord, help me to use this day wisely and to seek Your face for all I do.

~ *Amen*

Start Your Engine

Starting from the beginning, Peter told them the whole story: "I was in the city of Joppa praying, and in a trance I saw a vision. I saw something like a large sheet being let down from heaven by its four corners, and it came down to where I was. *Acts 11:4-5, NIV*

Peter's vision was intended to show that God had spread an even wider net than the believers originally understood. God was willing to save even the Gentiles and those who were not followers of the law. God provided a way for all of His children to know Him. This was an important revelation and helped the church to grow as people from all over the known world came to be baptized.

It's good to remember that when God is ready to start something new, He can rev up the engines simply by giving one person a piece of the puzzle. By the time the puzzle is complete, many people's lives will have been saved. God speaks to all of us and sometimes He even plays a small video that you can see in your dreams or in a vision.

He wants you to understand the point and then keep telling His story. You are a part of the puzzle that may bring others to salvation. You have been given the privilege to serve Him.

To accomplish great things, we must not only act, but also dream; not only plan, but also believe. ~ *Anatole France*

Sometimes You Win

Stand firm, and you will win life. *Luke 21:19, NIV*

Most of us expect that to "win" anything, a good job, a promotion, or even a dream vacation, we have to take action to move the ball forward. If we don't, we imagine that nothing will happen, and we'll be stuck. Perhaps! Sometimes though, you have to stand still. You must wait until God tells you to move. It's not easy because everything in you is geared toward finding more solutions and keeping the momentum going.

When you stand firm though, you've made the decision to stay the course. You're not going to let anything get in your way. You believe that everything is working together for your good and so you trust the outcome is in God's almighty hands.

Standing firm means that you've put your stake in the ground, you know what direction you're heading and you're going to keep your heart and mind surrendered to God as He leads the way.

Perhaps standing firm says that I believe with God in control, all will be well. Yes, standing firm in your beliefs may be all that you need to win today.

Lord, You know my heart and my goals. I pray that You will lead the way to the victory You intend for the work we're doing together. Thank You, Father! *~ Amen*

November

Sometimes You Lose

"What profit is it to a man if he gains the whole world, and loses his own soul? Or what will a man give in exchange for his soul?" *Matt. 16:26, NKJV*

Every day you make deposits and withdrawals in your spiritual bank account. You rise with a heart for the Lord, spend time talking things over and getting nourished. You know you're in God's hand and so you embrace the day with confidence.

Other times though, you don't take time for prayer or devotional reading. You don't know it at first, but before long, you have a sense of unrest, nothing goes as you expected, and you wonder if God has forgotten you. You feel like you lost, and you weren't even sure what the game was.

One reason you feel unsettled is that your soul is restless. Your soul is nourished and strengthened as it draws near to God. Your soul is refueled by His Spirit, so when you're having an off day, check your spiritual fuel gauge.

Your morning shower will cleanse your body, and a hearty breakfast will give you energy to take on the day, but neither of those will refresh your soul. Keep your heart and mind in Christ Jesus and you will never have to worry about the day. You will always walk in the victory of God's love and mercy.

Lord, I am so grateful that You feed my soul and keep me ever close to You.

~ Amen

Busy, Busy, Busy!

God gives some people the ability to enjoy the wealth and property he gives them, as well as the ability to accept their state in life and enjoy their work. They do not worry about how short life is, because God keeps them busy with what they love to do. *Eccles. 5:19-20, NCV*

You stay busy most of the time and it's good for you. God blesses the gifts of your hands and heart, and He inspires your work. However, if your heart is not into the work you do, it may be because the work is "soulless." It doesn't inspire you. You're busy, but busy with what?

When that happens, it's time to get back to God in prayer. Seek His guidance about what to do with your life that will engage your body, mind, and soul. Sometimes you have a job; other times you have work and the work makes your heart sing.

God brought you into the world to fulfill a specific purpose. He wants you to make a difference to others. If your job does not give you a sense of purpose, then take time to read the Word, pray, and listen. God will show up and guide you to the best ways to serve Him. He wants you to be busy doing the work that fulfills your spirit and your heart.

I long to accomplish a great and noble task; but it is my chief duty to accomplish small tasks as if they were great and noble.

~ Helen Keller

What a Great Day!

This is the day that the LORD has made.
Let us rejoice and be glad today! *Ps. 118:24, NCV*

Have you ever said, "Where did the day go? I don't even remember what I did!"

Most of us load up the day with yesterday's burdens, and never quite appreciate what today can bring. We're on overload before we even get started. Take heart!

The first thing you can do to stay in the present is to remind yourself that yesterday is spent, over, and there's nothing you can do to bring it back. Today wants you to stop turning around, stop trying to get back to something or someone, or someplace else. Today wants you to make a new plan and try again.

You also can't spend your today, trying to peek into tomorrow. That doesn't work either. Tomorrow might as well be as far away as the next century, because there is nothing you can do about whatever will happen tomorrow. Here you are then, back to today.

Make today count. Pray with intention and devotion. Give, rejoice, love, and be all that you were designed to be at this moment. Put your heart into your work, your soul into your prayers and your mind into all that God has given you for this one day. Own it! Make it your day to shine! Live this day to the fullest! Receive the blessings of God!

Today is tomorrow's yesterday. Make it count! ~ *Author unknown*

A Little Mixed Up

God is not a God of confusion but a God of peace. As is true in all the churches of God's people. *1 Cor. 14:33, NCV*

Confusion feels like a dark gray cloud hanging over your head, making it difficult to see what's happening around you. When you look up, nothing inspires your heart. When you look around, it appears that everyone else is just as mixed up as you are. When you look down, you only sense the blueness that has wrapped itself around your whole being. Perhaps what you must do is step away from the confusion and ask God to shine a light on your heart and mind. Ask God to show you what He would have you do.

If you don't get an answer that you can understand, then simply sit with Him. Be still! Let God draw near to you and wait for Him. He will guard you and guide you and help you find peace again. After all, He already knows the solution to your chaos and He knows everything will work out. Let Him simply rest with you until you feel His amazing peace, the kind of peace that goes way beyond your understanding.

You won't be mixed up anymore.

Lord, thank You for coming closer to me when I can't seem to find my way to You. Help me to be at peace today and leave all my concerns in Your hands. *~ Amen*

Rooting for You

May our Lord Jesus Christ himself and God our Father encourage you and strengthen you in every good thing you do and say. God loved us, and through his grace he gave us a good hope and encouragement that continues forever. *2 Thess. 2:16-17, NCV*

Here's a reminder. You are awesome. God knows exactly what troubles you, has a plan to help, and nothing about your situation is too big for Him to handle. He's with you now and every day of your life. Not only is God there for you, but your many friends are also thinking of you right now. Everybody is rooting for you.

John C. Maxwell said that "encouragement is oxygen for the soul." It helps you feel better so that you can take the steps needed to get to where you want to go.

Whatever is going on in your life today, here's some strength for your soul. Remember you are not alone, and you don't have to slay any dragons all by yourself. You are protected by the full armor of God, strengthened by His Holy Spirit, and loved by Jesus, the Son. You have everything you need to get through all that is ahead of you.

Pray for God's comfort and then give Him a chance to bless you in the best possible ways. After you're done, take a bow because everyone is cheering you on!

Lord, bless all my friends who need You today and feel all too alone to get things done. *~ Amen*

When Life Is Messy

The LORD hears good people when they cry out to him,
and he saves them from all their troubles. *Ps. 34:17, NCV*

Life is messy! You've seen it pile troubles up in a heap and not clean up very quickly. The piles get bigger and the relief does not come. It can be frightening and completely disheartening.

The good news is you can make a difference in how quickly the mess disappears. The first step is to confess your part in creating this pile of woe. Let God know you are sorry for your unwise choices. Let Him know your heart is broken, and you are ready now to clean things up.

If forgiveness is needed, do what you can to encourage forgiveness and compassion. Watch as God works to turn your sorrow into joy, moving in to help you make amends.

It's not easy to be at the front of the line, taking care of the messes that are made, but it's the best place to be. You are at the forefront of God's gifts of mercy and grace and He will strengthen your heart and mind in the process. After everything is cleaned up, He will guide you into making better choices. No mess is too big for God's love and forgiveness to overcome.

It's going to be a better day tomorrow!

Lord, thank You for coming into my life, bearing my sorrows, and helping me to clean up the messes I make. I praise Your name!

~ *Amen*

NOVEMBER 7

Just Do It...Again

I keep trying to reach the goal and get the prize for which God called me through Christ to the life above. *Phil. 3:14,* NCV

Once you take on the challenge that goal-setting offers, you must decide just how committed you are to the plan. You could try, even try again if you need to, but will you get up again for a third round if you still haven't reached the goal?

When you began your walk with God, you were inspired to achieve new goals with Him. You talked with God about what it would take to accomplish your mission. Maybe your first goal was to become a more intentional Bible student, so you could get to know Him better. Maybe one of your goals was to commit more time to prayer and serving others. You need God's help. He's the Coach.

Keep in mind that every time you set a goal, you're almost certain to experience a setback. Distractions and obstacles will come out of nowhere and you will have to determine just how serious you are about getting to the prize. You must just want to do it...again and again!

God bless you and give you an amazing victory in all you want to do for Him.

It is not your business to succeed, but to do right. When you have done so, the rest lies with God. ~ *C.S. Lewis*

Next Chapter Please

Brothers and sisters, whom the Lord loves, God chose you from the beginning to be saved. So we must always thank God for you. You are saved by the Spirit that makes you holy and by your faith in the truth. *2 Thess. 2:13, NCV*

You have a great story to tell. You are no longer wandering around the planet disconnected from the Creator, the Source, the One who designed the ground you walk on. You can add new chapters to your story whenever you choose because God gives you free will.

Create new chapters of your story by spending more time with God. Build on your friendship so you know His story and how it applies to your life. You learn more about God as you spend time in prayer, in His Word, and in praise and thanksgiving.

Think about your current life chapter. How will you add to your story? You can tell others what it means to have God as your Father. You can tell God how pleased you are to have this remarkable relationship with Him. This is the most incredible part of your life story. Thank God that He chose you and put your name in the Book of Life. The Author of the universe endorses you and loves you always.

Lord, thank You that I can rely on Your love and saving grace.

~ Amen

Happy Endings

"But those people who keep their faith until the end will be saved." *Matt. 24:13, NCV*

Don't you just love a story with a happy ending? All the conflicts are resolved, the good people are blessed, and the villains get their due. It delights your spirit when good overcomes evil and when love wins out over hate. Happy endings seem rare though.

You see the bad news rising as you watch the nightly television, or you see the posts that come up on Facebook or Twitter. So how do you stay positive in such a deeply troubled world?

For one thing, you know the end of the story. You know God prevails. God reigns. He is still in control and what He wants is what will happen. No ruler, no wealth or nobility is stronger than your Heavenly Father.

Rejoice when life is good and give God the glory. Pray when it's troubling, and know this day is not the end of the story. Today is just one page in the book of your life. No one knows when the final chapters will be written. Do your best to be a force for good. You are a light, a beacon in the world, desperately needed to offer the hope of the future.

May God bless you with great joy as you continue to live your amazing story of grace.

Lord, help me to remain steadfast and faithful, trusting that You are in control.

~ *Amen*

Ouch! That Hurts

No discipline seems pleasant at the time, but painful. Later on, however, it produces a harvest of righteousness and peace for those who have been trained by it. *Heb. 12:11, NIV*

When you stub your toe or get a splinter, the first thing you are likely to say is, "Ouch!" After all that hurts. You deal with the modest pain and go on with your life.

Sometimes in your spiritual life, you experience a little pain as well. It usually happens when you acknowledge the sins you've tried to hide from God. Of course, there is no hiding anything from God…ever! The "ouch" comes in when you own your mistakes and ask God to forgive you. God forgives those poor choices you made and gives you a clean slate.

There may be a few things that you are still holding on to, little sins that you haven't wanted to confess or commit to God, that you realize He's still nudging you to address. If you are experiencing anything like that, why not surrender any challenges you are not able to overcome on your own and let God help you. His discipline may hurt for a little bit, but it won't be long until you are fully healed. God wants you to make good choices and so He shapes and molds you with His loving discipline to help you become all that you were meant to be in Him.

Lord, forgive me the little sins that I try to hide from You and give me Your peace. ~ *Amen*

Can You Hear Me, God?

Therefore confess your sins to each other and pray for each other so that you may be healed. The prayer of a righteous person is powerful and effective. *James 5:16, NIV*

Some days, in your heart of hearts you believe God can listen, but you're not sure if you're really connected to Him. You wonder if He's too busy to receive more prayers, or maybe you've gone over your prayer quota and you just have to wait. It sounds silly to say, but your mind dreams up all kinds of reasons why God may be out of range.

As human beings, we don't really understand how God can process millions of prayer requests all at once, or how He can manage to make each individual prayer feel personally answered, but that isn't our concern. He doesn't ask us to figure out how He can do what He does. He only asks us to pray. He says to pray for each other. He even says to pray without ceasing.

If you're going through a dry spell in your prayer life and you're wondering if God can hear you, perhaps one thing to do is simply be still. Don't struggle with words. Just ask God to sit with you. Chances are good it won't be long before you start to talk to each other.

Prayer brings you closer to God, heart to heart.

Dear Lord, I will be still and wait. I will rest in Your Presence and give You praise. *~ Amen*

NOVEMBER 12

Wait for It!

We depend on the LORD our God;
we wait for him to show us mercy. *Ps. 123:2, NCV*

As human beings, we are not fond of waiting…for anything! When we're waiting for test results from the doctor, or for a check we need to pay our bills, or for nearly anything else, we're anxious. Waiting in a long line at the grocery store while someone sorts out their coupons, or waiting at the gas pump, adds to our concerns.

Perhaps more difficult than all the rest is when we're waiting for God to act on our behalf. We're waiting for Him to show up in a way that relieves our stress or our constant pressure. We're waiting for His answer about what direction we should go. We wait, and we wait some more.

The gift of waiting though is that it often brings clarity to what it is you really want. Having to wait for something lets you evaluate how important it is. God hears your prayers and knows you are waiting for Him to act. He's working out the details as you wait, preparing the answer that best suits your needs. His efforts are about favoring your life on earth, but even more, they are about favoring your life for eternity. If you trust Him, you'll find it was all worth the wait!

Thank You, Lord, for working on the details of my life, as I wait for You to act. *~ Amen*

Here Comes the Sun!

The sun has one kind of splendor,
the moon another and the stars another;
and star differs from star in splendor. *1 Cor. 15:41, NIV*

God made more varieties of plants and birds and fish and flowers, then we can even imagine. We could never have dreamed up all the ones that live on this earth, each with a unique purpose and in its own way, beautiful.

Now look at human beings. He created only two types, male and female, and yet within those two types are an infinite variety of aptitudes and attitudes. Each one is designed with His purpose.

Nothing is by chance, or randomly designed. God put His stamp of approval, His design on each one. When the sun comes up today then, remind yourself that you too are unique and special. You were created for a purpose and designed with incredible love.

You are the Light of the world and just like the sun that rises each day, God loves to see you shine. This is the day the Lord has made, and He wants you to celebrate all that you are because of all that He has done in your life. Let the sun shine into your heart today!

Lord, thank You for creating absolutely every living and breathing organism with exquisite detail. Thank You for creating me!

~ *Amen*

NOVEMBER 14

Are You So Sure?

My brothers and sisters, try hard to be certain that you really are called and chosen by God. If you do all these things, you will never fall. *2 Pet. 1:10, NCV*

This Scripture suggests that as you follow Christ you need to be certain and not try to guess about the work God has called you to do. We are told to make sure we have prayed and fasted and asked God for guidance.

Sometimes you know a person so well, you can finish their sentences. Putting your certainty to the test though, you can be surprised to discover that the person you knew so well did not make the expected response.

We must be careful about assumptions. When we make guesses about others, we have no guarantee that things will be as we think. However, there are things you can be sure about. You can be sure that God loves you and certain that Jesus lived, died, and was resurrected as payment for your sins. God never changes so He is the one certainty in your life. He will never leave you nor forsake you. He will never change His mind about how much He wants to know you and one day share an eternal home with you.

Be certain of your calling as a believer, and as a child of your Heavenly Father.

Set yourself earnestly to discover what you are made to do, and then give yourself passionately to the doing of it.

~ *Martin Luther King, Jr*

Where's Your Armor?

But let all who take refuge in you be glad; let them ever sing for joy. Spread your protection over them, that those who love your name may rejoice in you. *Ps. 5:11, NIV*

The changing seasons remind us how much we appreciate our armor of protection. Winter coats, boots and mittens make a significant difference to getting us out into the elements. However, no matter what climate you live in or what season of the year it may be, God has given you His armor to protect you:

> Stand firm then, with the belt of truth buckled around your waist, with the breastplate of righteousness in place, and with your feet fitted with the readiness that comes from the gospel of peace. In addition to all this, take up the shield of faith, with which you can extinguish all the flaming arrows of the evil one. Take the helmet of salvation and the sword of the Spirit, which is the word of God. *Ephesians 6:14-17, NIV*

With God's armor, you can take on the world because you are equipped to do His bidding. If your armor has gotten a little rusty, polish it up again with God's truth and love and you will shine His light in a world that desperately needs to discover He is there. Stand firm in your faith and go out fully dressed in God's protective gear.

Endurance is a key indicator of spiritual fitness. ~ *Alistair Begg*

NOVEMBER 16

Defenseless?

Defend my cause and redeem me;
preserve my life according to your promise. *Ps. 119:154, NIV*

Do you ever feel somewhat vulnerable as you step out into the world? Perhaps you have to walk to your office or your apartment from a big parking garage. It's lit up, but you still feel too alone as you walk along.

You must pay attention wherever you are, but you are not defenseless. You are not without strength to protect you. Turn your anxious thoughts into prayers, seeking God's protection and help; asking for His peace.

David was a king and though he had thousands of warriors he could call upon when he was feeling anxious, he chose prayer instead. He went to his Redeemer and Defender. He went to the One he had been talking to and believing in since the day he killed Goliath with a stone. David knew that with God on his side, he could face any giant that might come along.

Perhaps the best thing to remember is that God is with you, walking with you all the time, and He will guard you and give you peace when anxiety threatens your heart and mind. Your Defender created all that you see, and He invites you to put your hand into His. In fact, He has promised to be with you until the end of the age.

Lord, thank You for watching over me and the people I love. Keep us safe wherever we may go today. ~ *Amen*

NOVEMBER 17

Sinners and Other Strangers

But God demonstrates his own love for us in this:
While we were still sinners, Christ died for us. *Rom. 5:8, NIV*

Most of us cringe at the thought of our own sinfulness. However, those feelings of sinfulness are a gift to you. They remind you that you always need Jesus. If it weren't for the cross of Christ, there would be nothing you could do to be redeemed. You'd have no opportunity to save yourself.

God comes to us and does all He can to get our attention. He calls us into a relationship with Him, bringing us to Christ as we peek in at the child in the manger. He knows we can't help but fall in love with that radiant Being, sent to earth to show us how to live.

Baby Jesus nudges at our heart strings, but it's resurrected Jesus who gives us the gift of eternal life. We only have one small part to play. We must accept that Jesus is God's way to redeem us and that no other name exists under Heaven by which we can be saved.

So, here's the good news! You don't have to cringe any more. God loves you so much that He has cast your sins, no matter how big or how small, onto the shoulders of His beloved Son. He redeemed you once and for all, now and forever. Praise His Holy Name!

I more fear what comes from within me than what comes from without. *~ Martin Luther*

A Good Word

This will happen if you continue strong and sure in your faith. You must not be moved away from the hope brought to you by the Good News that you heard. *Col. 1:23, NCV*

Your hope is in the Lord and because of that hope, you might be called upon to be the voice of compassion, the "good word" for others. That's part of what faith does, part of what God shaped your heart to do.

Once you were separated from God by your sinfulness. You couldn't do anything to save yourself. God had to do it. He brought Jesus to earth to be the Savior and then took Him back to Heaven to be the Ruler for all time.

If you carry God's Word in your heart, then you are prepared any time to share love and light and possibility with others. You're ready to make a difference because you trust in God's actions on your behalf. Share the Good Word of God, and the good news of salvation and help those around you find peace with God. Let hope guide your heart and let kindness prevail in all you do.

"He has sent me to bind up the brokenhearted, [...] to comfort all who mourn, and provide for those who grieve in Zion—to bestow on them a crown of beauty instead of ashes, the oil of joy instead of mourning, and a garment of praise instead of a spirit of despair."

~ *Isaiah 61:1-3, NIV*

Quiet Your Soul

"By your patience possess your souls." *Luke 21:19, NKJV*

Patience is not a word that immediately brings joy to your spirit because you know what it means. It means you must wait. You wait for answers to your prayers or for events to happen, or to find quiet time to spend alone with God. You're always waiting for something.

Waiting doesn't have to be an unwelcome event though. You can turn it into the child-like faith you had as you anticipated a gift for your birthday, or as you waited for Christmas. Then you waited with excitement, knowing a reward would come.

You can still wait like that. When you go to God in prayer, seeking guidance or direction, wait with excited anticipation of the outcome. Wait, knowing that He will act at the right time, and the things you've prayed about will find the most perfect answer.

Open the door to waiting with patience, knowing that your soul rejoices in all that God is doing. Waiting may indeed bring strength for your soul.

"Abide in Me," says Jesus. "Cling to Me. Stick fast to Me. Live the life of close and intimate communion with Me. Get nearer to Me. Roll every burden on Me. Cast your whole weight on Me. Never let go your hold on Me for a moment." *~ J.C. Ryle*

Reach Up, Reach Out!

Why, my soul, are you downcast? Why so disturbed within me? Put your hope in God, for I will yet praise him, my Savior and my God. Ps. 42:5, NIV

It's easy to give God the glory when your life is going along well. After all, you can feel His Presence in your work and in your family. You recognize all that He has done to shape and mold you into the person you are. You feel good about everything and smiles prevail. Praising God feels natural to your spirit then.

Isaiah said that we must, "Put on a garment of praise instead of a spirit of despair." That's not easy to do, is it? When people in Isaiah's day were in deep mourning, they wore sackcloth and ashes. They wept before God and pleaded with Him to heal their miseries. Today, we don't do that, but we still put on a gloomy face and we struggle with even finding one reason for joy.

You can change all that right now. Put on the garment of praise, lift up your head and seek the God of hope, the One who knows you and loves you and has not abandoned you. He will renew your strength and give you infinite reasons to praise Him. Let your heart rest in all that He has done before, and all that He will yet do to bring you hope.

Thank You, Father, for raising my spirits and giving me hope.

~ *Amen*

It's Just Me, Lord!

And pray in the Spirit on all occasions with all kinds of prayers and requests. With this in mind, be alert and always keep on praying for all the Lord's people. *Eph. 6:18,* NIV

The invitation in this Scripture says you have the freedom to approach God in any way the Spirit leads. You're surrounded by opportunities to bring people you know to God's throne. It's a wonderful thing!

The Scripture also says to "be alert." When you're on the alert, it means you anticipate something, and you're ready for it to happen. You're fully awake to a possibility or an opportunity when it comes. When you're alert to God's Spirit, you're ready to help others.

Pray in the Spirit, that is, allow the Spirit to guide your thoughts as you pray for others by name. Be the voice for those who have not learned the beauty of prayer. Humble your heart to be a willing vessel of the Holy Spirit, ready to serve. The prayers of someone committed to God in all ways, are powerful.

You are blessed every time you spend time in prayer for yourself and for others.

The first rule of right prayer is to have our heart and mind framed as becomes those who are entering into converse with God.

~ *John Calvin*

Peace with God

Since we have been made right with God by our faith, we have peace with God. This happened through our Lord Jesus Christ. *Rom. 5:1, NCV*

Peace is what happens each time you say your morning prayers that renew your sense of power and purpose. You feel at peace because you trust the Lord for guidance and know that He walks with you throughout the day.

The sweetest harmony for any of us comes when we recognize what it means to be at peace with God. That kind of peace means you have surrendered your life to God, asking Him to live fully in your heart. Nothing is more important to you than serving Him and being His child.

Your faith is on a continuing growth pattern, learning and discovering more of what it means to walk with God, but you have been made right with God because He planned to bring you back to Himself. You have peace with God because God made it possible. God sent His Son, Jesus, to stand in the gap, to be your champion, your hero, and the only one who can save your soul.

Today, the peace that keeps your heart humming and your surrendered life joyful is the kind that God's Spirit pours out on those who love Him. May His peace sustain you all the days of your life.

Let nothing good or bad upset the balance of your life.

~ Thomas à Kempis

Living in Gratitude

LORD, I will thank you with all my heart; I will sing to you before the gods. I will bow down facing your holy Temple, and I will thank you for your love and loyalty. You have made your name and your word greater than anything. *Ps. 138:1-2, NCV*

David offered God continual praise. He knew nothing else in life was as powerful as a relationship with the Designer of the universe. David believed God sustained and delivered him in trials. By trusting God, David had killed a giant when he was just a child. As David grew up, he knew many giants would cast fears, doubts, illnesses, and troubles on his life. The only way he could truly slay those giants was to trust God. That's what David knew!

David also asked God's forgiveness when he knew he was wrong. He didn't hesitate. He put those wrongs before the God of his heart.

When you trust God with every detail of your existence, you are grateful because you know that God is with you. That kind of trust doesn't happen overnight, but if you are willing to bow down to the will of God, and reach up to God through every life experience, you will know what David knew.

God is with you. Give Him the thanks and praise and the glory that He deserves. Rejoice before the Lord and He will lift you up with love.

Lord, thank You for being the cornerstone of my life. *~ Amen*

Not Washed Up

I mean that you have been saved by grace through believing. You did not save yourselves; it was a gift from God. It was not the result of your own efforts, so you cannot brag about it. *Eph. 2:8-9, NCV*

Was there a time when you were all washed up? Maybe back then, you didn't know the Lord and you weren't sure whether you were saved or not.

Then, it happened. One day, your spirit and God's Spirit connected, and your eyes were opened. You started seeing God's hand at work everywhere you went, and you could literally feel His Presence. God invited you to be His child, and you accepted the invitation, and everything changed. You were saved, and you knew it. You were washed clean. You could go before God as His heir.

God loves you completely and now you live in His grace through believing. You are His child forever and all He wants from you is a devoted heart. He wants to know that you serve Him in all humility. When you know Who God is, you can help others get to know Him. You can help them get washed up and ready for the Savior, the gift of God. May God bless your life in every way today.

One loving soul sets another on fire. ~ *Augustine of Hippo*

NOVEMBER 25

For Goodness' Sake!

And we know that God causes everything to work together for the good of those who love God and are called according to his purpose for them. *Rom. 8:28, NLT*

This is one of the most positive thoughts in Scripture because it affirms that in all ways and always, God shows up for you.

God has your back and He is right there with you each time you seek His will and purpose for yourself or your loved ones. When you walk with Him, He is there to help you with all that happens in your life.

Sometimes His help means you get the promotion, you make the move, or you marry the right person. Other times, you aren't so sure what happened, but you know that even in the chaos God is with you. He's available to you, ready to hear your heart as you pray, ready to guide your spirit and keep you steadily on the path.

God is working out your life with you, and He wants you to trust that He knows exactly what He is doing. The stronger your relationship is with Him, the more you will understand what He does and what He has done to bless you and keep you.

Simply affirm, "God is with me; God is helping me; God is guiding me." Spend several minutes each day visualizing His Presence. Then practice believing that affirmation. ~ *Norman Vincent Peale*

Follow Your Heart

"A good person produces good things from the treasury of a good heart." *Matt. 12:35, NLT*

Jonathan Edwards advised his listeners and readers that their chief study in life should be about the matters of the heart. Edwards believed that the heart shaped your life. In the heart, God's image could be planted, and that image keeps you connected to Him.

Edwards also thought your perceptions of others were a result of the goodness of your heart and mind. In the heart, you develop behaviors and attitudes that you share with others. Your heart helps you determine right from wrong and understand the things God would have you do. Edwards also said that it was within the heart that a person's love for God, for holiness, and for all matters of salvation would live and grow.

These thoughts he uttered centuries ago, are still important today. When God is the center of your heart, He can protect and bless your life. When your heart produces compassion, and good ideas and love, you are wise to follow your heart. In truth, you are following God, who is at the heart of all you do.

Keep doing all the good and gracious things you can and let your heart lead you forward today.

Oh, study your hearts, watch your hearts, keep your hearts!

~ *John Flavel*

Everyday Grace

Each time he said, "My grace is all you need. My power works best in weakness." So now I am glad to boast about my weaknesses, so that the power of Christ can work through me. *2 Cor. 12:9, NLT*

You live in God's grace. It's a gift that you can't influence in any way. God sheds His grace on humanity as He chooses. Ephesians 4:7 says, "To each one of us grace has been given as Christ apportioned it." Grace then, cannot be earned or bought. It can only be given by God.

God watches over your life and the closer you are to Him, the more He can guide you. He offers His strength when troubles come. He is all powerful and nothing can deter His plans and His purpose for you.

One writer said that grace is what God gives us even when we don't deserve it, and mercy is when God doesn't give us what we do deserve. Grace then is not about you. It's about God! It's comforting to know that grace is like the air you breathe. It is always surrounding you.

At this time of thanksgiving, let God know how grateful you are that He loves you and strengthens you with the gift of everyday grace.

Grace is the free and undeserved goodness and favor of God to mankind. *~ Matthew Henry*

A Friend in Chaos

A friend loves you all the time,
and a brother helps in time of trouble. *Prov. 17:17, NCV*

Life can change quickly from peace, to total chaos, tumult, and uproar. When that happens, you have resources to help renew your strength.

The very first resource, of course, is God. Whatever is going on, put your troubles in His hands. Surrender your thoughts and feelings and seek His guidance. In His Providence, God has given you earthly helpers and advisors.

Some people comfort you and help you when trouble is brewing. They listen to your heart and pray with you. They bring you chocolate and laugh with you. These people are God's helping hands, the ones who want to show you how precious you are and how much you mean to God.

You are blessed when you have one good friend, or one amazing relative who will help when chaos comes. The thing to remember though is that your real friends and your beloved family will stick by you no matter what you're going through.

When friends and family cannot be there for you, God can be. God is available to be a friend, or a brother, as you embrace His love and call His name. With God's help, you'll find peace again in your heart and in your soul.

Some people treat God like a lawyer. They only go to Him when they are in big trouble. *~ Author unknown*

NOVEMBER 29

Prevailing Winds

"God makes his angels become like winds. He makes his servants become like flames of fire." Heb. 1:7, NCV

The gentle breezes of summer have faded away, and the chill of November winds whip through your warmest coat. You walk a little faster and wrap your scarf a bit tighter to stay warm. It's a chilling breeze and the prevailing winds influence everything about your life.

In Hebrews, God's angels become like winds. Perhaps the thought is that angels can appear out of nowhere, like the wind. They live and breathe and have their being in God, so they can move like the wind, blowing here and there as God commands.

Angels are messengers, employed by God for numerous reasons. They share "Good News" as they did the night Jesus was born. They spare people from catastrophe, as they did when they ushered Lot and His wife out of Sodom and Gomorrah. They can even break a guy out of jail as they did when Peter was in prison.

Joyful Christmas melodies speak about the work of angels, blowing like the winds as they share their messages. Be aware today, that somewhere around you, there may well be angels getting the work of God done. God has done great and marvelous things from the beginning of time.

Angels can fly because they take themselves lightly.

~ G.K. Chesterton

The New Moon

The Levites offered all the burnt offerings to the LORD on the special days of rest, at the New Moon festivals, and at all appointed feasts. They served before the LORD every day. *1 Chron. 23:31, NCV*

The Levites celebrated new moon festivals as a regular form of worship. The beginning of each month was considered sacred and was celebrated with feasts and burnt offerings.

We do not ritually observe new moon festivals in the Christian community, but we can see how the festival was beneficial. It served as a good way for families to worship and tell stories of what God had done for them over the previous weeks. They prayed and gave God a portion of what they had received from God's hand. The festival was a concrete reminder of all their blessings.

Today, give God your heartfelt gratitude for taking care of you and your family. Imagine how you would feel, if like the Levites, you called your family or friends together once a month, to celebrate in a festival of gratitude. God has even more for you to celebrate. May He be with you and delight your soul!

There is a famine in America. Not a famine of food, but of love, of truth, of life. ~ *Mother Teresa*

NOVEMBER 30

The New Moon

The Levites offered all the burnt offerings to the LORD on the special days of rest, at the New Moon festivals, and at all appointed feasts. They served before the LORD every day. 1 Chron. 23:31, NCV

The Levites celebrated new moon festivals as a regular form of worship. The beginning of each month was considered sacred and was celebrated with feasts and burnt offerings.

We do not ritually observe new moon festivals in the Christian community, but we can see how the festival was beneficial. It served as a good way for families to worship and tell stories of what God had done for them over the previous weeks. They prayed and gave God a portion of what they had received from God's hand. The festival was a concrete reminder of all their blessings.

Today, give God your heartfelt gratitude for taking care of you and your family. Imagine how you would feel if, like the Levites, you called your family or friends together once a month to celebrate in a festival of gratitude. God has even more for you to celebrate. May He be with you and delight your soul!

There is a famine in America. Not a famine of food, but of love, of truth, of life. Mother Teresa

December

Jesus Loves Me

Jesus answered and said to him, "If anyone loves Me, he will keep My word; and My Father will love him, and We will come to him and make Our home with him." *John 14:23, NKJV*

You are blessed with the love of Jesus and the love of His Father as well. Once your commitment was made, God and Jesus built a home with you. There's nothing better than when love builds a home.

Knowing Jesus loves you is far more important than the sweet song you sang as a little child. You are loved by the One who designed the entire universe. You are loved always and you're at home together. You can be yourself. You can talk to your Father any time you choose, telling Him about your day, or sharing your heart and the things that weigh on your mind.

Love means acceptance at every level. It means you're loved when you do amazing and great things, and you're still loved when you do foolish and embarrassing things.

It's a good day to say right out loud, "Jesus loves me!" Then look around your home and remind yourself that God is with you right where you are. He loves you and He is building a home with you. It's so good to know the amazing place where you belong.

May God bless your heart and your home today.

When Jesus is present, all is well, and nothing seems difficult.

~ Thomas à Kempis

Prayer Power

Therefore confess your sins to each other and pray for each other so that you may be healed. The prayer of a righteous person is powerful and effective. *James 5:16, NIV*

Whether you are an out loud, dynamic, over the top kind of prayer person, or a more quiet, steadfast, trusting prayer warrior, it's important to pray. The more you engage in conversation with God and offer gratitude and praise, or seek His advice and direction for your life, the more you build your relationship. The closer your relationship is with God, the more powerful your prayers will be.

God knows your heart and when you fall, or fail, or find yourself in circumstances that are confusing or difficult, He only asks you to come to Him. Come and share what is going on. You can trust Him to help you before you get to the "Amen."

When you pray with others, you feel God's power at work, generated and fueled by love. He has said, "Where two or three are gathered in My name, there I am in the midst of them." He's with you, hearing your heart speak, and giving you grace and power to receive His direction. Listen to Him and keep praying. Your prayers always matter to the One who loves you more than you can understand.

None can believe how powerful prayer is, and what it is able to effect, but those who have learned it by experience.

~ Martin Luther

More Questions than Answers

Now when the queen of Sheba heard of the fame of Solomon concerning the name of the LORD, she came to test him with hard questions. *1 Kings 10:1, NKJV*

Wouldn't it have been fun to be with Solomon and the Queen of Sheba when she came to visit and quiz his knowledge? No doubt, she had her leadership team help her come up with the tough questions, designed to stump Solomon, so she could assure herself he didn't have as much wisdom as had been reported.

It's the nature of human beings to want to stump the scientists and scholars and theologians and others who hold powerful information. Sometimes we want to do the same thing to God. We ask Him the hard questions, the ones we cannot wrap our arms around. Of course, no question is too hard for God, but the answers still may not come. God knows what we can handle.

It's good to come to God with your questions. He will give you insight into discovering answers for yourself when He knows your heart is ready. He loves you so much that He won't burden you with more than you need to know.

Your life is in God's hand and He knows how much to reveal to you at any one time. Keep asking Him the questions.

Some people think God does not like to be troubled with our constant coming and asking. The only way to trouble God is not to come at all. *~ D.L. Moody*

The Present

For I consider that the sufferings of this present time are not worthy to be compared with the glory which shall be revealed in us. *Rom. 8:18, NKJV*

It's December and what often feels like the busiest time of the year. You're doing your best to finish strong, managing work, home, and the holiday spirit as best you can. You're looking at projections for the coming year, and at the same time reviewing everybody's Christmas list to see what surprises you might share on the big day. Safe to say, you're busy.

Today, stop right where you are. Focus on this moment and this day only and let go of any concerns for yesterday or tomorrow. This is the day the Lord has made, and He is with you. He wants you to get the most from today, staying present in each thing you do.

The present moment is where you can listen with your heart to a friend, or a family member, allowing only that conversation to occupy space in your mind. As one writer so aptly put it, "There's no time like the present."

Today is the gift you must unwrap, the one that will have its own sweet surprises and its own concerns. Be in the now, because God is in the know and He only wants you to take one day at a time. Keep walking with Him!

Yesterday is gone. Tomorrow is uncertain, but today is a gift, Unwrap your gift wisely. It is your present.

Beginnings and Endings

He said to me: "It is done. I am the Alpha and the Omega, the Beginning and the End. To the thirsty I will give water without cost from the spring of the water of life." *Rev. 21:6, NIV*

The old year is closing and the New Year looms ahead of us. Some of us are happy to see this old year end, because beginning again inspires hope.

The One who began everything, our Creator and Redeemer looks to the future as well. He alone knows when He will choose to shut down the work He began so long ago. He is the Alpha and the Omega, the beginning and the end. Everything about planet Earth is in His control. The wonderful part of God's plan is that He offers to each of us a chance to receive His gift of the water of life. One drink of this water and we get to live with Him in the future. We will be part of His family and live in perfect peace and love.

As you look to one year ending and another one opening, go past your own circumstances. Remember you have already received the Living Water. You have every reason for hope. Be assured that you are known and loved and as this year ends, you are part of something amazing as the future unfolds.

Lord, may I finish the end of this year with joy and gratitude for all that has been and for all that is yet to be. *~ Amen*

When to Quit

Jesus told his disciples a parable to show them that they should always pray and not give up. *Luke 18:1, NIV*

"Don't give up!" is good advice if you're dreaming big dreams and you're working hard to make them come true. After all, success never comes without hard work and a few obstacles.

The advice to not give up is given because any important work requires persistence. Jesus wanted His followers to know that He realized the work they would be doing would be hard and dangerous. He knew they would face difficult obstacles, and they would be hauled off to prison. His advice to them was to pray, pray, and pray some more because persistence in prayer and a positive attitude would get them where they hoped they would go. No doubt, He would offer that same advice to you.

If you're not on solid ground with God today, give up on your old direction and take a new course! Give up any pride or any sense that you had to be right in your approach and give God a chance to show you what is right. Listen with your whole heart to what God wants for you. Don't give up on the dreams you and God created together!

All things are possible to him who believes, less difficult to him who hopes, more easy to him who loves, and still more easy to him who perseveres in the practice of these three virtues.

~ *Brother Lawrence*

Embrace Today

Guide me in your truth and teach me, for you are God my Savior, and my hope is in you all day long. *Ps. 25:5, NIV*

What if you embrace today with only one thought? You will only go where God wants you to go and you will act on His advice.

You may do these things already, but the difficulty with our intentions is that life intervenes. We find ourselves running here and there, solving problems, and trying to get things done. It's good, but it isn't the same as waiting for God's voice before you act.

King David often asked God to lead him and to teach him what he needed to know. He wanted to do what was right in God's sight. He wanted to live in truth, God's honest truth, because he knew it was his only hope.

Your hope rests in the love of God. It is the hope that gives you peace as you rise to each new day, knowing that you are not expected to manage life by yourself. Just for today, stop and put your plans in God's hands. Let Him guide you to the best possible outcomes. Celebrate the blessings you receive and His amazing power and Presence. Embrace today! Embrace God's love for all that you do.

Keep yourself as a pilgrim and a stranger here in this world, as one to whom the world's business counts but little. Keep your heart free, and always lift it up to God. ~ *Thomas à Kempis*

Keep Listening

"My sheep listen to my voice; I know them, and they follow me. I give them eternal life, and they shall never perish; no one will snatch them out of my hand." *John 10:27-28, NIV*

A French theologian wrote that, "God never ceases to speak to us, but the noise of the world without and the tumult of our passions within bewilder us and prevent us from listening to Him."

We may agree that we're not especially good listeners. We listen with one ear as our children tell us stories, or even as our spouse shares what happened during the day. Our attention is divided, seldom ever truly focused on the one who is speaking.

At prayer time, we talk to God about everything on our minds, but don't wait for Him to talk with us. We don't hear God's voice as He nudges us, or as He offers a Divine insight. We're too busy. We're not focused.

Jesus said His sheep would recognize His voice and follow Him, because they won't follow any other shepherd. They know He is the only one to listen to. He's the Shepherd who protects them, watches over them, and determines the safest way to find clean water and a place to rest.

Listening is a skill every believer needs to develop. Listen with both ears and with all your heart. He's always speaking to you.

Lord, I am here, ready to listen to Your voice. ~ *Amen*

Have It Your Way

"But my people did not listen to me; Israel did not want me. So I let them go their stubborn way and follow their own advice." *Ps. 81:11-12, NCV*

Have you ever felt like God stepped aside and let you create a mess? Oh, He did not abandon you, but He allowed you to make the foolish choices, because You had already made it clear you didn't want to hear what He had to say.

When God's people didn't listen to Him, He allowed them to live in their own stubbornness. He let them follow their own plans. They had a pattern of stubborn behavior that kept them away from God until they got into a mess.

You don't have to beg God to be with you. He wants to be with you. However, He won't barge in or intrude. He will not come in unless you invite Him to be at the center of your thoughts and actions.

You don't want God to let you "have it your way." You don't want Him to back off and watch as you create a mess of your life. You don't want your stubborn self to be on the throne of your life. If you are trying to do things your way, stop! Ask God to come back to your heart and mind and reign over you so that you are fixed on Him in all that happens. God is good and only wants the best things for you.

He who stands upon his own strength will never stand.

~ Thomas Brooks

Be Prepared

John the Baptist is the one Isaiah the prophet was talking about when he said: "This is a voice of one who calls out in the desert: 'Prepare the way for the Lord. Make the road straight for him.'" *Matt. 3:3, NCV*

John the Baptist was hand-picked to get people's hearts ready for Jesus, the Messiah. John drew people to him and baptized them in the name of the One who was yet to come. He was humble and didn't strive to make his own name great. He was opening the door, making the way for Jesus to come in.

Like John the Baptist, we are preparing the way for the Lord. We bear witness to what God has done and tell others about Jesus. We don't put obstacles in the way of any person who might be searching for the Lord. Instead, we make a straight path so they can receive Christ as their Savior.

At this season of Christmas, we are reminded again of the gift of God that comes in the form of an infant who wraps Himself around our hearts. The world is every bit as desperate for Him as it was back in the days of John the Baptist, perhaps more so. At the Christmas season and all through the year, let us open the door for Christ to come in and prepare the way.

Dear Lord, please let Your Spirit move me to share Your love with those around me today.

~ Amen

Stay Alert

Be alert. Continue strong in the faith.
Have courage, and be strong. *1 Cor. 16:13, NCV*

Somehow, it's easier to put your faith on display at this time of year. It's somewhat of a freeing experience to wish "Merry Christmas" to neighbors and friends, not really considering whether they share your beliefs. Of course, you're always free to share your faith. As you put up your nativity scene, pray people will be inspired by it and ask you what your faith is all about. Be strong in your approach to the season so as the new year begins, you keep telling your faith story.

With each Christmas light you use to adorn your house, remember the Light that came into the world, for all people, so that they could be saved. Shine your light with great joy and share the Good News of Christ. Stay alert because God will bring people to you that need to know His story of truth and love.

Your faith may help someone else understand more fully why they put up a Christmas tree, and why they sing carols of angels and shepherds. You can make a difference in your neighborhood simply by being an example of love and light. After all, Jesus comes to us at Christmas and invites us to recommit our lives to Him, prepared to follow Him into the New Year.

The birth of Jesus is the sunrise in the Bible. ~ *Henry van Dyke*

Sparkle and Shine

Let your light shine for all to see.
For the glory of the LORD rises to shine on you. *Isa. 60:1, NLT*

Jesus is the Light of the world and no one needs to fear the darkness when they trust in Him. He lights the way for them and provides guidance for the things they do. He is the North Star for believers.

How can you add sparkle to light up the hearts of those you meet? You may lead someone out of the darkness just by being yourself and helping them to see God's love at work. Your light is like the candle that lights all the other ones around it.

Consider what it means for the glory of the Lord to rise and shine on you. God's glory is His holiness, His brilliant light, His incredible Presence. His glory goes before Him and surrounds Him always. He graciously offers a portion of Himself to you, causing your spirit to connect with His and giving you more sparkle than you could ever have on your own.

God gives you His Light so that you can shine, and others can see that He is near. It's a great day for you to be the flame, the candle, the beacon, the sparkly light that brings brilliance and joy. May you live each day sharing God's glory.

Words which do not give the light of Christ increase the darkness.

~ *Mother Teresa*

DECEMBER 13

Honoring Your Creator

This is what the LORD says—your Redeemer and Creator: "I am the LORD, who made all things. I alone stretched out the heavens. Who was with me when I made the earth?" *Isa. 44:24, NLT*

Christmas brings its own joy and glory. We put nativity scenes in church yards and angels atop Christmas trees. We sense that human beings are striving to be a little kinder and a bit more thoughtful to each other. We see once again all that God has done and are reminded that He did it all without any help from us.

The earth is the Lord's and He reigns. He alone brought us into being. He alone is our Creator. How do we honor God with our lives? What can we do to show Him that we recognize His sovereignty and all that He has done for us?

Perhaps you could bring a little gift to a child who will spend the holidays in a hospital bed or read the Christmas story to those whose hearts long to hear it. The opportunities are endless for you to honor God by doing something for the least of His children. A kind word, a smile, a gesture of love in any of its forms will make the holidays brighter for those around you and will give God pleasure at the choices you've made.

Lord, help me to honor You with my whole heart and mind and soul. I celebrate Your kindness and Your love for all people.

~ Amen

Helping Hands

She extends a helping hand to the poor and opens her arms to the needy. *Prov. 31:20, NLT*

Between Thanksgiving and Christmas, charitable organizations thrive, bringing gifts of joy and gladness to many people who simply cannot take care of themselves. We are God's hands and feet and so we are the only way those in need can receive His care.

You've always been a generous person and whether you've been able to give gifts of financial donations or gifts of time, you've done your part. You are a blessing and God loves that you're a cheerful giver. This year pray specifically for the people you are choosing to help. They may be homeless through no fault of their own, greatly in need of hope and possibility. They may be people with chronic illness or in great need for a variety of reasons, and so they have no choice but to accept the charitable help of others.

As you think about the ones to whom you're giving gifts of love, remember that they are also children of God. They are people that He cherishes and offers His plan of salvation. They are your brothers and sisters in Christ.

Thank you for extending a helping hand and blessing those around you with your generous spirit and your kindness. May God bless you and keep you for all that you do for others.

Too many have dispensed with generosity in order to practice charity. ~ *Albert Camus*

The Message of Hope

Never be lacking in zeal, but keep your spiritual fervor, serving the Lord. Be joyful in hope, patient in affliction, faithful in prayer. *Rom. 12:11-12, NIV*

J. I. Packer said the Christmas message is that there is hope for a ruined humanity—hope of pardon, hope of peace with God, hope of glory—because at the Father's will Jesus Christ became poor, and was born in a stable.

As we get closer to Christmas, what possibilities lift your spirit and give you energy just to think about them? Maybe you hope for a new home or for a better job or for a relationship to be repaired, strengthened or renewed.

We are reminded that God Himself is the author of hope, the One who tries to open our eyes to see His hand at work in our lives. He offers the only hope that gives us the way to everlasting life. God did not wrap His hope in a fancy package tied with sparkling bows and colorful papers. He placed His gift in a feeding trough, wrapped in cloths, and adored by a mother's love. God brought His hope to the world so that every person who would tiptoe to that manger and cast their eyes on Him, would have hope.

Be joyful in your hope today and let your faithful love serve as a light to those around you. The hope of the world has come to you!

Without Christ there is no hope.

~ C.H. Spurgeon

The Spirit of Love

The fruit of the Spirit is love, joy, peace, forbearance, kindness, goodness, faithfulness, gentleness and self-control. Against such things there is no law. *Gal. 5:22-23, NIV*

The holiday season often gives us a powerful picture of what it means to have the fruit of the Spirit. We see joy in the faces of young and old alike, filled with anticipation of the delights of Christmas. Some will visit family, others will gather loved ones around a brightly lit tree. Each family will find a way to make the season merry.

We hope that with God's love we'll be a little kinder and be more giving and generous. We challenge the negativity that permeates the news and dampens our sense of peace. For this one season, we let all that negativity go and usher in the nativity of love. With child-like faith, we come back to the manger.

This year, may you receive even more of God's grace and mercy. See Him in the face of each person you love. God has given you a spirit that reflects His own, one that brings gentleness and peace, mercy and hope, forgiveness and forbearance as you head into the year to come. May you feel the blessing of all God has for you today.

The word which God has written on the brow of every human being is hope.
~ Victor Hugo

Here Comes the Son

I write these things to you who believe in the name of the Son of God so that you may know that you have eternal life. This is the confidence we have in approaching God: that if we ask anything according to his will, he hears us. *1 John 5:13-14, NIV*

As you prepare for the birth of baby Jesus, imagine His teenage mother, riding on a donkey, looking for a shelter, ready to deliver at any time. She is not at home because she had to go to be registered for the census with her husband, Joseph. She's been through amazing things in the past few months and she is still not certain what it means to be carrying, "the Son of God." All she knows is God is with her no matter how things look, or how uncomfortable she is.

Hold this part of the story with you as you continue to prepare for the holiday. Consider what it means that the Son of God is soon to be born into the world. His life means that everyone who believes in His name will be given a gift…the gift of salvation.

This one life makes a difference to all humankind. You have every reason to be confident in your relationship with God because you have embraced His Son. No gift under your tree means more to your heart than this one. May God be praised!

Christians believe that Jesus Christ is the Son of God because He said so.

~ *C.S. Lewis*

Waiting for the Lord

When the men came to Jesus, they said, "John the Baptist sent us to you with this question: 'Are you the One who is to come, or should we wait for someone else?'" *Luke 7:20, NCV*

As Jesus began His ministry back in the days of John the Baptist, there were many, including John, who had a belief that the Messiah would come any time. They wondered if Jesus might be the One they had been waiting for. Like kids at Christmas, they waited with hope and anticipation that they would have a better life and happier times once the Messiah began to reign. They had been waiting for a long time. They were joyful because they felt sure the countdown had begun to the Messiah's arrival.

The countdown to Christmas has begun and we now know that Jesus is the One we have been waiting for. He is the gift of Christmas, the One who will make a difference in our lives forever. He is the treasure, the most amazing present we could ever receive. As you wait for Christmas this year, draw even closer to your loved ones and to your Father in Heaven. The celebration of His birth will be that much sweeter. Celebrate His life, for the waiting will soon be over!

Christ came when all things were growing old, and He made them new.

~ Augustine of Hippo

DECEMBER 19

The Treasure

And when they had come into the house, they saw the young Child with Mary His mother, and fell down and worshiped Him. And when they had opened their treasures, they presented gifts to Him: gold, frankincense, and myrrh. *Matt. 2:11, NKJV*

The wise men who visited the baby Jesus had been studying the stars, anticipating the birth of the Savior, and they knew nothing could bring them more joy than the moment they laid eyes on the baby King. It was glorious to them and they humbly fell on their faces when the sacred moment arrived. They had traveled across the desert sands with treasures to show their love for the Messiah. As extravagant as the gifts were, they knew they were humble gifts at best. After all, the best gift was Jesus Himself.

It's always fun at Christmas to come up with little treasures to give to the people we love. We picture the smile on their faces, that moment of delight as they receive it. We anticipate Christmas morning with great joy.

No matter what gifts you give or receive this Christmas, there is no treasure as valuable as the love you share. God gave us the gift of Jesus because He loves us so much, He wanted to be sure that we could get back to Him one day. We know that the greatest treasure around any tree is Jesus. His love blesses our hearts as we gather together.

The person who has God for his treasure has all things in one.

~ A.W. Tozer

Celebrate Your Faith

Take delight in the LORD, and he will give you the desires of your heart. *Ps. 37:4, NIV*

No matter how busy you are or how much work it is to get your house decorated and your Christmas cards out, there's something very special about the celebration of Christmas that brings delight. Of course, you may not feel the delight until things slow down. It comes in peace as you sit by a nicely lit tree with soft background music, or you're at Christmas Eve service setting your spirit free as you sing carols. The joy comes when you realize that even with the shopping and the wrapping and the get-togethers with friends and family, you know that Christmas is sacred.

Christmas is the beautiful, hallelujah of your faith; it is the sweet recognition that you have received God's gift of love and that everything you do around the holiday itself has significance. You love to let God know how much it means to you that Jesus was born and that you follow Him every day.

Take heart over Christmas and let the sweet delight of the season radiate from your spirit. Sing with the angels and give glory to God for all that He has done. Dance a little, enjoy special moments with others, and take delight in all that God has for you. Christmas is His celebration of joy and love and He did it all just for you.

May the Christ of Christmas be yours! *~ Author unknown*

Peace Be with You

"When you enter that home, say, 'Peace be with you.'
If the people there welcome you,
let your peace stay there." *Matt. 10:12-13, NCV*

The writer of Matthew knew that having real peace, the kind that only God can give, is an amazing gift. A home that is filled with peace is one where love decorates the hallways and kindness brings honor to the living spaces. You know that peace of mind and heart is a worthy gift at any season of the year, but it is one that is particularly welcome at the birth of the Christ child.

No doubt, Mary would have enjoyed finding a home filled with peace, with a suitable atmosphere to deliver God's Son. Of course, we would imagine that even in a shelter designed to protect animals, a spirit of peace prevailed. No matter what else Mary was feeling, she likely felt God's peaceful Presence as she looked into the eyes of her baby boy. His amazing gaze would have filled her soul with love.

Wherever you may be this holiday, along with a tin of cookies, carry the gift of peace to those you meet, gracing their homes with the peace only God can give. Say to each one, "Peace be with you!" and continue to live in infinite grace and joy.

If God be our God, He will give us peace in trouble. When there is a storm without, He will make peace within.

~ *Thomas Watson*

DECEMBER 22

Angels and Shepherds

When the angels left them and went back to heaven, the shepherds said to each other, "Let's go to Bethlehem. Let's see this thing that has happened which the Lord has told us about." *Luke 2:15, NCV*

The Christmas story seems wrong-side out. If we were telling the story we'd have a beautiful princess and a protective prince. We'd have kings who brought amazing presents and we'd certainly have angels lighting up the night sky.

As we look at it again, maybe the story is right-side out. We do have a beautiful princess named Mary. We have her protective husband, Joseph. We have an amazing star to guide the way to Bethlehem, wise men with exotic presents, and a stable turned into an enchanted place as shepherds and angels looked on. It was a beautiful and sacred beginning of the life that would change the eternal hope of every human being.

Yes, God might have given Mary and Joseph more fanfare, better lodging, or less stressful conditions. You may hope He would do that for you. In fact, He does that when we answer His call as Mary did. He stays with us for the rest of our life journey. You are being escorted each day by the living King of glory.

Lord, thank You for leading me forward and blessing my life so richly each day.

~ *Amen*

DECEMBER 23

That Shining Star

After they had heard the king, they went on their way, and the star they had seen when it rose went ahead of them until it stopped over the place where the child was. When they saw the star, they were overjoyed. *Matt. 2:9-10, NIV*

The astronomers who followed the star to Bethlehem believed that it was a guide and a sign they were headed in the right direction.

The Bible doesn't offer a follow-up story about how the lives of the wise men were changed after they visited Bethlehem. We only know that they did not return to Herod but went back to their own countries by other routes. Imagine what happened in their hearts and minds as they each returned to their own kingdoms.

Chances are good the shining star stayed in their minds for the rest of their lives. A glimpse of the Savior gave each of them a purpose for living. Now they had the story to tell of the living God. They knew that nothing would ever be the same again.

Now, centuries later, we still need to follow the star to Bethlehem. We just need one glimpse of the Savior to have our eyes opened to all that God is doing. From way back when to this very moment, God has been leading and guiding us to find the Savior, for He is our amazing shining Star!

It is much better to be drawn by the joys of heaven, than driven by the sorrows of earth. ~ *Author unknown*

DECEMBER 24

The Eve of Blessing

So Joseph also went up from the town of Nazareth in Galilee to Judea, to Bethlehem the town of David, because he belonged to the house and line of David. He went there to register with Mary, who was pledged to be married to him and was expecting a child. While they were there, the time came for the baby to be born, and she gave birth to her firstborn, a son. *Luke 2:4-7, NIV*

As human beings, we keep forgetting who is in charge. We make our plans and we act as though everything will be done as we wish. We imagine we know what steps to take, and then discover we can do nothing on our own. We must wait on the Lord and move in the direction He would send us.

Despite the chaos, the weariness of traveling, and the fact that they could not find a place to stay, the perfect time came for the baby to be born. They finally found a shelter. They wrapped their baby in warmth and love. They knew God had blessed them, brought them to safety and that His plans would be their guiding light from that day forward. The same thing is true for you. Follow in the way God leads you and He will bless you with glorious light.

We are to order our lives by the light of His law, not our guesses about His plan. *~ J.I. Packer*

The Light in the World

The true light that gives light to everyone was coming into the world. He was in the world, and though the world was made through him, the world did not recognize him. He came to that which was his own, but his own did not receive him. Yet to all who did receive him, to those who believed in his name, he gave the right to become children of God. *John 1:9-12, NIV*

Welcome to Christmas, you amazing child of God! The light is shining all around you, all through you, and is born anew in your spirit because Jesus has placed His Holy light inside your heart.

As you celebrate all that Christmas means to you, remember the angels who sang at His birth. Look at the gifts beneath your tree and remember the efforts the wise men made, risking their lives to see the baby in the manger. Look at the glowing lights around your neighborhood and remember that God's light is for everyone.

Embrace those you love, knowing that nothing can change the love God has for them as each one comes to know Him better in the coming year. It's an amazing day and everything about it is for you. The light of the world shines for you and what a glorious gift it is!

May God bless you and keep your light shining everywhere you go.

All the Christmas presents in the world are worth nothing without the presence of Christ. ~ *David Jeremiah*

Hope for Tomorrow

The Word became flesh and made his dwelling among us. We have seen his glory, the glory of the one and only Son, who came from the Father, full of grace and truth. *John 1:14, NIV*

The Light of the world is sparkling brightly, bringing you His truth and grace and offering you new possibilities. His glory is the power of love unleashed, uncensored, unstoppable because He shines through you.

If you are still weighed down by the troubles you've collected during the year, then come to the Light. Seek God's favor to wipe the slate clean and give you hope to start again. Renew yourself in Him and unwrap the gift of His love. He came for you and came to bring you light and newness of life.

Fill your heart with Scriptures that give you hope and challenge you to build a stronger relationship with your Savior. Pause and reflect on the good things God has done. Take each good thing and praise Him, trusting that He sees you right where you are and knows everything you need.

He is with you today, tomorrow and always. Nothing can separate you from His intentional and unconditional love. You are His! You are a delight to His heart. Rest in that thought and He will renew your hope.

Count your blessings, build a pile—
For blessings counted, make you smile.

Seeing the Light

The people walking in darkness have seen a great light; on those living in the land of deep darkness a light has dawned. *Isa. 9:2, NIV*

Have you ever tried to understand something, but you simply didn't get it? Then one day, out of nowhere, the light dawned. You got it! You suddenly could see what everybody was talking about. It was a shining moment for you.

Some people still are waiting for the light to dawn on their faith. They simply do not understand the Bible, or the hope of Jesus. They are walking in the dark. They don't even know that they are blind and that only God's Spirit can awaken them.

It's wonderful to see the Light and know that God is with you. It changes your focus and perspective and helps you to live in a way that is more generous and loving. His Light is your guide and your promise any time you walk through a dark place. His Light is with you forevermore.

Remind yourself that you are the only Bible some people will ever read. You may be their opportunity to discover the hope of Jesus. You are a friend who can lead them out of the darkness.

Let your light continue to shine!

We can forgive a child who is afraid of the dark; the real tragedy is when an adult is afraid of the Light. *~ Author unknown*

The Prince of Peace

For to us a child is born, to us a son is given,
and the government will be on his shoulders.
And he will be called Wonderful Counselor, Mighty God,
Everlasting Father, Prince of Peace. *Isa. 9:6, NIV*

These words from the prophet, Isaiah have been sung in church choirs, made blessedly familiar by Handel's *Messiah*, and are a glimpse of the present and the future all at once. Jesus, born in a stable in Bethlehem is no ordinary child. He will grow up to be the ruler, the head of all governing bodies on earth and in Heaven. The names that are given to him are extraordinary, beyond measure for no one like Him has ever come to earth before, or since. He reigns! Isn't it amazing that Isaiah could talk about Him in such a way hundreds of years before Jesus was even born.

God wants to bring us back to Himself. He wants us to come home again someday and know that He loves us more than anything. He wants us to love His Son, the Prince of Peace.

The blessing is to remember the Mighty God, the Wonderful Counselor and the Everlasting Father are with you always. You can share your heart in intimate detail, for they are with you always. In Christ, you have been given the peace that passes all understanding.

Keep your heart in peace. Let nothing in this world disturb it; everything has an end. ~ *John of the Cross*

Gracious Goodness

Simeon took the baby in his arms and thanked God: "Now, Lord, you can let me, your servant, die in peace as you said. With my own eyes I have seen your salvation, which you prepared before all people." *Luke 2:28-31, NCV*

When Mary and Joseph went to the temple to offer a sacrifice for the birth of Jesus, they encountered a godly man, named Simeon. The Holy Spirit had told Simeon that before his death, he would hold God's gift of salvation. He would see God's Son.

Mary and Joseph, surprised by many things that occurred around the birth of Jesus, must have wondered at Simeon's prayer. Holding the infant in his arms, Simeon thanked God for the blessing of seeing God's salvation for both Jew and Gentile. It was an unforgettable moment!

As you leave the old year behind, remember how blessed you are to carry the future in your heart. Proclaim God's goodness. Like Simeon, you have seen the salvation of the Lord firsthand.

Begin each day with praise and thanksgiving.

Peace does not mean the end of all our striving,
Joy does not mean the drying of our tears,
Peace is the power that comes to souls arriving
Up to the Light where God Himself appears.

~ *G. A. Studdert Kennedy*

Happy Days Are Here Again

He will bring you joy and gladness, and many people will be happy because of his birth. *Luke 1:14, NCV*

Think about the things that truly make you happy. You have been given numerous blessings through the year that is ending and sometimes it's helpful to remember each one.

Did you rise each day from a warm bed, protected and sustained by nutritious meals and the laughter of people you love around your table? Did you worry about things that never happened? Did you discover that your friends are still there for you, ready to listen to your heart and share stories of their lives?

Maybe you found comfort in your faith in a new way, or you were blessed unexpectedly by someone from church or even a stranger. You breathed in the sunshine and the rain, knowing that God was in control and that you could count on Him to be with you any place you had to go.

No doubt your own blessings go way beyond these suggestions, and it's likely that each one brings a smile to your face. Be happy today. Know that nothing will happen to you that is a surprise to God because He goes ahead of you, ready to guide your steps. Thank Him for your blessings and end the old year with a sense of peace and joy.

Concentrate on counting your blessings and you'll have little time to count anything else. ~ *Woodrow Kroll*

You Win!

Loving God means obeying his commands. And God's commands are not too hard for us, because everyone who is a child of God conquers the world. And this is the victory that conquers the world—our faith. *1 John 5:3-4,* NCV

You're finishing the year with a win. You're victorious! Your faith has brought you this far and it will carry you joyfully on to the year ahead. You and God make an amazing team, and nothing can change that. He has sustained you since the day you gave your heart to Jesus.

Now you can find strength for your soul and be encouraged in everything because you know you are not alone. You have the full blessing of the Trinity; the full power of the Creator of the universe and you can call upon that power any time. Your prayers are heard and your life matters.

Go ahead and close the door on the old year. You are free to let it go and feel the blessing of the fresh winds of joy that the new year will bring. You've done well, and God is delighted to have you as His child. He promises to be with you always, to bless you and keep you every day of your life.

Doesn't it feel good to be a winner? Now go out and make your Father proud!

God always causes me to triumph in Christ Jesus.

~ Adapted from 2 Cor. 2:14

About the Author

KAREN MOORE is the best-selling author of over 100 inspirational daily devotionals.

Karen is a keynote speaker for writing conferences and women's groups. She worked in the greeting-card industry and teaches greeting card writing online.

Karen has also worked as a book publisher for children's books and Bibles. She is married and lives in Richmond Hill, Georgia.